I0141562

Life in the Wilderness

Discovering God's Certainty in Uncertain Times

Charles A. Haun

CAH PUBLISHING

Copyright © 2014 by Charles A. Haun

Life in the Wilderness
by Charles A. Haun

Printed in the United States of America

ISBN 978-0-692-26485-0

All rights reserved. No part of this document may be reproduced or transmitted in any form, by any means (electronic, photocopying, recording, or otherwise) without the written permission of CAH Publishing.

Unless otherwise indicated, Bible quotations are taken from the King James Version of the Bible.

Scriptures quotations marked (NASB) are taken from the New American Standard Bible®. Copyright © 1960, 1962, 1963, 1968, 1971, 1972, 1973, 1975, 1977, 1995 by The Lockman Foundation Used by permission. (www.Lockman.org)

Scripture quotations marked (NIV) are taken from the THE HOLY BIBLE, NEW INTERNATIONAL VERSION®, NIV®. Copyright © 1973, 1978, 1984, 2011 by Biblica, Inc.®. Used by permission. All rights reserved worldwide.

CAH PUBLISHING

PO Box 916552
Wekiva Springs Rd. • Longwood, FL 32779-99998

Dedication

⸺✦⸺

To all those throughout the years who have supported
Teaching All Nations, the ministry
of Charles and his wife, Violet.

Thank you for your friendship, love, and prayers.

Table of Contents

Acknowledgments

My heartfelt thanks to the board members of *Teaching All Nations*: Jane and Richard Woodard, Jake Luffy, Violet Haun, and Renay Crowe. Their support and prayers made this book possible. I would also like to thank my family for their helpful advice and love.

A special thank you to my sister Renay Crowe for her research, which was vital for the publication of our father's book. Also, to Helena M. Mariades, Th.D., for her personal support as a treasured friend, counselor, and author. Her guidance and prayers made all the difference in this book being started and completed. I owe a debt of gratitude to Kathy Curtis, another precious friend, for her faithful words of encouragement and generous gift of time, and editing and typesetting talents. Many thanks to Kelly Jadon for her valuable assistance with editing and writing.

I would not have been able to compile this book without the help of my mother, Violet Haun. Her love and passion for this project was priceless and kept me motivated. Her desire was that her husband's writings would be available for many to read and enjoy. For years, she stood faithfully by his side and continues to exhibit the same strength of character.

Last, I wish to express my appreciation for my dad, Charles Haun, the author of this book. The wisdom that he gained through countless hours of studying God's Word, in which he lived daily and taught to others, continues to touch me and many others with the love of Jesus Christ. I know he would want all the glory to be given to God.

Brenda Haun

Introduction
My Dad, Charles Haun

———❦———

Deep in the night hours, a glowing light spilled from my father's office doorway into the hallway. There I stood quietly listening. *Was he writing? Studying? Praying?* All I heard was silence as I strained to get a glimpse of him. I yearned to know about my dad's relationship with Jesus Christ. Much later, I learned that while in prayer he spent most of his time sitting silently before God. My dad, Charles Haun, was one who lived to commune with the Lord. He understood the value of just listening to Him. Thirty-five years later, I am working on publishing his book that you are now reading. I can't help but wonder if the chapters were being prayed about and written during those late hours in his office. In the process of compiling *Life in the Wilderness*, I learned that this had been my dad's desire: to have his popular series of eight *Wilderness* booklets, which were based upon his experiences and studies, organized into one book.

Both the Old and New Testament acknowledge the need for an understanding of the wilderness. The pasture and dry places without water are a part of living life. The walk with God at times leads us away from comfort to uncertainty. But that's the thing that uncertainty teaches—that God's adequacy is certain.

Life in the Wilderness covers eleven wildernesses in the experiences of the children of Israel. Each chapter unfolds the obstacles, tests, training, progress, victories, and the meaning of each wilderness. The objective is to show the reader how God takes a believer from the point of "Being Willing to Follow" to "Living Heaven on Earth."

You will get to know my dad in his many personal stories that are woven throughout this book. He was a courageous man, who lived in the security of knowing Jesus Christ, as he stood in front of the headhunters on the Amazon River in Peru and as he used his bare hands to grab a fifteen-foot water boa. Through times of pain and sickness, and a close-to-death moped accident, my dad was aware of God's nearness.

As he traveled all over the world, Dad was faithful to his calling from God. A few of the places my dad lived or visited outside of the United States were Peru, England, Holland, Nicaragua, and Israel. He stood behind pulpits, taught Bible school students, and sat in living rooms sharing the Word of God with grace and simplicity. As a result, many lives were transformed.

I don't remember a time that my dad worried. In *Life in the Wilderness,* Dad tells of the trust in God he gained during a personal two-year-long spiritual wilderness. He also writes about an experience while living in Israel when he took a short excursion by foot into the wilderness of Judea.

Dad writes, "Where is the Wilderness of the Red Sea, the Wilderness of Shur, the Wilderness of Etham, and the Wilderness of Sin? Some of the wildernesses and experiences of the children of Israel will be located for you on Bible maps, and some will not. There is little profit in seeking the physical and the geographical locations. The Wilderness of Etham and the Wilderness of Shur are believed to be the same location. The pinpointed locations of other wildernesses are simply unknown. The important thing is not the location, but the name and the events associated with the name. This will get us to the core of God's intention: to communicate His message of hope."

What a treasure it was to have a father who daily lived what he taught to others. I would have to write a whole other book in order for me to share how much he had beautifully affected my life as a father and as a minister of God's Word.

During Dad's life, there was one common thread—a willing and yielding heart toward Christ, even in the wilderness seasons of his life. My dad remained faithful to his Savior as he entered Heaven at the age of sixty-nine in July of 1996. During the time of my dad's passing, my family and I heard from many who remembered the first occasion they had heard him speak or stated that he had been like a father to them. Several spoke of his steadfastness and about how his ministry had impacted them, which continued to help them many years later.

These are just a few quotes that reflect his care and ministry to others:

> Pastor Jake Luffy recalled, "We (his students) would say of Charles, 'He no longer lived, but Christ lived in him.' Charles became the grace of God to us because he was what he was by the grace of God. His Christian life was not one of human emotion or human sentimentality, but rather, one of a deep commitment born out of love for his Master."

> A friend and ministry confidant, William Pepper, wrote, "Many who knew Chuck witnessed some of the areas the Lord so appreciated in him—foremost, his rising to be alone with God and his diligences to analyze the Word. Also, the heart of a poet occasionally reflected in his writings. He had a strong love for his family and compassion for so many. Ministry always seemed to flow from him. He touched so many lives."

> "I heard Charles Haun teach for the first time in 1974," explained Jane Woodard, a friend. "I was so greatly touched in that meeting that I found myself sitting on the edge of my chair and physically leaning forward to catch every word. The outward physical effect of the teaching did not even come close to the deep inward impact it was having on my spirit. His teachings concerning the trials of this life were foundational in eventually bringing me to a place of repeated victory. Once during the early years of our friendship, I talked to him about a particularly fierce trial I was going through. I expected to get some sympathizing words. Instead, he laughed with joy at what I could spiritually gain and pushed me back into battle! Charles' words always directed me deeper into God with exceptional clarity."

May this book be a blessing to you, as it has been to so many. Pastor Wade E. Taylor puts it this way, "Charles had a special gift of making the barren wilderness, which exists in some measure within the lives of each one of us, a more understandable and acceptable place. And along with this, Charles showed us not only the way out, but he took us further into the land of promise."

As you read, my prayer is that you will also quietly listen to what God has to say to you and, if it is the case, about your life in the wilderness. Expect to discover God's certainty in uncertain times.

Brenda Haun

Chapter One
Willing to Follow
in the Wilderness of Paran

⸻∞∞⸻

The Wilderness of Paran will have features which differ from other wildernesses. This is true in the case of every wilderness. They all differ from one another in some aspects. We shall not be considering the physical characteristics of the Wilderness of Paran. This work will focus upon spiritual aspects which are taken from the Bible.

SO AWFUL?

In Christian circles, believers have been given quite a variety of thoughts on spiritual wildernesses, some of which may be correct, and some incorrect. However, a person's experience in a spiritual wilderness may not fit anything that he has been told. For example, the totally terrible thing which was reported to me, is not nearly as bad as I was led to believe. Most believers have the idea that the spiritual wilderness experience is practically unbearable. If such a person is found in the wilderness, his built-in attitude would immediately translate the experience as terrible. It is almost impossible to convince him that it is beautiful, and a wonderful place in which to be. The wilderness does not feel good nor does it appear beautiful. He may have a very difficult time with the wilderness. He may have difficulty believing that it should be part of the Christian's spiritual training. He may find it virtually impossible to discover its positive aspects. If he would give his attention to the Word of God and to the wisdom and experiences of others, he would indeed learn the ways of God in a wilderness experience.

WILL YOU UNDERSTAND?

Most (if not all) believers have experienced a spiritual wilderness. These have a foundation or platform upon which they can better understand (or understand for the first time) its divine arrangement and purpose. If you have never experienced a spiritual wilderness (which is highly unlikely) you may have extreme difficulty understanding this area. Even some who have passed through many wildernesses have a difficult time understanding. This is mainly due to the fact that they do not wish to own wildernesses as part of their Christian experience.

The believer somehow assumes that he must understand everything today. Therefore he presses for meanings which do not exist; or he will insist upon enlightenment which is beyond his experience and capacity to know and to carry. The result of such persistence is misunderstanding. The real damage in this is the assumption that a true understanding has been attained. To avoid the dangers entailed in such practice, we must first be content not to understand. Secondly, we must be willing to lay aside what we may or may not believe. Thirdly, we must be willing to hold, or contain, "the mystery of the faith in a pure conscience" (I Timothy 3:9). That is, we must be willing to hear that which we do not understand, receive it, and hold it within ourselves, without doing anything with it for the time being.

Most of that which Jesus taught His disciples was not grasped by them at the time. Later they understood what they received. What we do not understand today, we are to hold in a pure conscience for the future.

The very fact that we experience a wilderness does not necessarily mean that we recognize it as such. Some may never have been told that their difficult experiences are called wildernesses. They may have been given other names. My intention is not to label these experiences, for a label may help, or it may hinder. My purpose is to help believers in their walk with God, regardless of what their difficult situations may be called.

Keep in mind some characteristics found in these difficult times I refer to as wilderness experiences. A partial list of so-called negative difficulties is: testing, proving, tribulation, persecution, suffering, spiritual dryness, and darkness.

For example, whenever the consciousness of God's presence is lost for a period of time so that prayer and communion seem to become meaningless, the believer is in a wilderness; he is in dryness. There is no consciousness of God's blessings and movings upon him in his wilderness.

There are also positive characteristics in the wildernesses. The Wilderness of Paran is "glory" or "beauty." This is the meaning of "Paran," a Hebrew word (6290 in *Strong's Concordance*).

Most of us do not look upon the wilderness as a place of glory and beauty. In order to see the wilderness in such gratifying terms, we must first become aware of God's intentions in bringing us into the wilderness. Once we come to this awareness, we can then begin to understand why and how glory and beauty can be in a wilderness.

The characteristics found in the meaning of the Hebrew word "Paran" are a general description of all the wildernesses as they relate to the believer's life. Complete descriptions of the wildernesses are not found in the meanings of the Hebrew names. Scriptures which directly and indirectly relate to the wilderness in question will add to the description. The Word of God will tie things together for us, and give us the picture God wants us to see and understand. The Bible is called the "Good Book." It is "gooder" than most people realize. From the Bible we shall see what is moving in the wildernesses. God's direction and purposes in the wildernesses can be discovered in His Word.

God's direction can be seen and somewhat understood as the Israelites first approach the Wilderness of Paran, "And the children of Israel took their journeys out of the wilderness of Sinai; and the cloud rested in the wilderness of Paran" (Numbers 10:12). This was not their choice, rather it was God's choice; it was God's direction for them. The Israelites simply followed the cloud, stopping where it stopped, moving when the cloud moved. Here the cloud stopped in the Wilderness of Paran. The wisdom of God is in His direction. If we find His direction, we find His wisdom. We must follow in order to find.

LESSONS

The first lesson to be learned is to follow the cloud. We must learn to follow what we know to be the direction of God. Many of us spend so much time and effort in worrying about what we do not know, that there is little strength and opportunity left to follow God in what we do know. As we learn to walk in the known will of God, we will spare ourselves much trouble and anguish.

The second lesson to be learned is not to complain and question God as you follow. The children of Israel were always complaining about these wilderness stops. "Well, why did the cloud stop here? Doesn't God know that there is no water here, and that this is the wilderness?" "Why does God lead us into the wilderness? To kill us because there are no graves in Egypt?" As they followed the cloud, they did not recognize the wisdom of God in leading them to these specific places. Therefore they did not recognize God's purpose in each stop. If we do not learn the second lesson (learn not to complain) we will never see the meanings in "Paran." We will miss the beauty and glory in the wilderness.

DON'T MISS IT!

The brightness of the glory of God, the cloud, the burning fire by night, rested in the Wilderness of Paran. The tribes of Israel lived under this cloud. But one can live under the glory of God and never see it. Consider how many people missed the Glory of God as Jesus walked this earth to teach and perform God's wonderful miracles.

Today some believers will miss the glory of God—in the wilderness. There are many things we would never want to miss. Vacation! Would we want to forego our vacation time? Payday! Who would want to miss payday? Christmas! Few believers would want to miss Christmas.

We want money, convenience, comfort, health, happiness! We want a nice home and car! When a Christian gives these things greater priority than the glory of God, he has come short of the glory of God. He will miss the beauty and glory in the Wilderness of Paran. We will miss seeing the glory of God if our vision is fixed on our fears. Fear will keep us from looking toward the wilderness. Let us not be afraid of the wilderness.

Seasons in the wilderness will become the occasions when God imparts certain divine meanings and revelations and richness to us. The wilderness will be the place of our greatest progressions in God. There are certain things which God can bring to us only as we properly relate to His glory in the wilderness. There are certain aspects of the work of God in us which must be accomplished in the wilderness and nowhere else. These cannot be done in the Promised Land. They cannot be done in Heaven. They cannot be done in prosperity. They cannot be done in health. Wherever they must be done, we must follow God to the place and respond to Him there.

Certain aspects of God's care and character are seen only in difficult places. How can we know Him as Healer unless we become sick? How can we see Him as Provider unless there is a need?

Most of us will not render to God complete surrender and cooperation when we are in good times. Wherever we must be to have God accomplish His work in us, we must follow God to that place and respond to Him there. This was true for Abraham, and for us as well.

THE WORKSHOP

The wilderness is God's workshop. He has designed it for us. He brings us to it, "even every one who is called by My name, whom I have created for My glory" (Isaiah 43:7). We are brought there to see His glory, to relate to it, to learn from it, and above all, to be conformed to His image. We would prefer God to work on us in His workshop of green grass and still water. Although these have their places in our Christian experience, certain changes in us are not accomplished in these lovely and pleasant places. We do not seem to linger long in the pleasant places.

The children of Israel followed the cloud to green grass. The name of the place was "Hazeroth." The stem of this Hebrew word "Hazeroth" (2698) means "green," "grass," "leeks," "enclosure," and others.[1] This Hazeroth must have been a luscious place. *The International Standard Bible Encyclopedia* refers to it as "the best pastures" (page 3067 b). To those camping there, this would have

---

[1] Benjamin Davidson, *The Analytical Hebrew and Chaldee Lexicon of the Old Testament* (Cary, NC: Oxford University Press, 1959).

been most pleasing. We don't like to camp in the desert or in the wilderness, but rather in an oasis where there is a carpet of green grass and a fish-filled stream. How long do we camp in the green grass beside the still waters? Not very long.

We must follow the cloud. It moves from Hazeroth, as recorded in Numbers 12:16, "And afterward, the people removed from Hazeroth and pitched in the wilderness of Paran." The cloud did not tarry long over the green grass, but moved to the wilderness of Paran. The lush grass must be left behind. Leaving green grass and entering a wilderness like Paran is most discouraging.

Everything seemed to be to Israel's advantage in pleasant Hazeroth. However, not everything was fine and correct in the hearts of the people. This is where the murmuring against Moses was so strong that Miriam became leprous because of it.

Wildernesses, not utopias, are the workshops of God. In a utopia God cannot work into His people the dedication needed to fulfill His purposes. Adam and Eve, more than anyone else, except the angels in Heaven who fell, prove this truth. They did not respond correctly in their paradise.

The green grass of Hazeroth is desired by all, but does not fully and totally meet man's spiritual needs. The leadership directly under Moses failed in the green grass. There, "the anger of the LORD was kindled against them (Aaron and Miriam); and he departed" (Numbers 12:9).

The workshops of God are not in places of pleasantries where everything always goes well. The potter's wheel is not always an abundance of money. The anvil of God is not necessarily a state of unfailing good health. What kind of Christians would emerge from a utopia where there is never a threat, never the valley of the shadow of death? Where there is no battle, there can be no victory. If there is no victory, there is no overcomer. We can live in a utopia as long as the angels who fell did, and not be any better for it. Aaron and Miriam loved the green grass of Hazeroth as much as anyone. It did not cause them to respond to God properly. His glory and His beauty were not manifested through them there.

Green grass fades and the flower withers, but whoever does the will of God abides forever. Our physical well-being, all the things of this present life with which God could possibly bless us—these material blessings—fade away. We buy a brand new car, and what do we have? In time, a piece of junk. If we wait long enough, we will see the car take its place with others in the junkyard.

Everything passes away. A building may be ever so sturdy, but it won't remain forever. We may buy a suit with flaring lapels and soon we have to buy one with modest lapels. Dispose of all the wide neckties because the narrow ones are back in style. Back and forth, back and forth the fashions of this world are always passing away. Nothing is permanent; nothing here is established, "But he that doeth the will of God abideth for ever" (I John 2:17b).

We must release all these things that shall pass away, and follow the Master. We must not cling to the things of this life. Jesus said that these things do not hold the essence of life (Luke 12:15). Life does not consist of these things of this present world, although most people suppose it does. God, in opposition to this philosophy, is always attempting to draw us away from that which is temporal toward that which is eternal.

THE GLORY CLOUD!

People frequently ask me, "How did you like Peru (or Jerusalem, or wherever I may have lived)?" I really don't know because it's beside the point. It is not the town or the house in which we live. The focal point is the cloud. I would rather abide under the Shekinah.[2]

It doesn't matter where we may be or under what circumstances we may be living, just as long as the Shekinah Glory of God abides upon us. The condition of the wilderness is immaterial, as we live under the shadow of the Almighty.

---

[2] "Shekinah" is a Hebrew word used in Jewish theology to refer to a visible manifestation of the presence of God. This particular form of the work is not found in the Bible; forms close to it are. The word means "to dwell," "to abide," "to remain." In this work, the term "shekinah" is used to describe that which abides, whether or not it is visible. Glory of God in a small humble dwelling than to live in a luxurious mansion without the Glory. If we live under the abiding (Shekinah) cloud of God, it will make little difference whether we are in the wilderness or in Heaven. It is the glory of God which is to make an impact upon us and overshadow our life.

Live under the impact of God, not under the impact of some problem or some sorrow or some catastrophe. Live under the influence of faith, not wonderful feelings or the lack of them. Your life will be fulfilling and satisfying under the abiding presence of God.

We are by nature creatures of sense. The natural man thus limits his findings of truth to such matters as can be appreciated only through sense perception. He must see and feel before he will believe, thus closing the door to the realm of the spirit, where faith moves, discovering truths of higher, spiritual value. The faculties which operate in the realm of the natural are God-given. They are intended to function for the comfort of man in his natural realm in the physical world. But these absolutely fail when he tries to use them to discern God in His spiritual relations and manifestations. God has provided faith for this purpose. Through faith we may enter into a new realm where there are spiritual verities and spiritual laws operative.

The life of the Christian is supernatural— that is, above the natural. It is neither entered into nor lived by natural means. The process of weaning man from the limitations of the human and introducing him to the life of the spirit and faith is extremely trying to the flesh. There must be this necessary process of adjustment if we are to truly live the spiritual life and fully enter into the possibilities of development that God has provided for us.

Let us welcome each stroke which sets us free, and like bold adventurers in faith let us discover and possess the rich prospects in God.[3]

---

[3] John Wright Follette, *Smoking Flax And Other Poems* (Asheville, NC: Follette Books, 1971), 34.

Then welcome each rebuff
That turns earth's smoothness rough,
Each sting that bids nor sit nor stand but go!
Be our joys three-part pain!
Strive, and hold cheap the strain;
Learn, nor account the pang; dare, never
Grudge the throe!

—*Robert Browning*

God brings us into the wilderness to meet with us. He desires to share His glory with us. There is nothing more meaningful upon this earth than God's approach to us and taking up His residence in us. He desires to manifest Himself to us and to live with us and walk in us. There are times when wonderful feelings and goose bumps will accompany such manifestations of God. But most of the time there will be no wonderful feelings. Most of the time God will meet with us in the wilderness where the wonderful feelings are absent, and where there is no water.

The secret of our success in this life is God. If our focal point is Heaven as a place after our physical death, then we will miss the best thing in life. Here, in this life, God wishes to be with us. That is better than our Heaven after death, which is beyond our present location. God is better than a believer's future Heaven, any day of this week, any present time, any present place. God will be better than Heaven, even after we get there.

Some believers live and talk as if their future Heaven is better than God. I've never found it so. But of course I've never been to Heaven. I live here on earth. That is where I will focus my living, instead of attempting to live in the future. I will focus upon the secret of success in the now life—the now God.

When I was interviewed on a live television program, the interviewer opened with what he thought was a rhetorical question. He asked, "Aren't you excited about going to Heaven?" Without hesitation, I honestly answered, "No." The man's mouth gaped open in frozen silence; he lost control of the interview. There was no way he could backtrack; it was already being viewed by thousands. In an instant I saw that he was not going to recover quickly. I immediately rescued him, saying that my excitement was in God now.

GET THE PICTURE!

Our excitement, joy, satisfaction, contentment should not be sought in circumstances or wonderful feelings, but in God. He is very exciting and satisfying, even in the wilderness—particularly in the wilderness. We shall see this as we trace the Wilderness of Paran through the Word. We shall attempt to see God Himself as fully as our limitations allow, and seek to have as complete a picture of the Wilderness of Paran as possible.

Some of this picture emerges as we look into this cloud which stopped in the Wilderness of Paran. It began to operate in the very beginning of Israel's deliverance from bondage. In Exodus 14:20 it does a very unusual thing, "And it came between the camp of the Egyptians and the camp of Israel; and it was a cloud and darkness to them (Egyptians), but it gave light by night to these (Israel)." Here, the glory of God is a place of darkness to some, a place of confusion, a place in which they can find no understanding.

What are some people going to do with the glory of God? How will some people relate to it? The Egyptians did not relate to it very well, nor do most unbelievers today. The unbeliever is not expected to appreciate the glory of God. What is unexpected is that the children of Israel did not relate to it very well. Yes, even some believers have no or little conception of the glory of God. They may not be aware of their particular relationship to that aspect of God. The glory of God can approach a believer in a form unknown and unrecognized and is therefore unwanted by that believer. It may not occur to him that God is attempting to enrich his life.

The Egyptians saw the manifestation of God's glory at the hand of Moses. They finally admitted it was the hand of God. But even though they recognized God's doing, they did not come into submission and obedience to Him. Therefore, the cloud was darkness to them at the Red Sea. If we walk in disobedience to God, unwilling for His work to be accomplished in our life, the glory of God will be a headache to us. If we walk in obedience to God, willing for His work, that which He brings to us will become light, beauty, and glory to our life.

Let us learn from these two groups. One group saw darkness; the other saw light. These two opposites stemmed from one cloud. Do you get the picture?

POINT OF VIEW

What we see depends upon our point of view. Our point of view is the direction in which we habitually look, "And it came to pass, as Aaron spake unto the whole congregation of the children of Israel, that they looked toward the wilderness, and, behold, the glory of the Lord appeared in the cloud" (Exodus 16:10). The gaze of the Israelites had just been on meat, which they desired, but did not have. Only when they looked toward the wilderness did they see the glory of God. The glory of God was not in the meat that they desired.

The reason why many of us, on different occasions, miss seeing the glory of God is that we are looking toward that which we desire. We are viewing Canaan Land when we should be looking toward the wilderness.

If the glory of God is appearing in the wilderness, and we are gazing at the Promised Land, we may see the Promised Land, but we will not see the glory of God. When the glory of God has come to the wilderness, it is time to give the wilderness our attention. God brings you into the wilderness specifically to see His glory. He wants to bring to our vision His love, mercy, grace, longsuffering, provisions, and purposes.

Although many are brought to the wilderness to see the glory of God, not all see it. The direction of our vision at any particular time in our lives will determine what we shall see. It will also determine what we are not seeing of that which God wants to show us. We shall miss seeing His goodness as we constantly gaze at unfulfilled desires and long for the comforts of the flesh.

The wilderness was the place of opportunity. Here, from the Wilderness of Paran, the Children of Israel could have moved into greater opportunities. The possibility of taking the Promised Land was theirs. God Himself actually initiated the conquest of Canaan at this time from this place, as seen in Numbers 13:3, "And Moses by the commandment of the LORD sent them from the wilderness of Paran: all those men were heads of the children of Israel."

The wilderness may not be seen by some as a launching pad into an orbit of spiritual reality and living. But the wilderness is that, and more. It is a place of opportunity.

A particular opportunity is seen in verse 2 of Numbers 13, "Send thou men, that they may search the land of Canaan, which I give unto the children of Israel." These men are going to search and discover. They are moving toward that which God had promised them. In this, many things will be discovered, and revelation will unfold. The Israelite spies are going to discover things which they never thought existed in that promised area. What do they discover? They discover the fruits of the land. They return from the Promised Land to Moses, in verse 26 of chapter 13, and show him their discoveries. They say to Moses in verse 27, "We came unto the land whither thou sentest us, and surely it floweth with milk and honey; and this is the fruit of it." This was quite a revelation for these people who left the fertile waters of Egypt.

Foundations are necessary for revelation. The more abundant the revelations, and the fuller and richer they are, the more the need for greater and stronger foundations. God will often bring us through difficult places simply to establish in us a sufficient foundation and strength for the revelation, which He desires to bring to us. Foundations are built by irrevocably trusting God and responding properly to Him in all your situations, whether pleasant or unpleasant.

Ten of the twelve spies did not have a foundation sufficient enough to support their revelation. Instead of great faith coming to them from the revelation, they were filled with fear and defeat. Two spies caught the truth in the revelation and were filled with faith.

The foundation for revelation must be built. Without it God will never be able to put into our souls certain truths and revelations, and the means of living them. Therefore we must be willing for the undergirding foundation to be built in us. Unwillingness for this particular work of God will cause great loss of the riches of God.

Come, let us go into the wilderness with willing hearts. There we will learn of His riches, and glean for ourselves unimaginable wealth.

CONTRASTS

In our willing walk with Him we will learn and receive of Him. But we must stay with Him. He may lead in various and unlikely situations of great contrast. This will be necessary for learning and receiving.

A great contrast is seen in Numbers 13. The twelve men leave the wilderness and go into a land which flows with milk and honey. From the wilderness to abundance could be a pleasant contrast for all. From nothing to abundance would certainly magnify the blessing of plenty. If God wants to illustrate to us light, He can take us into darkness, and then into light. That would make an impression upon us. If He wants to put joy into our soul, He could take us through sorrow, and then plunge us into joy. That certainly would get the job done.

God will bring us through great contrasts in order to emphasize certain qualities, and establish them in us. If we are taken from joy into greater joy, that second joy will not be too much emphasized. But if we are brought from sorrow into greater joy, it becomes greatly impressed upon our life. God certainly knows how to impress us. Often He will reverse the contrast. If He wants to impress upon us a degree of the sorrow His Son experienced, He will bring us into great joy, then plunge us into sorrow. That way, we shall not only learn about the Man of Sorrows, we shall experience some of His sorrow. It will change us. It will equip us to comfort those who sorrow. The contrast of light with darkness will teach us many things and enrich our spiritual life.

When I entered Bible school as a first year student, the Lord was like a bright light to me. His presence was so near and intense that I could neither eat nor sleep on a regular schedule. I loved the light. But after several weeks in that wonderful climate it all lifted, and I found myself in total darkness and dryness. I was impressed. I was terrified. I learned darkness and drought. I learned many things which can be learned only in a wilderness. I learned that God is faithful to me, even in a desert land, and that He could be my light, even in darkness. But the greatest event spanning those two years in the wilderness was the treasure of darkness I gleaned for myself. I came out with a complete trust in God. So complete that it defies description. So complete that I would expect no one to believe its extent. This treasure of perfect trust was worth the two years of darkness.

There are two areas of blessings which relate to the wilderness. One concerns the blessings that are within the wilderness; the other the opportunities for blessings based upon the wilderness itself and our proper responses. The Promised Land was the opportunity for blessings based upon how the children of Israel responded to God in the wilderness.

There was no way the Israelites could get from Egypt to Canaan without going through the wilderness. After the wilderness, a dip into the Land-of-Milk-and-Honey revealed the blessings, "And they came unto the brook of Eshcol, and cut down from thence a branch with one cluster of grapes, and they bare it between two upon a staff; and they brought of the pomegranates, and of the figs. And they went and came to Moses, and to Aaron, and to all the congregation of the children of Israel, unto the wilderness of Paran, to Kadesh; and brought back word unto them, and unto all the congregation, and shewed them the fruit of the land" (Numbers 13:23,26).

A NEW LOOK

We have such an abundance of inheritances and other blessings, that we presently have no idea how many and how great are God's provisions. From the land of plenty and blessings, the wilderness is usually looked upon as an unhealthy and undesirable place. This is particularly true for those who have experienced failure in the wilderness (in their dry times). Indeed, the wilderness is a place of possible failure. This is not the fault of the wilderness, and certainly it is not the fault of God. Nor is failure to be blamed upon the enemy. The failure of a believer in the wilderness is the fault of that particular believer.

Certain saints coming to the wilderness will focus their attention upon its unpleasantnesses to such intensity that they see these unpleasantries magnified many times. The real problem is not the wilderness with its difficulties, but with the self-centered view of the believer. Actually, in most cases the view has been turned self-ward. Thus, it can be clearly understood how some folks create for themselves more unpleasantness than is actually in the picture. Because of a great sense of self-worth and self-preservation, we may consider a situation as very dangerous. If we could turn our vision away from self and focus upon God, our view would change altogether. With this different point of view, we would discover God's purposes. Then, the situation we feared as dangerous would be seen as God's arrangement for the purpose of bringing blessings to us.

If we were suddenly confronted in the wild by a lion, and we had no protection nor defense, we would normally regard that as a dangerous situation. Samson found himself in this very situation. Upon meeting him, the lion roared (Judges 14:5). In the natural, that would be considered dangerous. But if this situation is viewed from God's point of view, the lion does not look like an insurmountable object. The one who intended to defeat and eat Samson became Samson's source of food (honey). In verse 14 we read what Samson said about this, "Out of the eater came forth meat, and out of the strong came forth sweetness." God works desperately to change our point of view in order to impart to us His own faith and strength.

What we see is what we become. The apostle Paul states this in II Corinthians 3:18, "But we all, with open (unveiled) face (our change of view) beholding as in a glass (mirror) the glory of the Lord, are changed (being changed) into the same image from glory to glory, even as by the Spirit of the Lord." Thus, in order for the victory and strength which are in the Lord to become ours, we must look in the right direction.

My family and I encountered dangers while serving as missionaries among the headhunters at the headwaters of the Amazon. One day several children were playing in shallow water when a 15-foot water boa approached them, unseen, swimming under water. A boa of such size is capable of eating a child. A neighbor of the boarding school in Pucalpa, Peru, where our children attended, lost their six-year-old son to a 16-foot water boa.

As the boa swam unnoticed toward the children, an Indian woman came to draw water and saw the snake from her elevated position. She screamed a warning to the children. They all immediately rushed out of the water to safety. No child was permitted to play in the water from that point onward.

After a few days, our four-year-old daughter, Brenda, was playing in a dugout canoe floating in the shallow water, but tied to a small tree stump. Standing on the rear platform of this 18-foot dugout, she lost her balance and fell into the water. This attracted the boa's attention. As Brenda was scrambling out of the water, a domesticated white duck entered the water. The boa was swimming toward Brenda. The duck came between the boa and Brenda. The boa grabbed the doomed duck and disappeared below the water's surface.

With Indian fishing spears we searched for the snake in three or four feet of water. Locating it, the Indians pierced two spears through its scaly skin. The snake immediately released the duck, which popped to the surface quite dead, and coiled himself around bottom grass. We attempted to dislodge him by pulling on the spears. He desperately clung tightly to the grass. We lost one spear, but finally pulled him loose from the grass. With the one spear remaining in his flesh, we hauled him to the surface. But he exerted more strength and was pulling himself loose from the last spear. It was apparent he would escape. Then he would have further opportunity to kill one or more of the children. I sensed that God did not want us defeated in this situation. Therefore, I could not permit the snake's escape. Without any hesitation, I jumped into the water and with my bare hands grabbed the snake by its tail. Danger was no concern of mine. I had a great sense of the power and sufficiency of God. I had no fear.

Seemingly, this 15-foot boa was helpless in my hands. At least he did not attempt to attack me. He did excrete on me; but no matter what he did, I would be the victor. With little effort, I flung him out of the water onto the dry ground where he was easily killed.

HOW BIG IS GOD?

How big are the dangers, the storms, the circumstances in our life? How do we view them? The way these Israelites viewed the wilderness and even the Promised Land, determined defeat for them. If we view things centered upon self, naturally the giants in the Promised Land will be bigger than we. The lion will be stronger. The boa will be insurmountable. And the wilderness will be a situation which will kill us. But if our view focuses upon God, the giants are grasshoppers as compared to the size of God. The lion is weak. The boa is conquerable. The storm cannot destroy. The danger is safe.

In the wilderness, all too often, our vision is sorely limited. We see the lack and the difficulties. God's provisions cannot be seen very clearly, if at all. Many believers do not know that God can provide a table for the needy, even in the wilderness. The provisions and power of God do not determine whether we fail or succeed in our walk with God. His provisions and power are always at hand and without limit. The ability of God to work in and through us is not the determining factor in our failure or success. God is more than able—always.

UPON OUR SHOULDERS

The way we look at things will determine whether we fail or succeed. Does the enemy have enough power to cause defeat in our life? No way!

In the wilderness the children of Israel were fighting the Amalekites. At one moment the Amalekites would be winning. Then, at another moment, there would be a change and the Israelites would be winning. Why? Was it because the power of the enemy was strong at one moment and weak at another moment? No! It was Moses! When he had his hands up, Israel was winning. When his hands dropped, the enemy was winning (Exodus 17:11). It didn't depend upon God. It didn't depend upon the enemy. It depended upon Moses. God has provided all things. Now the question is, "How do we relate to all of God's provisions?" How do we view the overall circumstances of life in light of God's provisions? Do we look at things as centering upon ourselves, or do we look at things as centering upon God?

The Christian in the wilderness should not focus on: (1) himself, (2) the enemy, (3) what God does for him, (4) what God provides for him. The Christian should focus on God Himself. If anything in our life is in focus over and above God, we are out of bounds and in danger. Since all things move out from God, then let us have HIM as our focal point.

ONLY VICTORY

As we follow this advice there will be only victory; there will not be defeat. If we find ourselves in a situation which, in our view, is bigger than God, what shall we do? We shall faint! We shall fall! This very situation is the place to which God has brought us for the sake of greater opportunities in Him. But alas! It becomes our place of failure and defeat. Why? Because God is not our focal point. The fault is not in God. Nor is it in the situation itself. The fault is not in another person; the fault is in us. The failure and defeat are our own doings.

The children of Israel were brought into a situation designed to bring them many blessings. What did they see in it? We are told in Numbers 13:28, "Nevertheless the people be strong that dwell in the land, and the cities are walled, and very great; and moreover we saw the children of Anak there." It seems that they are seeing everything but God. Ten of the twelve spies saw the Promised Land strongly defended by unconquerable enemies. They report back, "The Amalekites dwell in the land of the south: and the Hittites and the Jebusites, and the Amorites, dwell in the mountains: and the Canaanites dwell by the sea, and by the coast of Jordan" (Numbers 13:29).

Where does such an attitude lead? In the case of the report of the ten spies, it dragged others to their level, and led to defeat. "Wow! Did you see that?" "Yes! How terrible!" "What are we going to do?" "I don't know. It looks hopeless." Everything is in the picture but God. The unpleasant situation fills the vision. God is not seen. It reminds me of the disciples counting the loaves of bread, the fish, and the people (John 6:9). But they did not count Jesus. Without HIM there is no answer to the situation.

Even today most Christians believe that the enemies own and rule everything. There is unbelief as to who owns the land. How often do we hear, "The angels of the Lord! Oh, the angels of the Lord are everywhere around us!"? We do not hear that as often as we hear, "Oh, demons are here; demons are there!" According to Scripture, "The angel of the LORD encampeth round about those who fear him, and delivereth them" (Psalm 34:7). There are more angels than demons encamping about us. Some believers have given the earth to Satan and wicked people. At least this is their faith. But it is not according to the Word of God, "The earth is the LORD'S, and the fullness thereof; the world, and they that dwell therein" (Psalm 24:1). Why don't we emphasize that which the Bible emphasizes? Mostly it is because the ungodly emphasis has been carried on and established through many generations.

It is the same story today among many believers as it was among the ten spies searching out Canaan. The ten tell on themselves in Numbers 13:31, "We are not able to go up against the people; for they are stronger than we." The power and might of the enemy which the Bible de-emphasizes are emphasized by so-called believers.

Take a fresh look at the God of Joshua, of Samson, of David, of Elijah, of Daniel, of Paul. Change your point of view if it is incorrect. Look upon the provisions of God. See His care and concern for you, "Open our eyes, O LORD, that we may see." You shall succeed. You shall win. The apostle Paul was certain of this. He wrote, "Thanks be to God, who giveth us the victory through our Lord Jesus Christ" (I Corinthians 15:57).

The youth, David, was certain of victory. He faced Goliath with the words, "You are coming to me depending upon your great stature and strength. I am depending upon God" (I Samuel 17:45). David saw a power and might far above that of Goliath's. King Saul's men of war saw Goliath's strength to be above God's. The ten spies Moses sent out saw the giants of the land to be stronger than God. Both the warriors of Saul and the ten spies were portraying a lie. They could not do otherwise, for that was their vision. They all testified to what they saw. They all were deceived and defeated. David saved the day for Saul's men, but the ten spies caused their families and friends to die in the wilderness, defeated.

The Children of Israel were brought into the Wilderness of Paran for the specific and expressed purpose of going onward to possess the Promised Land. That was the purpose of God. When we are brought into a wilderness by God, we are not brought into that wilderness to be overcome by circumstances. God has no intention of feeding us to wild beasts. He does not bring us into a wilderness to fail by unbelief, or to faint and die from weariness. God does not make the wilderness a part of our lives to defeat and discourage us. He does not bring us into the wilderness to kill us, as some of the Israelites thought concerning themselves. We are brought there to take advantage of the opportunities which God has placed there for us.

WE NEED THIS WAY

The wilderness is a part of our development. It is necessary for our growth. It is God's method for getting His provisions to us. It is that which the Lord uses to bring spiritual enrichment into our lives. It is a means God uses to develop our faith and trust in Him. The wilderness is an essential part of the Christian life, whether we like it or not. He brings us to the wilderness so that we may see His glory moving in this particular unlikely and unpleasant place. Let us look for the glory of God in the wilderness. Let's not look at other things. If we do, we will miss the cloud and the glory. Certainly the difficulties and the giants will be there, but looking at them as insurmountable problems and unconquerable enemies will lead us to defeat. Let us lift our eyes from the ground and look heavenward. Helen H. Lemmel expresses this well in her hymn, "The Heavenly Vision":

> Turn your eyes upon Jesus,
> Look full in His wonderful face;
> And the things of earth will grow strangely dim
> In the light of His glory and grace.

"Turn your eyes upon Jesus." That's the best advice we shall ever receive under any circumstance. Once we have our blessed Lord in proper view, everything else falls into proper perspective. Then the whole realm of Heaven is before us, seen in true value. His glorious person and abundant provisions come into clear and correct focus. We see the victory before it comes. All that we shall ever need is in Him. Come, let us follow our Beloved into the wilderness. There we shall come under His sheltering wings and draw from His endless provisions. There a thousand needs will be met. There we shall behold His wondrous beauty and glory. And from there we shall go into even broader blessings, brighter beauty, and grander glory.

PRAYER

Father, we are grateful to You for your bountiful supplies. Your provisions are more than we will ever use. We ask that You would instill faith within our hearts to believe You, to believe for your provisions; to believe, Lord, that You will meet our hearts in every situation. Oh, that we might believe that You came to the wilderness before we got there! Oh, that we could believe that You are everywhere, that wherever we are, You are there. God, help us to believe it, not with our heads, but with our hearts. Oh, that it might grip us! Oh, that we may live as if we believe that You are in this difficulty, that You are in this circumstance, that You are in this wilderness. Help us to believe that You are really with us. May faith in these truths of the wilderness grip our hearts in such intensity, that we will have a song in the wilderness, in the night, where You are. Amen.

Chapter Two
Discoveries and Beginnings
in the Wilderness of Beersheba

———∞∞∞———

WANDERING

The first biblical reference to the Wilderness of Beersheba is in Genesis 21:14, "And Abraham rose up early in the morning, and took bread, and a bottle of water, and gave it unto Hagar, putting it on her shoulder, and the child, and sent her away: and she departed, and wandered in the wilderness of Beersheba."

The Wilderness of Beersheba relates to the Christian life in many ways. For Hagar, it was a place of wandering. She lost her way. Trying to make it through, she spent her resources. It was not because of disobedience upon her part; that would be another story. She simply did not know where she was or how to find her way out. It was part of her lot in life. It was to be a means of fulfillment. And so it is in the Christian's life. Wandering is the first of many aspects encountered in the Wilderness of Beersheba.

Wandering is the first element to occur in the spiritual wilderness of Christian living. It is designed and arranged by our heavenly Father. The wandering itself is necessary. Its purpose is to bring the believer to the end of his supplies, and into the other benefits found in the wilderness.

The wandering is designed to bring one to the realization of his inadequacies, and that he has no clear and certain direction apart from God. Wandering is worth the trouble if it can bring such revelations. This wandering can relate to the unbeliever. He is without the salvation provided by Christ Jesus, and without an inclination to follow the Lord. But the wandering also relates to the believer, one who has been trusting in the Lord, at least in some areas.

DISCOVERY

The Wilderness of Beersheba is to be a place of discovery, after first being a place of wandering.

Like all wildernesses, the Wilderness of Beersheba is a classroom in which the Lord attempts to teach the wanderer. The first truth to be learned in this classroom is Jeremiah 10:23: "Nor is it in man who walks to direct his steps" (NASB). If we do not discover this truth in the Wilderness of Beersheba, we will not move into the directives of God.

The second truth to be learned is John 15:5, "Without me you can do nothing."

THE FIRST KEY

Between the wandering and the discoveries there are two key aspects. Before the first discovery can be made in your wandering, you will need the first key. The first key to discovery is despair. What an awful key! It is too horrendous and personal to be viewed as a key, let alone used as one. But don't worry. You do not have to recognize despair as a key. God, without your understanding, will still turn the lock on your door of opportunity.

Discoveries cannot be realized if you are supplied with forty heavily laden camels. You have enough food and water, a large and sturdy tent, servants, and gold. All your heart could desire, you have.

Somehow God separates you from your bountiful provisions (if indeed you had them in the first place). You have very little. Please accept this little bottle of water and a few loaves (fist size) of bread. This limited provision (strength) is not going to last for many days. It is not supposed to last long. It is designed only for the purpose of getting you deep into the wilderness. It is not designed to take you through the wilderness. You cannot get out on your low provisions and failing strength. Thus you are allured (tricked?) into traveling into the wilderness, as expressed in Hosea 2:14, "Therefore, behold, I will allure her, and bring her into the wilderness, and speak to her heart."

You are given enough by your heavenly Father to get you into the wilderness. You go into the wilderness on the strength of the provisions given, following the Lord. (He will be there to meet with you.) There in the wilderness your greatest discovery will be the most insignificant in your own eyes. You will discover your own weakness.

Entering the wilderness is done with the strength which one already has. There in the wilderness that strength is spent. Then, when the one who entered the wilderness comes out of the wilderness, she is leaning on her beloved. She has exhausted herself. She has spent the provisions and strength which enabled her to journey into the wilderness. This is necessary; this is what God wants; this is His plan. Therefore God cannot send you into the wilderness with a great supply.

Some refuse the wilderness as part of their Christian living. They miss that which God had planned for them. They were to come out of the wilderness with additions of great riches. God designed to enrich their lives. When the one in the Song of Songs went into the wilderness she was not leaning on her beloved; when she came out, she was, "Who is this coming up from the wilderness, Leaning on her beloved?" (Song of Songs 8:5, NASB). "Leaning on the Beloved" (of invaluable worth) was gained in the wilderness. This picturesque arrangement, as far as the will and the desire of God are concerned, is absolutely essential.

Discovery! Revelation! How wonderful they are! They are so tasty that we consider ourselves as having arrived and eaten the total provisions of God. Actually, after despair, we have just made the very first and foundational discovery. We are just getting started. There will be other discoveries made with the second key.

THE SECOND KEY

After our discovery of our own weakness, the next key comes into the picture. The second key is adjustment. We must adjust to our meager supply. Once we discover that we do not have enough, we must then direct our steps accordingly. This means that we cannot attempt to depend upon our limited supply. Neither should we continually gaze upon its inadequacy. Our direction must be adjusted toward the Lord. Then we discover the wonderful relationship of leaning heavily on Him.

Hagar had no opportunity to lean heavily upon forty camels loaded with supplies. If we have such an opportunity, there likely will be no learning to lean on our Lord. With meager provisions, Hagar soon discovered that she was in a place of need and despair. That is a good discovery. What is surprising about it is that it took Hagar so long to make that discovery. She should have known that her supplies were insufficient before she left Abraham.

I don't think I would have departed from Abraham with a bottle of water and a few loaves of bread. My first experience with the physical wilderness was a short walk into the Wilderness of Judea. We as a family lived at its edge in northern Jerusalem. A friend and I planned to walk an hour into the wilderness. We thought that two hours away from home was not long enough to require provisions. Therefore we took no water. After an hour and a half, thirst and dehydration were so severe in our bodies that we had doubts about making it home alive.

With such an experience in my life, I'd say to Abraham, if I were in Hagar's place, "Hey, what are you trying to pull here? Come across! Consider the wilderness situation." Of course I would spoil God's intentions and plan. Wouldn't we all ruin the ultimate fulfillment which God has in mind if we could always have everything we think we need? If we could have all that we want when we want it, how would the intentions of God be fulfilled?

Hagar did not seem to have good foresight. When it comes to the spiritual life, we also lack foresight. She took that which Abraham offered her, and went with Ishmael into the wilderness. There she wandered. Soon "the water was spent in the bottle, and she cast the child under one of the shrubs. And she went, and sat her down over against him a good way off, as it were a bowshot: for she said, Let me not see the death of the child. And she sat over against him, and lift up her voice, and wept" (Genesis 21:15-16).

DESIGNED LIMITATIONS

Hagar experienced dire need and despair. This was an absolute necessity. The foundation making this experience possible was the meager provisions. With great provisions you may never discover your real need. Hagar needed God more than she needed water, the most essential element of life. This discovery becomes basic to other discoveries and to all that God has for you.

Let us say that you begin your Christian walk with an eight-ounce bottle full of faith. Because of your health and wealth you never need much faith. Then your supplies of health and wealth suddenly vanish. You discover that your faith is not sufficient to carry you through. In desperation you seek the Author of faith. You discover the Fount. You draw from the well. The bottle of faith you carried is forgotten.

Your bottle, full of faith, long-suffering, and grace, does not carry an unending supply. You may experience a situation more difficult than all the others you have previously faced. It drains your bottle, leaving you empty, destitute, and in need. Then you make a discovery: you didn't have as much as you thought you had. Any person can have infinite patience if his patience requires only a little output. So if he has two ounces of patience per day and needs only one ounce per day, he thinks that he has an infinite amount of patience. But let him get into a place where he needs four ounces per day. Then what? Then there's a discovery made, the discovery of weakness and insufficient supply.

You go into the wilderness with your bottle. It contains whatever God's grace and wisdom dictate for that particular time and place. Whatever you have, whatever you move with, will be very limited.

The reason behind the limited supply is your focal point. You focus upon that which God has given you. This must be adjusted. God Himself must become your focal point. Therefore God's unlimited supply must presently be limited.

The Lord sends you with that limited supply. And you go as though you have it all, more than enough to see you through. At least it gets you into the wilderness; the supply has fulfilled its purpose. But it is soon spent. Then you start crying the blues and begin to wonder what's going on. "Why haven't I enough love, why haven't I enough faith?" Your love and faith are spent. You discover that you really did not have all the faith that you thought you had. Now God might be able to bring you to the place of discovery to which the apostle Paul was brought. Listen to him, "I am crucified with Christ: nevertheless I live; yet not I, but Christ liveth in me; and the life which I now live in the flesh I live by the faith of the Son of God" (Galatians 2:20). I think he lost what little faith he had and discovered that his faith was not as great as he judged it to be. Paul discovered that his faith did not hold him as well and as long as the faith of Jesus Christ could. Remember that Jesus said to Peter in Matthew 14:31, "Why is it that your faith endured just a little time?" ("Little faith" is translated from a compound Greek word [*Strong's* number 3640]. It is composed of the word "faith" [*Strong's* 4103] with a prefix which is translated "briefly" as well as "little." The prefix [3641] can carry either thought.)

When your faith comes to the end of its ability to move, as in Peter's case, then of course there's always that faith of which Paul wrote, "the faith of the Son of God." Habakkuk is a tremendous witness to this. He writes, "The just shall live by His faith" (2:4), The same reality which gripped Paul's life also gripped the prophet's life when he found himself in very difficult situations.

Habakkuk refers to one who has much (2:5-6). Of this one he says, "Behold, his soul which is lifted up is not upright in him" (2:4). If man is depending upon his own strength and power, as in this case, that soul is lifted up and is not upright as far as the ways of God are concerned. Thus, there is nothing within that man sufficient enough to carry him very far along in a life pleasing to God.

Man in himself is lacking. His shortcoming is conclusively and straightforwardly expressed by the apostle Paul, "For all have sinned and fall short of the glory of God" (Romans 3:23, NASB).

God has provided for the weakness of man. All the elements needed for man to fulfill God's expectations will be given to him as he turns to God for them. Every need is met in God when man looks to Him as the source in his day-to-day living.

"The just will live by His faith." Man is to unite with God and draw from that source all that he needs. In this way man becomes able to fulfill the tasks and purposes God has in mind for him. The apostle John graphically records this fact:

John 15:4-8 (Amplified)

"Dwell in Me and I will dwell in you. Live in Me and I will live in you. Just as no branch can bear fruit of itself without abiding in (vitally united to) the vine, neither can you bear fruit unless you abide in Me. I am the Vine, you are the branches. Whoever lives in Me and I in him bears much (abundant) fruit. However, apart from Me—cut off from vital union with Me—you can do nothing. If a person does not dwell in Me, he is thrown out as a [broken off] branch and withers. Such branches are gathered up and thrown into the fire and they are burned. If you live in Me—abide vitally united to Me—and My words remain in you and continue to live in your hearts, ask whatever you will and it shall be done for you. When you bear (produce) much fruit, My Father is honored and glorified; and you show and prove yourselves to be true followers of Mine."

We who dwell in Jesus will draw from the Vine; the just shall live by His faith. His faith becomes our faith. His faith is sufficient for all events at all times. He may bring us into situations where our own faith cannot sustain us. We must remember that His faith can sustain us, wherever and in whatever. And with this thought in mind, Habakkuk closes his testimony in the glow of God's faith:

Habakkuk 3:17-19

"Although the fig tree shall not blossom, neither shall fruit be in the vines; the labor of the olive shall fail, and the fields shall yield no food; the flock shall be cut off from the fold, and there shall be no herd in the stalls; yet I will rejoice in the Lord, I will joy in the God of my salvation. The Lord God is my strength, and He will make my feet like hinds' feet [*even though they are not; even though we are coming far short of that*], and He will make me to walk upon my high places." [*He will bring me to the places of His desire, and will give me all that is lacking.*]

Habakkuk comes to the place where he can say, "Well, so what if things around me (my situations) are bad! I'll still trust the Lord to be to me all that I need. And even though things get so bad that there doesn't seem to be a way out, still I'll believe that God will be more than my sufficiency in such circumstances." This is a most precious discovery in time of despair.

41

WHERE IS GOD?

God brought Hagar to the place of need and despair. This situation caused her to make a discovery. It was in her hour of greatest need, when she expected only death. God came through and revealed His sufficiency to her at that place and time of nothingness. There, at that place, then, at that time, Hagar made a discovery.

Hagar could never have made her discovery unless she had become desperate and had cried out in despair. The very place of need and despair was the place where God was. God is at the end of your bottle of water. This is where God hears. This is where God speaks. This is where God is discovered in greater fullness.

Hagar would never have come into these wonderful experiences with God if she had never entered the Wilderness of Beersheba. She never would have known Him as she did apart from her despair in the wilderness.

GOD HEARS

The wilderness is the place where God hears, "And God heard" (Genesis 21:17). It is not necessarily true that Hagar or the lad was crying **unto** the Lord. They certainly were crying. But the Bible does not state that they were praying to God or crying to the Lord. She lifted up her voice and wept due to the fact of her situation.

In the absence of a prayer or cry to God, there is an amazing thing about God. He is aware of our heartaches and tears. Even though we do not take them to Him or express them to Him, yet He is aware.

A girl, a Bible school student, stood in the office of the Bible school she was attending, and at which I taught. She owed most of her tuition for the past quarter. She was informed that she would not be allowed to begin the coming quarter until her past bill was paid. There was no way she could come up with the money. She left in tears, not in prayer, in tears. She was just heartbroken. She went into her bedroom and fell on her bed and wept and wept, not unto the Lord, but simply in her own sorrow. After a little while someone came to her and said that her school bill had been paid. She did not ask God to take care of it. She wept only because she was in distress over her disappointment and inability to continue in school. And God said, "I see those tears; I hear the cry." Even though it may not be addressed to Him, God will look into that situation and move on the basis of what He sees. God's intense care and concern for us are amazing.

In the Bible God moves on behalf of others without an approach being made to Him, without a prayer said. There is the story of the widow of Nain. She was walking along with her only son on the brier, ready to be put into the grave. She wept her heart out, not to God, she just cried because of the situation. Jesus comes along and has compassion and raises her son (Luke 7:11-15). She didn't request that. She didn't ask God to do that.

Likewise God may come to you in your hour of distress, when you are beside yourself. You feel and believe that He is a million miles away. You cannot pray; you just have a good squall. God sees. He hears. He arrives. He has compassion. He meets your need.

He heard a voice, a sound ("voice" and "sound" are from the same Hebrew word [6963]). He heard this sound coming from the Wilderness of Beersheba. Someone's crying! The results of God's hearing the lad were the angel of the Lord speaking to Hagar, and her discovering God. She discovered that God cares for her. The angel said, "Fear not, for God has heard the voice (sound) of the lad where he is" (Genesis 21:17). Don't be afraid; God has heard and has come to take care of you in your distressful situation. Isn't God a nice person? He is very thoughtful of us, more so than we realize.

Isaac went to Beersheba, "And the Lord appeared unto him the same night, and said, 'I am the God of Abraham thy father: fear not, for I am with thee and will bless thee and multiply thy seed for my servant Abraham's sake'" (Genesis 26:23,24).

To Isaac, who went up to Beersheba, God appeared at night. Isaac discovered God, just as Hagar did, in the Wilderness of Beersheba. Watch! Be alert! Be aware! Are you in a wilderness now? Could it be the Wilderness of Beersheba? God is there. He is sitting there beside you as you cry. Your Provision has come.

PLACE OF BEGINNINGS
The nation of Ishmael began in the Wilderness of Beersheba, "Arise, lift up the lad, and hold him in thine hand; for I will make him a great nation" (Genesis 21:18).

That situation did not look like a beginning of a great nation, did it? It did not look like the beginning of a little nation. It did not look like the beginning of a family. There's the mother. There's the lad. No water! No water in the wilderness is death. It looked like the end. But God said, "Oh no, that's not the end; it's just the beginning. I will make him a great nation."

With Abraham the Wilderness of Beersheba was a place of beginnings. There a covenant is instituted and a city founded, "Thus they made a covenant at Beer-sheba; then Abimelech rose up, and Phicol the chief captain of his host, and they returned into the land of the Philistines" (Genesis 21:32). "And Abraham planted a grove in Beer-sheba, and called there on the name of the LORD, the everlasting God" (verse 33). A grove is planted. Others will take advantage of this grove. A city will develop. Beginnings which are blessed by God have longevity. I have visited this very physical place, the city of Beersheba.

Most Christians coming into the Wilderness of Beersheba think that they are going to die. They are not going to die. This wilderness is a place of beginnings, not endings. They don't end their lives in the Wilderness of Beersheba, they experience beginnings. At least they are not supposed to die there. Some people may end their lives there. They could die there because of unbelief. But it is a place of beginnings. It is a place where believers are to find greater degrees of living, a place where treasures are discovered.

LIFE

Discoveries and beginnings are the characteristics of the Wilderness of Beersheba. Life is among the things discovered, which results in new beginnings, "And God opened Hagar's eyes, and she saw a well of water" (Genesis 21:19). In the wilderness a well of water is life. It meant life to Hagar. Life! It is the greatest treasure of man!

Isaac also finds life in the Wilderness of Beersheba, "Now it came about on the same day, that Isaac's servants came in and told him about the well which they had dug, and said to him, 'We have found water.' And he called it Shebah; therefore, the name of the city is Beersheba unto this day" (Genesis 26:32-33, NASB).

Each finds his own well of life. Abraham was at this well before his son Isaac. But it was not passed on to Isaac. Perhaps an enemy had filled it with earth. Or maybe the well Abraham discovered went dry. Whatever happened, it became necessary for Isaac to make his own discovery.

Life can become quite a discovery for one dying in the wilderness. A new beginning! Jesus Christ, the Fountain of life, the Giver of eternal water can be discovered. "The water that I shall give him," Jesus offers in John 4:14, "shall become in him a well of water springing up to eternal life" (NASB).

REST

Isaac came to Beersheba after living in Gerar, a distance of about twenty-two miles. Gerar was the capital of Abimelech, king of the Philistines. Isaac's experience in Gerar was one of strife over wells. When Isaac moved far enough away from Gerar the strife ceased. He finds enlargement in Rehoboth (meaning "room, space"). He has comfort, a large household, and great holdings of cattle. Yet he leaves this area for Beersheba.

A walk with God entails the leaving of comfort, and the making of one's way toward uncertainty. "He leadeth me beside the still waters," is a well-loved passage of Psalm 23. The Hebrew verb ("nahal" [5095] translated "leadeth") indicates more than "to lead." "Nahal" is saying that the Shepherd brings a person from one place of water to another place of water.

"We have found water," Isaac's servants said. God leads a person to that. Appearances may deny that there would be water there. But the Shepherd Who leads and guides knows where there is water. And water is life.

The place of water is also a place of rest. The strife over wells which Isaac experienced in Gerar is over. This rest is reflected in the name "Sheba" which means "seven." From this word comes the Hebrew word "shabat" (sabbath), the day of rest.

Rest is a renewing. This relates to the Wilderness of Beersheba as a place of beginnings. The **New Covenant** is in the picture here. This is enfolded in the name "Sheba," also meaning "oath" (*Strong's* numbers 7650-7652), having to do with repeating an agreement seven times. Abimelech comes to Isaac at Beersheba to make a covenant (Genesis 26:26-31), or to **renew the covenant** which he had made earlier with Abraham (Genesis 21:32).

Abraham discovered water at Beersheba, and that led to a covenant. Isaac discovered water at Beersheba, and that led to a covenant. Hagar discovered water at Beersheba, and that led to a covenant. The covenant made to Hagar contained the adequacies of God, its Maker, and is represented by the well. This replaces Hagar's spent bottle of water, which represents her inadequacy. The truths moving in this story are reflected in the Gospel of John, chapter 4. Jesus met the Samaritan woman at the well. Jesus said to her, "I can give you water and you won't get thirsty any more." In the New Covenant this "well of water springing up into everlasting life" is provided for the "whosoever" in John 3:16. The well in you is provided for your own sake. It flows out from you for the sake of others.

The well replaces Hagar's bottle of water. It replaces, as it did in the life of the Samaritan woman, the coming again and again to those things which temporarily satisfy. The meager supply, the dissatisfying supply, the insufficient supply, is inundated by the Well. The focus is changed from the supply to the Supplier.

A DWELLING PLACE

Ishmael and his mother found a dwelling place in the Wilderness of Beersheba, and later in the Wilderness of Paran, "And God was with the lad; and he grew, and dwelt in the wilderness, and became an archer" (Genesis 21:20).

Why not live in the Wilderness of Beersheba? There's a well of water there. Do you want to leave and go elsewhere? That's a great risk you take, to leave the well on your own initiative, to take your own direction. You have only this bottle. If you go out from this well you most certainly will come into a far worse predicament. Again the water would be spent from the bottle. But here, in this place, you have the Well. You cannot take the well with you. (Some try.) But you can stay with the well. Don't insist that the Shepherd follow you; follow the Shepherd. Stay with the Well.

The Wilderness of Beersheba became for Ishmael a dwelling place. He was brought there. He made the necessary adjustments to that situation which was quite different from the conditions in Abraham's tents. After his experiences (the need, the meager supply, the revelation, the provisions), he made an adjustment. And in this place, a new, strange and desolate place, Ishmael lived under the blessings of God. The second key was used, that is, adjustment was made and further discoveries followed.

You too are able to live in the wilderness. God is there; revelation is there; provision is there. What else do you need? Must you insist upon having a rose garden without thorns? Do you want to set up some other type of situation which is more to your liking? Rather than attempting to change your situation, you change. All that you need is now existing where you are. Do not press forward with your desire to alter your circumstances, believing that your needs will be met through such means. Adjust! Live! Let that place in which you now are, not another place, become for you a dwelling place. Live there until the Shepherd takes you elsewhere.

ENLARGEMENT

The adjustment is made, the dwelling place is found, after severe testings. Abraham underwent a severe test in offering Isaac to God. After this he "returned to his young men, and they arose and went together to Beersheba" (Genesis 22:19). Abraham takes up residence at Beersheba after the test, the trial. It is also after the provision of the ram caught in the thicket (Genesis 22:13). In the case of Ishmael it is after the provision of the well (21:19). After testings and trials, after the discovery of provisions, after adjustment, contentment, and satisfaction, Beersheba is found to be a good dwelling place. It is not so good at first sight that everybody has flocked there. It's not crowded. Those in Beersheba find that they have a lot of elbow room.

Isaac had trouble finding elbow room in other places, "And Isaac's servants digged in the valley, and found there a well of springing water. And the herdmen of Gerar did strive with Isaac's herdmen, saying, The water is ours: and he called the name of the well Esek; because they strove with him. And they digged another well, and strove for that also: and he called the name of it Sitnah. And he removed from there, and digged another well; and for that they strove not: and he called the name of it Rehoboth (enlargement); and he said, For now the LORD hath made room for us, and we shall be fruitful in the land. And he went up from there to Beersheba" (Genesis 26:19-23).

The further removed you are from the striving masses, the roomier life becomes. Isaac moved from Gerar to Beersheba, which became his dwelling place. This, as well as Rehoboth, is a roomy place. There's nobody there who is going to give him a rough time, nobody to say, "Hey! That well is mine!" The strivers don't even know the well is there. I wonder if it has anything to do with the "secret place" of Psalm 91.

There is a lot of room in God. And there is a relationship between roominess and our covenant of life with God. We noted that Beersheba was the place of a covenant between Abraham and Abimelech. And we saw that it was the place of a covenant, so to speak, between God and Ishmael. Also we can sense a covenant between God and Isaac when God met Isaac at Beersheba. The covenants came only after adjustments had been made. The entrance into the New Covenant is the beginning of a new relationship which, in God, is an enlarged place for the believer.

Enlargement is what Israel sought and was promised from the time of their deliverance from Egypt. And Beersheba relates to this enlargement, the inheritance of Israel: "from Dan to Beersheba," the extent of the Promised Land, as far as Israel possessed.

Jacob's abode was at Beersheba. That is where his father and mother lived. The family was there; the present inheritance was there. This was a place of godliness. But "Jacob went out from Beersheba, and went toward Haran" (Genesis 28:10). He goes to a place where he has no inheritance. He leaves the place of the worship of God and he goes out to another place, to a place of idolatry. He leaves the place where his father, Isaac, blessed him with the inheritance.

THE PLACE OF RETURN

Many years later Jacob (Israel) returned to Beersheba, "And Israel took his journey with all that he had, and came to Beersheba, and offered sacrifices unto the God of his father, Isaac" (Genesis 46:1). Back to Beersheba, the place of return, the place of renewal. It was the place of his blessing and inheritance. It was the place Jacob left. But Israel (Jacob's new and God-given name) returned to Beersheba and offered sacrifices unto the God of his father Isaac. And God spoke to Israel, just as He did to the others at the same place. Beersheba is the place of covenant, the place of revelation, the place of inheritance, and the place to which the one who left must return.

Don't leave Beersheba; you will have to return. The process of returning may be costly. It cost Jacob the dearest and nearest to his heart, his wife Rachel (Genesis 35:19). It further cost him great bereavement when he was deprived of his son, Joseph (37:35). Although the path of Jacob in chapter 35 headed in the direction of Beersheba, he did not then arrive. Later, the death of his father caused him to travel yet closer to Beersheba. But not until the news of Joseph's being alive did Jacob finally arrive in Beersheba. It takes some people so long to return. Once there, it becomes a place of renewed dedication to God, and the renewing of God's covenant with the one who has returned.

Beersheba is a place of a return to the altar. Isaac "builded an altar there, and called upon the name of the LORD" (Genesis 26:25). So when Jacob returns to Beersheba he returns to the altar, he returns to the sacrifice, he returns to the place of seeking God (Genesis 46:1). Beersheba is the place of return. May this always be true in our lives when we realize that we are on our own paths, going our own ways. Let us go back to the altar, to our surrender, and do again our first works.

TESTINGS

To get to where God wants His child may be a rough road for some. We are to become willing to go through all that is necessary in order that God can bring us to the places of His choosing. We must become willing to travel with just a meager supply. Jesus said, "Take nothing for the journey, no staff, no bag, no bread, no money, no extra tunic" (Luke 9:3, NIV). God sends us forth to meet our testings. He doesn't send us with so much that the testings become meaningless. He sends us with little enough that the testings are real, and with just enough that we don't die.

When we discover our dire need, what do we do? We probably cry. We do not know how to approach God intelligently. At least at first we don't, and so we cry like little children. But when we

49

stop our crying and adjust, we make our discoveries. We discover that which God wants us to discover. We come out of the testings in His power and with more spiritual riches and greater richness of character.

Hagar cried because she thought that she and her child were going to die. The lad may have been too young to think of death, but he cried for water, the necessary element for his life, "God heard the voice of the lad" (Genesis 21:17). We do not hear of Hagar's having any more children. But in the voice of the lad, God heard the cry of all the children, and children's children, all who would issue from Ishmael. God hears good. He heard the voice of the "bloods" (in the Hebrew text) of Abel (all those who would have issued from him) crying from the ground in Genesis 4:10.

Even for Jesus, the wilderness is a place of testings and discovery; and there He finds a greater degree of living, "Being full of the Holy Ghost, he returned from the Jordan, and was led by the Spirit into the wilderness" (Luke 4:1). Jesus is full of the Holy Ghost, yet He goes into the wilderness. And what does He meet there? His testings; He meets testings! How much power does He have when He goes into the wilderness? Not much, if any. He does not go into the wilderness in the power of the Spirit. The Spirit "drives" Him there (Mark 1:12). He is not going into the wilderness with much supply; He is going for a testing, a real, genuine testing. He is going to get hungry. He is going to feel this thing. It is going to be a temptation, not just a farce acted out by Someone with infinite power. It is going to be a real test, not just a sham or an empty show. It is going to be reality as our Savior is plunged into the depths of feeling distress and agony. Jesus, in all His infirmity of the flesh (Romans 8:3; Hebrews 2:14; 4:15), will feel true temptation. He will be "touched with the **feeling** of our infirmities."

Jesus did not go into the wilderness as the Son of God. No, He did not. Satan addressed Him, "If you are the Son of God, turn these stones into bread." Jesus answered that inference with "man." He said, "Man shall not live by bread alone," not, "The Son of God shall not live by bread alone" (Matthew 4:3-4).

Jesus did not go into the wilderness with a great power to blow Satan away when he made his approach. That is exactly what some of us would like to do. We would like to bowl him over with the power and authority we have. If we had our way, we would destroy Satan, wipe him out of existence, or send him to the Lake of Fire right now. If we were God we would just toss him out of existence and that would be the end of him. Don't be foolish. Don't be foolish. Jesus did not meet him that way. Jesus did not say, "Who do you think you are? I'll blow you over! I'll show you! I'll bind you by my power." No, Satan came to bare down upon the Son of Man in all the aspects of His (Jesus') feelings and desires. Did not Jesus desire glory? Watch how He prayed, "Glorify me with the glory that was mine with You before" (John 17:5). Jesus had that hunger aspect in Him, and Satan bore down upon that hunger. "I'll give you glory. See the glory of these kingdoms? I'll give you all of this," Satan offered (Matthew 4:8-9). There was a hunger in Jesus to come into that which God had provided for Him. That which Satan showed Him of the kingdoms of the world is that which God had provided for Him (Revelation 11:15).

We all hunger for that which God has offered. It is not an illegitimate hunger; it is a legitimate hunger. There in the wilderness Jesus hungered (Matthew 4:2), "If you are hungry, then eat."

"No, I have to live hungry. It's not the time for eating yet. I have to go hungry. This son of man aspect of me must be subjected and touched by means of this meager supply. I cannot come into the fullness of kingship and power and glory."

Jesus feels. He is so weakened by His encounter in the wilderness that angels must come to sustain Him, to minister to Him, to strengthen Him (Matthew 4:11). It so weakens Him. But it strengthens Him. He comes out of that severe testing, not with the meager supply which He had when He entered into it, but with more. He goes into it with a bottle of water. He comes out with a well, "And Jesus returned in the power of the Spirit." The testings end only "when the devil had ended all the temptation" (Luke 4:13). Jesus does not throw the devil into the Lake of Fire. He does not permanently bind him. There is simply a withdrawal for a time, "He departed from him for a season."

But Jesus was triumphant; He destroyed the devil (Hebrews 2:14), as well as his works (I John 3:8). He won the victory in the wilderness, "And Jesus returned in the power of the Spirit."

Jesus did not go into the wilderness in the power of the Spirit. Remember how He went in, "And Jesus being full of the Holy Ghost, returned from Jordan, and was led by the Spirit into the wilderness" (Luke 4:1).

Notice how Jesus came out from the wilderness, and what happened, "And Jesus returned in the power of the Spirit into Galilee: and there went out a fame of him through all the region round about. And he taught in their synagogues, being glorified of all" (verses 14-15).

He did not engage in this ministry before His wilderness experience. This ministry came afterward. First He had to meet his testings, His trials. Peter says, "After you have suffered awhile God will strengthen you, stablish you, make you perfect" (I Peter 5:10).

We are brought into that which Jesus experienced. We enter into that which Hagar entered. There we meet the testings and the trials, and the other difficulties—head on. We walk the way the children of Israel walked, the way of the wilderness. There, as it was with the children of Israel, we meet our trials and testings. We come into situations which are impossible, which threaten our very existence, our very life, and we don't have much strength. We do not have adequate provisions. We discover that we lack.

Why, do you suppose, does God bring us into difficulties? He does this in order to squeeze stuff out of us. Bad attitudes, unbelief, independent self-sufficiency, pride, and such things are to be squeezed out of us. This will make room for Him to put into us the things which He wants us to have.

To have the stuffings squeezed out of us is quite an experience. Just think what our tube of toothpaste goes through every day. Soon there isn't anything left in it, so we throw it away. But God doesn't. He takes the empties and fills them with something better than they had before. He is going to beautify us. He is going to glorify us, and put the radiance of Himself in us, put in us His own beauty, His own grace, His own power, His own glory. Can we see that? Will it become part of our vision? All of His quality goes in when all of self has been squeezed out.

Peter experienced the squeeze and came to realize, "I am not as good as I thought I was" (Mark 14:29-31,68-72; John 21:15-18). Peter had to admit his weakness. That way, he would learn, and come to the purpose which God intended for him. Peter discovered that he lacked. We discover that we lack. But we can lean; we can lean upon our Shepherd. And we can be brought up out of the Wilderness of Beersheba with so much more than we had when we went into it.

Go into the Wilderness of Beersheba, cry your tears, get upset, get uptight, get confused, get all turned around, have a good cry. Don't worry. God will be around before you die. You must make your adjustments. You will make your discoveries. God will give you what He has for you in Beersheba. And that will be quite a prize package!

REMEMBER

The Wilderness of Beersheba is a place of wandering, despair, discoveries, adjustments, beginnings. It is your place of lack and weakness. But you must always remember that it is the place where God hears you. This is where God draws you into a richer life with Him.

In your adjustment, the wilderness becomes your satisfying dwelling place. Do not attempt to leave this place on your own. If you leave the wilderness before God's time, you will only have to return to rebuild the altar and renew your dedication to God. That can be rather costly. Rather pay the lesser cost of obedience; follow Jesus and remain in the will of God.

PRAYER

Our Father, we're so grateful to You for Your love. We're grateful to You for Your manifestations to us, when You come to us in our situations, trials, and circumstances. We thank You that we can see into Your recorded Word by the revelation of the Holy Spirit. You show us what You have set before us, in the path where we walk.

You provide the light which is at our feet. You provide what little light that may shine ahead of us, that we may know the way in which we are walking. We ask You for courage, and we ask for a willing heart to go Your way in order that we may be properly molded by You. Encourage us with a vision of the end results. Encourage us with revelation of the glory, the beauty, and the strength which will be due us at the end of the tests, at the end of the trials. When we face our tribulations and temptations and difficulties, may we face them with You, depending upon You, Lord. Uncover for us the discoveries which we cannot make for ourselves. Reveal to us that which we cannot see by our own efforts. Do in us, Lord, that which we cannot do, for Your eternal glory. Amen.

Chapter Three
Necessary Anchors
in the Wilderness of Etham

―∞∞∞―

The wilderness is part of God's physical creation; it is also part of His divine arrangement as applied to Christian experience. Any critic can relegate these times of dryness, distress, and difficulties in Christian experience to Satan or to disobedience. Human logic can easily arrange Scripture to suit itself. However, the apostle Paul applies the wilderness experiences of Israel to the Christian experience, "Now these things happened to them as an example, and they were written for our instruction" (I Corinthians 10:11, NASB). The entire setting of "these things" which "happened to them" is in the wilderness (verses 1-10). Two significant verses (12 and 13) relate the success of Christian living to understanding, learning, and applying the lessons of the wildernesses.

In the first of these two verses, Paul gives warning to one who is already standing, "Therefore let him who thinks he stands take heed lest he fall" (verse 12). He would of necessity have to be standing in order to fall. The term "thinks he stands" does not refer to one who is deceived in believing that he is standing while he really isn't. He is standing.

To those who are standing in a victorious Christian life, Paul gives warning to pay attention to what he is saying. Many believers learn nothing from the experiences of Israel in the wildernesses. Paul plainly indicates that without this learning there is the possibility, if not the certainty, of falling from victorious living. Understanding and learning from the failures of others bring us into an awareness necessary for the success we desire in our Christian life. Jesus warns us of unawareness in Luke 21:34, "Take heed to yourselves, lest at any time your hearts be overcharged with surfeiting [dissipation], and drunkenness, and cares of this life, and so that day come upon you unawares." Paul echoes this warning in I Thessalonians 5:3 (NASB), "While they are saying, 'Peace and safety!' then destruction will come upon them suddenly like birth pangs upon a woman with child; and they shall not escape." "Suddenly" is from the same Greek word (*Strong's Concordance* number 160) used in Luke 21:34 (translated "unawares"). The meaning is "unawareness."

The second significant verse immediately following Paul's reference to Israel's wilderness experiences is known by memory by most believers, "No temptation has overtaken you but such as is common to man; and God is faithful, who will not allow you to be tempted beyond what you are able; but with the temptation will provide the way of escape also, that you may be able to endure it" (I Corinthians 10:13, NASB). In its context, this verse relates to the experiences of Israel in the wildernesses as related and applied to our Christian walk today. Many believers have failed to recognize and therefore understand the lessons and purposes of the wildernesses. As a result, some of these believers, if not most of them, continually fail in victorious Christian living. It is hoped that this book will aid in preventing failure, and bring those already in failure out of it and into victory.

OUT OF EGYPT

"Out of Egypt" is a term used among believers to indicate a born-again experience and/or deliverance from this present world's philosophies. The believer should remember that once one comes out of Egypt he is headed for the wilderness. As soon as the children of Israel came out of Egypt, "they took their journey from Succoth, and encamped in Etham, in the edge of the wilderness" (Exodus 13:20).

The Israelites left slavery. But they also left pleasant things. Egypt was a pleasant land. It is often referred to in parallel to "pleasures of sin," (Hebrews 11:25). That parallel certainly applies. But there is an opposite parallel of Egypt's lushness, which is a believer's life of great blessing and joy. When God's people left Egypt they left a land of pleasant greenery, a "well-watered land." About 500 years prior to Israel's exodus from Egypt, and prior to Sodom and Gomorrah's destruction, the lushness of the Jordan Valley was compared to Eden-like Egypt, "And Lot lifted up his eyes, and beheld all the plain of Jordan, that it was well watered every where, before the LORD destroyed Sodom and Gomorrah, even as the garden of the LORD, like the land of Egypt, as thou comest unto Zoar" (Genesis 13:10).

EDEN ALWAYS?

A newborn babe in Christ finds that he is in the garden of the LORD, well watered everywhere. His spiritual and physical senses are dramatically touched by the spiritual water and greenery. His spiritual taste buds have experienced the goodness of the Lord. He, in his elation, is totally unaware that he is on his way to the wilderness.

Egypt, to whatever it is likened, is tasty. The children of Israel left the land which produces great-tasting melons. The best watermelon I ever ate was in Egypt. My taste buds still long for that watermelon. The Israelites, once in the wilderness, longed for those melons, along with other foods of flavor, "We remember the fish, which we did eat in Egypt freely; the cucumbers, and the melons, and the leeks, and the onions, and the garlick" (Numbers 11:5).

That which is behind the Israelis and that which is ahead of them are in great contrast to each other. The people leave a land of pleasant greenery. Now they are on their way to a place of stark contrast, a land in which none of their comforts and palatable delights are found. They are on their way to the Wilderness of Etham.

Your beginnings in God are as delightful as the goodies of Egypt. You have the pleasurable sense of God's closeness and His unusual and frequent manifestations of Himself to you. All this is a prelude to your journey to the wilderness, to the land of stark contrast. But you are happily unaware of that which lies before you.

FOUR ANCHORS

Who would ever think that anchors would be needed in the wilderness? There are floods in the wilderness. Flash floods in the wilderness have turned over vehicles and taken human lives. But the floods for which we need anchors are of another kind. We can be drowned in the wilderness by distress, discouragement, and the like.

The need of four particular truths, which I will here refer to as anchors, is not apparent to most who are on their way to the wilderness for the first time. Unawareness was the case as it related to the physical aspect of my first experience with the wilderness of Judea. I planned a two-hour walk. I was not aware that within ninety minutes in the wilderness I would need water. So I took no water, and suffered dehydration for it.

These four truths are very important. These anchors will save you from drowning in despair; they will save you from dying. Less serious, they will spare you many a headache.

The apostle Paul was aboard a ship in a storm when his life was in possible danger from threatening rocks in a shallow sea, "Then fearing lest we should have fallen upon rocks, they cast four anchors out of the stern, and wished for the day" (Acts 27:29).

If we have something which will hold us in difficult times, it becomes a tremendous benefit in our lives—a real lifesaver. Remember that the angel stood beside Paul in the ship that night and said to him, "Fear not, you will appear before Caesar" (verse 24), storm or no storm. By this time the sailors had lost all hope of being saved. "And when neither sun nor stars in many days appeared, and no small tempest lay on us, all hope that we should be saved was then taken away" (verse 20). But the angel gave Paul hope, and he passed it on to others. Yet a danger was feared: "fearing lest we should have fallen upon rocks...."

In our progress into God, in our spiritual journey, there should be a concern about falling upon the rocks, and our making shipwreck of our lives. There are dangers. The child of God faces them daily. This is why the apostle Paul urges us to take heed in I Corinthians 10:12 (referred to in the first paragraphs). We should be concerned when we are standing, concerned enough to take heed to the Word of God, to the things of God, to the Spirit of God, to the leading of God. We should take heed so that we are able to prevent ourselves from falling upon the rocks. Let us avail ourselves of the anchors God has provided for us.

These four anchors from the ship in which Paul traveled kept that vessel from possible destruction during the long and difficult night. They may have saved the lives of those sailors, soldiers, and prisoners who were aboard ship with Paul. They probably enabled

Paul to fulfill the words of the angel to him, to fulfill the will of God. They will certainly do as much for you.

These four anchors I have for you are four truths found in the book of Exodus, and relate to Israel's first trip into the wilderness. These can become the four anchors which you might cast, and which will hold you from being dashed upon the rocks during the lashing storm.

Any storm in your life can last a long time—months or years. God expects you to endure the storm, "Thou therefore endure hardness, as a good soldier of Jesus Christ" (II Timothy 2:3). "Endure afflictions" (II Timothy 4:5). "Blessed is the man that endureth temptation" (James 1:12). "He that endureth to the end shall be saved" (Matthew 10:22). The fours anchors are designed to help you to endure.

The Israelites move out from Egypt. They camp in Etham at the edge of the wilderness. At this point we will begin to pick up the anchors. May the Holy Spirit make them a part of your life.

FIRST ANCHOR

And the LORD went before them.
Exodus 13:21

The first truth in this subject of Etham, the first anchor, is, "And the LORD went before them." On your way to the wilderness it is good to know that the LORD goes before you, not behind you. When the Lord is behind you it seems to indicate that He does not want to be involved in what you are doing.

I was brought by the Lord into an intense and pleasant prayer pattern. The Holy Spirit always flooded it with the Lord's presence and power. The personal joy was so great that three hours in such an atmosphere seemed like merely thirty delightful minutes. It lasted only several short weeks. Then the Lord left it. What a disappointment! I attempted to force its reinstatement by forcing myself to be on my knees daily for long periods of time. But the Lord was no longer interested in continuing this past pattern. He wanted to bring me into another prayer pattern. After some days in my attempt to get the old pattern moving, the Lord came and stood behind me and asked, "What are you doing on your knees?" He certainly did not want to be involved in what I was doing.

"And thine ears shall hear a word behind thee, saying, 'This is the way, walk ye in it,' when ye turn to the right hand, and when ye turn to the left" (Isaiah 30:21). No voice behind you is a good sign. Some believers are distressed over the fact that they never hear from God. Don't be too concerned. In disobedience, out of the will of God, the Word says, "You shall hear." That's true, and that becomes necessary. But what about a walk of obedience? God's speaking may be very infrequent or nonexistent in a walk in His will. Once you are in God's will, there is no need for His speaking unless there is a change in His will. You simply continue to follow in obedience.

He goes before you as you follow in obedience. You have heard Him in directing you. On the other hand, you may not have been conscious of His leading. Something got you going on the right track. You may hear His voice in front of you as you go in obedience. Or you may not hear His voice as you continue on the proper path. Do not be overly concerned about His silence. Rather focus your attention upon the first anchor—He goes before you.

The Lord goes before you. The Lord is there. That's a fact! If He goes in front of you, then He arrives before you arrive. He goes before you. This is a needy and valuable anchor. We should recognize, feeling or no feeling, that the Lord is present, and that He got there before we did. This is a tremendously valuable truth to the person who finds himself in the wilderness.

It would be to your advantage to know (before you wake up and discover that you are in the wilderness) that you are on your way to the wilderness. For if you know that you are on your way to the wilderness, it would help cushion the shock of the wilderness when you do arrive in that land of stark contrast.

Let us suppose that you know that you are (or were) on your way to the wilderness, and that you know the Lord is (or went) before you, also on His way to the wilderness. The conclusion that He steps (or stepped) over into the wilderness before you do (or did) is inescapable. This will be an anchor for your soul. It will hold you in the difficult places. Your Shepherd goes ahead of you. What great comfort!

If the Lord goes before you, He knows the circumstances to which you are coming. He knows every place which you experience in the whole of your lifetime. He has been leading you; He has gone ahead.

I was visiting with and ministering to a group of Navajos in Arizona. There I discovered that they tended sheep. This was usually the women's job, to shepherd the flock. This area near the Grand Canyon is not particularly blessed with beautiful green pastures. One day I followed an aged shepherdess and her sheep. I wondered if that old gal knew what she was doing. I saw no pasture for the flock. But after a couple of hours, we arrived at suitable pasture. As I talked to the shepherdess I found out that she always goes before the sheep. She knows where she is taking the sheep before she takes the sheep there. She had already scouted the area a day or two before. She had already determined the proper place to bring her sheep. Although it might be a little rough getting there, her charges are going to proper pastures.

The Lord is my Shepherd who goes ahead; He knows where He is leading me. He goes there before He begins to lead me there. He walks ahead of me as He leads, "When he puts forth all his own, he goes before them, and the sheep follow him" (John 10:4).

So you have come into the wilderness. This is the barren place between lush pastures. This is the place between the well-watered land and the land of milk and honey.

He allured her into the wilderness (Hosea 2:14). By His wonderful approaches He allured her. He did not lay all His cards on the table. There are hidden factors. She did not know where she was going.

It is His mercy and love for us which keep certain factors hidden from us. If we knew that we were going into the wilderness, chances are that we would balk and turn into another path. But the Lord is clever, and entices us. "Come, come right this way," He seems to indicate. This is the initial invitation; this is the initial leading into the wilderness. Remember that He has already been there. He is always a step or two ahead of us—at least that.

God is with you; He goes before you. I pray that this truth will so come into you that you will know God is with you even though your feelings and your mind say that He is not. May your heavenly Father cause this truth to grip your heart so forcefully that you can live in the reality of it. When you permit Him into your heart with this truth, you will have an anchor that holds your soul as you journey through the wilderness.

In order for truth to be an anchor, it must grip your inner being. It is not to be gathered simply by mentally assenting to it, although that certainly will help. One must remember that truth is not mental gymnastics of some sort. If you are to have faith in the truth, and if you are to gather truth, it will be by the Holy Spirit, by His work and revelation. On your part it will necessitate an ongoing surrender to the ways of God. More and more the truth will grip you. Regardless of the circumstances or the situations in which you find yourself, you will know and live the truth. It will be a sure anchor for your soul.

SECOND ANCHOR

To lead them on the way (NASB).
Exodus 13:21

"The Lord is leading," is the second anchor or truth. He was leading the children of Israel in the way which they should go. This is one of the greatest securities (a most trusted anchor) that you could ever have. To know that you are following in the way which God is leading is of unspeakable value. If you find yourself in a certain place, and you have been obedient to the best of your knowledge, you can have confidence that God has led you there. If you belong to the Lord, you are under His care. "For all who are led by the Spirit of God are sons of God," writes the apostle Paul to the Romans (8:14, Amplified).

The leading of God does not always necessitate the consciousness of it. It is better to get your anchor from the Word of God than from your consciousness or feelings.

When you are brought by God to a place which does not seem to your consciousness or reasoning to be the plan of God, you will need the God-has-been-leading-you anchor. It is the sure Word of

God: "He leadeth me" (Psalm 23:2). His divine arrangement may not look like His leading. But when this second anchor or truth becomes yours, the winds of doubt can blow their fiercest without adversely affecting you.

Do not attempt to lead yourself. He is leading. Do not attempt to go in a direction which you have chosen. Do not of your own prerogative decide that this is the way in which you are going to go. If God gives you the prerogative to choose a direction, that's another story. That's okay. But do not take the prerogative yourself.

You may find yourself in a situation where you **must** make a choice without any awareness of God's leading. If you have been walking in the righteousness of God, the very choice you make will be the leading of God without your being cognizant of it. Your habitual walk in righteousness will simply continue; your decision will be the proper one.

The children of Israel followed the cloud. It was not the way which they chose. It was the way which God chose. If you can follow the leading of God, you put yourself in a great advantage. If, at the same time, you can be truly convinced in your heart that you indeed and in truth are following the leading of God, you put yourself in a greater advantage. This is a tremendous anchor for the soul. It will hold you firmly in dreadful storms. Your anchor will safely hold, regardless of the velocity of the storm. Your anchor holds! Instead of being dashed upon the rocks, you are safely going through the storm. God has led you, and is still leading you. Know it! Believe it! "For He who has compassion on them will lead them, And will guide them to springs of water" (Isaiah 49:10, NASB). God said it. It is His word. It is certain.

When you come to know the Lord as your personal Savior, you come to the One Who is to be your Shepherd. He carries the lambs in His arms. He faithfully shepherds the sheep. This is not an arrangement which accrues only to the one who has been matured in God for twenty years. The leading of God is not for only those who have had long experience in walking with Him. The Shepherd does not shepherd only those who know Him so well that they seem to have no problem in knowing the will of God. Leading is arranged for you at the very beginning of your coming into the relationship to Jesus Christ as Savior, as Shepherd. First, He has led you out of death into life. Certainly from that point you could trust Him to continue leading you in His own paths, along His own ways for your betterment and for your well-being. He led you out from death even before you knew Him. Certainly He can lead you as His child.

Having such an abundance of appropriate passages in the Word of God, you certainly should know that God is leading you through Christ Jesus, your Lord and Savior. When the leading seems so strange that you do not believe it to be His, you still have His Word to assure you. Jeremiah has shared his experience with us, "He [the LORD] hath led me, and brought me into darkness, but not into light" (Lamentations 3:2).

When you come into a difficult area, look back to the fact that you did not move into it on your own prerogative (if that is the case). God led you there. This difficult area seems to be an unreasonable leading of God. It is not unreasonable; it is proper. But you are unaware of its correctness when you open your eyes and see nothing but darkness. It is not necessary that you understand that your present plight of darkness is appropriate. It is only necessary that you understand that the LORD has led you there. You may wonder, "Well! How did I get here? Did I disobey God; did I sin?" No, you got there by obeying God, not by sinning. You arrived there by following the leading of God. That is how you find yourself in the wilderness. How do you think the children of Israel got into the wilderness? Do you think they decided, "Well, let's take a trip to the wilderness?" Oh, no! They did not want to go to the wilderness; they wanted to go to the land flowing with milk and honey. Who wants to go to the wilderness!

The Israelites followed the cloud. The cloud led them, not to the land which flowed with milk and honey, but, to the wilderness. What a bummer! That's the time you need an anchor. If you can understand that God has led you this way, you will have the anchor you need. You do not have to understand why. If you can know that God cares for you, you can trust Him to lead, and you can trust His leadings. You can also believe that you are brought along the paths of His choosing. You can believe that God is still there with you, leading you in spite of the circumstances.

When this truth of God's leading grips you to a sufficient degree and intensity, then, regardless of the situation or storm, your anchor holds. You are secure, held by truth. God has planned truth especially for you. It comes to you, not to slay that which He wants kept alive, but to bring His qualities to your life and preserve them there. Truth has come to you for the purpose of holding you securely in its certainty. Truth comes to you to liberate you from bondage, and to allow you to function freely in God. Regardless of where you find yourself as the result of the leading of God, you can be free from the circumstances. "Even though I walk through the valley of the shadow of death," records Psalm 23:4 (NIV). In the valley of the shadow of death you have certain anchors which hold you fast. Even there you can have certain pillars of faith, certain truths. Truth will hold you steady as you go through a most trying and most difficult place.

THIRD ANCHOR

And the LORD went before them by day
in a pillar of a cloud,
to lead them the way;
and by night in a pillar of fire, to give them light;
to go by day and night.
Exodus 13:21

Anchor number three, a light in darkness, is a very necessary and most comforting anchor. Of all the paintings I have seen of the Israelites crossing the Red Sea, not one portrayed this third anchor or truth. Did you know that they crossed the Red Sea at night? God requires night travel. The children of Israel left Egypt at night. They crossed the Red Sea at night. God expected them to travel at night. You should know this. It is better to know it than not to know it. Some day you are going to wake up in the middle of the night and wonder why you are traveling. Of course, you may not believe that you are traveling. You may simply think that you are wandering aimlessly in a particularly distressful situation. But you are traveling. It is proper to be traveling at night. It would be good to know this before you discover the many difficulties which are related to night travel.

God takes you onward, traveling in the dark. "It is so dark. How can God expect me to see where I am going?" God expects you to travel at night, but not without a light. God expects you to have a light. He does not send you on a night trip without a light. What kind of God would that be? He is not that way. He provided for the Israelites a pillar of fire by night. He led them by day and by night. At night they had a light.

The most difficult point of time is between the plunge into the darkness and the finding of your flashlight. If you could understand that God gives light, then you have your third anchor. God will provide for you a light in your darkness. This is an anchor which will help prevent you from falling upon the rocks. There are some people who do not know that God has provided them a light to walk through darkness. They go stumbling on and stumbling on and falling into all kinds of unpleasant messes, and getting cut and bruised and crying the blues. Why should they be doing that? They have a light available to them. But they do not know that, so they attempt to move and struggle in darkness without realizing that God has provided them a flashlight. They do not believe that there could be a light in their intense darkness. They believe many things which are not true—I have sinned, I have backslidden, God is displeased with me, etc. How readily some believe the suggestions of the Liar, while being so slow to believe the Word of God. But for those who believe the truth, this third anchor is available.

MY ANCHOR

Months before I entered Bible school as a student, and months afterwards, the presence of the Lord was very intense in me. I could neither eat nor sleep on a regular schedule. I did not complain; it was most wonderful. Suddenly the consciousness of God's presence vanished from within my being. I thought I had sinned, or had permanently backslidden. I could not put my finger on any particular point of disobedience, but I knew it had to be there somewhere. Prayer and the Bible were meaningless to me. I was floundering in the dark. God was nowhere to be seen or touched.

I struggled on for weeks attempting to break through my darkness. There was no progress.

I was about to give up. Then one of my teachers, Walter Beuttler, in a Sunday morning chapel service, ministered on "walking by faith, not by feeling." That helped me for another couple of weeks. Still I had no light. The blackness got worse, if indeed that were possible. I became more discouraged. What's the use! There was only one thing to do: quit school.

The plan: attend Sunday morning chapel. Eat dinner. Pack. Attend the Sunday night service. Sleep. Arise at 2 a.m. and quietly carry my stuff to my car and sneak off the grounds and head home.

The plan was executed. I attended morning chapel. Again it was Walter Beuttler who was ministering. He spoke on "waiting for God." Now my plan was slightly modified. Instead of going to dinner, I went to my room. All of the students were in the dining room. I had this opportunity to be alone and to "wait for God." But I had no expectation, not even a glimmer of hope was in my heart. But I thought it wouldn't be right not to give God an opportunity.

I sat at my desk with my arms folded. "Here I am, God," I informed Him. I did not know where He was. I would let Him know where I was. "I suppose You know I'm leaving school early in the morning." I continued, "If there is anything You would like to say before I go, this is Your chance."

God did not keep me waiting long, less than a minute. He spoke words by the Holy Spirit in the pit of my stomach. "Isaiah 43," was all He said. It was as clear as a morning church bell. It was as sharp as a razor. It was as distinct as a full moon on a cloudless dark night.

I had no idea what Isaiah 43 was about, and I was not interested in it. So I said to the Lord, "Lord, I'm in real bad shape. I need something from the New Testament." So I waited for some New Testament reference He might give.

Again, He did not delay; in seconds, He spoke. It was the same clearness, the same sharpness, distinctly enunciated in the pit of my stomach. And it was the same words, "Isaiah 43."

I was slightly disappointed that the Lord did not give me a New Testament reference. But I thought it would not hurt to turn to Isaiah 43 to see what it contained. Since no verse was given to me, I started to read from the first verse:

> But now thus saith the LORD that created thee, O Jacob, and he that formed thee, O Israel, Fear not: for I have redeemed thee, I have called thee by thy name; thou art mine.
>
> When thou passest through the waters, I will be with thee; and through the rivers, they shall not overflow thee: when thou walkest through the fire, thou shalt not be burned; neither shall the flame kindle upon thee.
>
> For I am the LORD thy God, the Holy One of Israel, thy Saviour: I gave Egypt for thy ransom, Ethiopia and Seba for thee. Since thou wast precious in my sight....

Tears so blurred the words that I could read no further. I repented of my distrust and unbelief. My whole plan was blown to bits. I stayed in school. But now I had a light. I was still in darkness, and would be for two years.

Job wrote, "By His light, I walked through darkness" (29:3). God gives us a light. The batteries do not wear out, the bulb does not burn out. It is an ever-ready light, not the Eveready we buy at the store, but an ever-ready light, a truly ever-ready light. I have an Eveready, which is not ever ready. But when you deal with God you deal with a light, which is ever ready, ever ready. And the light is yours, an anchor for your soul.

FOURTH ANCHOR

He took not away the pillar of the cloud by day,
nor the pillar of fire by night, from before the people.
Exodus 13:22

This fourth anchor, this fourth truth, is "He took it not away." It was ever ready. It was ever there, ever ready to serve, ever effective.

God is and will forever be faithful; He does not burn out; He does not grow dim. He is here; He is leading. He provides a light for your darkness, and He does not remove it in mid journey. It does not dispel the darkness; that is not its purpose. But you can walk through darkness with this light.

If this truth of the faithfulness of God (the fact that He does not remove the light) can indeed grip your heart, you have your fourth anchor. God is faithful! Forever! Every moment of the day God is faithful to you. Although the consciousness of His presence may be removed, He, the Light, never leaves you nor forsakes you, "For the Lord himself has said, I will never leave you nor forsake you" (Hebrews 13:5, Lamsa). God is forever faithful, "I will not take it away by day or by night."

This truth does not have its foundation in you; it does not depend upon you. Whether you can feel God or not, whether you can see anything or not, whether you can hear anything or not, will not change this truth. This is an anchor, not because of you, but, in many cases, in spite of you. God declares that He will always be with you, never to leave you nor forsake you. Your sin will not change this. Your unfaithfulness will not change this. "If they break my statutes, and keep not my commandments; Then will I visit their transgression with the rod, and their iniquity with stripes. Nevertheless my lovingkindness will I not utterly take from him, nor suffer my faithfulness to fail" (Psalm 89:31-33). It is true that you may forsake God. It is not true that God forsakes you.

"Yea, though I walk through the valley of the shadow of death, I will fear no evil; for thou art with me; thy rod and thy staff they comfort me. Thou preparest a table before me in the presence of mine enemies" (Psalm 23:4-5). How can He prepare a table before you if He is not there? He is there! You may be so conscious of the enemy that you cannot sense God nor see the prepared table. Your circumstances and difficulties may be so intense and trying, that they push out of you the awareness of God's nearness. You are very sure that God has forsaken you; you just know it! At such a time you need the fourth anchor.

The Word of God is not to be disavowed. The Word of God is true. It does not convey to you false statements and principles. Therefore, when you come up with suggestions from your own heart which are contrary to the Word of God, what are you going to believe, yourself or the Word? The apostle John wrote, "If our heart condemn us, God is greater than our heart, and knoweth all things" (I John 3:20). The Word of God says that God does not condemn you, "For God sent not his Son into the world to condemn the world, but that the world through him might be saved" (John 3:17). Jesus said to the woman taken in adultery, "Neither do I condemn thee: go, and sin no more" (John 8:11).

God is not in the condemning business. Man is. So then, if my heart condemns me, and God does not condemn, who am I going to believe? "God is greater than my heart." That being the case, I will believe God. I will not believe the suggestions which have come from me, nor will I believe any of the suggestions which come from the enemy. I certainly hear the suggestions; I cannot help that. But to anchor my soul in those suggestions is to miss the anchor which God has provided for me—the faithfulness of God.

This fourth anchor, the faithfulness of God, will hold you to such an extent that you can go to sleep in the storm. If you know that God is faithful to you every moment of the day, you can rest in great peace. Your peace and rest can be so complete that the tranquility can give you a guilt complex. Your extreme rest can make you feel guilty. It seems to you that you are not carrying your proper load and fulfilling personal responsibilities. The newness of it all gives your conscience an uncomfortable feeling. You never before realized how "easy" His yoke could be, and how "light" His burden could be (Matthew 11:30).

Do you know where the sea of glass is? It is before the throne (Revelation 4:6). Do you know what the sea of glass is? It is a sea which is smooth; it is never disturbed by waves. You never see a storm on the sea of glass; it is only calm. This condition is before the throne of God. It is not in the world. You can so relate to the rulership and dominion of God, so live in Him, that you will live in tranquility, even though there is a storm. That is not denying the storm. You can have peace in time of war, and you can have war in time of peace. You can be in a storm when everything is calm, or you can be calm when everything is stormy. It all depends upon where you live. It depends upon which is gripping your heart, the storm or the faithfulness of God.

This tremendous truth of the faithfulness of God can carry you through the wilderness. This anchor can hold you steady through the storm. This enlightenment can take you safely through the darkness. Knowing of His care and concern can lift your heavy load and bring you comfort.

HIS UNFAILING FAITHFULNESS

The disciples came to Jesus in the storm and woke Him and said, "Master, carest thou not that we perish?" (Mark 4:38). Don't you care, God? Many times believers have this attitude, which may or may not be expressed. "God, what's the matter? Don't You know what's going on? There is a storm. Don't You care about us? Don't You know we are going to perish?" Tell God; tell God; tell God. Inform Him. He is so ignorant. You don't have to do that. God knows more than you know. If you know anything about the faithfulness of God, you know that the ship is not going to sink.

I was on a missionary trip in Costa Rica which entailed air travel. The Cessna 180, in which I was traveling, held four people and limited luggage. The pilot crammed the luggage compartment until the baggage intruded upon passenger space. In the back seat, built for two, he put three men. In front sat the pilot and a woman who weighed about 250 pounds. The runway was in a bowl, mountains on all sides. The Cessna rolled down the strip straining to its very limits, and yet it wasn't able to get off the ground. As the mountain raced toward us, the pilot broke out in a cold sweat. And was he sweating! I said under my breath, "God, if this plane doesn't go up, You don't go up either," for He was with me. I relaxed. If God was faithful to me right now, He would get this plane off the ground some how, some way. Without a foot to spare it left the ground and banked around dangerously close to the mountain.

Never worry about the faithfulness of God to you. The truth of His faithfulness can be so real to you that it can carry you through very trying and dangerous situations.

From Costa Rica I went to the headwaters of the Amazon in Peru, and ministered for years among the headhunters. I was alone when I met some Indians, three canoes full of them. I knew that they were out to kill someone; I knew by certain signs. There were no women or children with them. All of them had their weapons. All were well painted. I figured that they did not come to kill me, nor to raid the village at which my family and I lived. Otherwise they would have made a sneak attack. I was not disturbed over the situation. I knew the faithfulness of God.

When I went to this particular headhunting tribe for the first time, I went alone, taking no food provisions with me. I discovered that there was some disease which was wiping out that particular group. When I arrived, a dead body was wrapped and suspended on poles above a smoking fire. Some had died before that young man, and some would yet die. Only three Indians were not affected by it. All the others were so affected that they could hardly leave their hammocks. Except for a pot of yuca (cassava) cooked days ago, there was no food to be had. The Indians were unable to hunt and garden; they didn't want food; they were too sick to eat. Therefore, I was hungry my entire week's visit except the day I caught two fish and killed a wild duck.

One day a small boy of about five years of age got out of his hammock to go out into the area of the forest the Indians used for the toilet. But he could not make it, and therefore defecated upon the dirt floor of the hut. Besides ailing with whatever it was which was taking their lives, the boy's stomach was bloated because of worms, and he had dysentery. The dogs began to eat of the feces. The Indians do not feed their dogs anything, due to the belief that doing so would ruin them as hunters. Even scraps from a meal are thrown into the river rather than allowing the dogs to have them. And so they eat almost anything. An Indian woman chased the dogs away from the feces. On the way out of the hut (which has no walls) these dogs got into the cooked cassava. They got about three good mouthfuls before the woman chased them from it. This perhaps reminded the Indian woman that I might be hungry also. So immediately she went to the pot and dipped out some cassava (like mashed potatoes) from where the dogs had been eating. (I don't know how the dogs could make a withdrawal of cassava without making a deposit of human feces which surely was on their whiskers.) The woman handed this stuff to me in a small red clay bowl. I held it up to the Lord and I said, "Lord, do You see this? Do You know what's in it?" I gave Him a minute or two to take in the situation. I then said to Him, "I am going to eat it." And eat it I did. But I knew that He had brought me to those Indians at that time, and in that situation. I knew that God was faithful. I knew it as surely as I knew there was a nose on my face. I knew that God was faithful, and that He was faithful to me—personally to me. I ate it. I did not get sick; I suffered no ill effect, nothing. My anchor holds! "Hallelujah to the Lamb, His child fore'r I am!"

> And it holds, my anchor holds;
> Blow your wildest then, O gale,
> On my bark so small and frail,
> By His grace I shall not fail,
> For my anchor holds, my anchor holds.
> —*W. C. Martin*

The day that the 15-foot water boa constrictor struck at the children in the tribe is covered in detail in chapter one. The instant I jumped into the water to grab the snake with my bare hands I knew that God was faithful. If David could grab a lion, why could I not grab a boa constrictor? The thought of being harmed did not cross my mind. God is faithful to me. Every moment God is faithful. I had absolute confidence in God. I did not hesitate to jump into the water and clamp the fleeing boa in my two hands. Most men, I can say with reasonable certainty, would not plunge into water to grab a large boa without aid. No warrior would face Goliath. Why? Because none knew how faithful God was. But someone came along who had known by experience the truth that God is faithful. This truth was part of David's life. It had lived with him in the field, among his sheep. He would meet the giant through the faithfulness of God, just as he had delivered his sheep from the lion and the bear.

If this truth, the faithfulness of God, can become part of your life, then you can meet any situation at any time and be victorious. God is faithful to you in whatever thing you have to meet and overcome. It presented no problem to me to jump into the water after the boa. I did not think about it; I knew, without thinking, that God was faithful, and that, through Him, I would overcome. I knew it in my life. David knew, and writes, "For by thee I have run through a troop; by my God have I leaped over a wall" (II Samuel 22:30).

Nothing stops you if you know that God is faithful to you at all times. He was and will be and now is faithful. Do not hope that He will be, or that He might be. No, no, no! That is not the anchor to which I am referring. You have to **know** that He is faithful. This becomes the anchor for your soul. This will help you when you come into the wilderness, into the trials, into the testings, into the difficulties, into things you must overcome.

DO YOU HAVE THESE FOUR ANCHORS?

1. The Lord goes ahead of you.
2. Your Shepherd is leading you.
3. You travel at night with a light.
4. God is forever faithful to you.

If you have these four truths, they will be of tremendous benefit to you as you function and live in God's divine arrangements.

DRIVEN

Etham is the place, "at the edge of the wilderness of Etham," where God sees to it that you are overtaken. He is going to see to it that you get pushed into the wilderness. That is one form of His leading. He brings the children of Israel to the edge of the wilderness in order to get them into it, "And they departed from Succoth, and pitched in Etham, which is in the edge of the wilderness" (Numbers 33:6).

Okay, you are right on the edge now. God would just love to give you a little shove, and shove you right into the wilderness. Yes, He would just love to do that. Some will not want to believe that God does that. But I want to show you something which Saint Mark records in his Gospel, chapter 1. If you don't think that God will be pushy at times, you better have a close look at verse 12, "And immediately the Spirit driveth him (Jesus) into the wilderness." Whoof! That is hard; that is very, very hard. It wasn't, "If you please, would you come this way." It was not that. It was a push, "And he was driven into the wilderness."

Even loving Saint John brings out the pushiness of God. Jesus says, "He putteth forth his own sheep," in John 10:4. The Good Shepherd puts forth His sheep. This is a strong Greek verb, a very strong verb. The Greek word means that He thrusts them out. The word ("ekballoo," numbered 1544 by Strong) is also translated "cast out" and is applied to those cast out into outer darkness, to devils, and to ones forcibly being expelled from an area. This is the same word which is translated "driveth" in Mark 1:12. The **Loving** Father, the **Holy** Spirit, the **Good** Shepherd—pushy?

If sheep are not willing to leave the fold, force must be applied. That is very pushy. He does not say, "Now sheep, if you please; will you leave your comfort for the unknown?" No, no, no! He puts them forth. There is a force there.

The children of Israel are on the edge of the wilderness. God would like to give them a push, and push them into the wilderness. Why, do you think, did He bring them to the edge of the wilderness? For the specific purpose of giving them a push. Pharaoh is the one God uses to shove them. God used the Egyptians to drive His children into the wilderness, "But the Egyptians pursued after them, all the horses and chariots of Pharaoh, and his horsemen, and his army, and overtook them encamping by the sea" (Exodus 14:9).

At this particular place, at the edge of the wilderness of Etham, God will see to it that you are overtaken. Yes, **He** will see to that. It is His doing. Look at verse 4 of Exodus 14, "And I will harden Pharaoh's heart, that he shall follow after them [God will do this!]; and I will be honored upon Pharaoh, and upon all his host; that the Egyptians may know that I am the LORD. And they did so [followed after the Israelites]."

There you are, your back to the wall. There is no way out. Well, isn't that just wonderful! What are you going to do? Why not try trusting in God? Did you ever think about that? Why, do you think, is your back to the wall? Do you think that it was just an accidental happening? Oh no! This is divine arrangement. This is ordered of God. This is God's doing.

God gives the Israelites a shove into the wilderness by means of Pharaoh (Exodus 14:10). The Egyptians forced them on their way, "And they departed from before Pi-hahiroth, and passed through the midst of the sea [the crossing of the Red Sea] into the wilderness, and went three days' journey in the wilderness of Etham, and pitched in Marah [bitter]" (Numbers 33:8). Pharaoh executes the shove; God executes the crossing of the Red Sea; and now they are in the wilderness. Now they are on their way to the testings and the refining processes of God. "Oh, I thought that we were going to the Promised Land. God, didn't You make a mistake?" No, no; no mistake was made. God led them, gave them a shove into the wilderness, and they went three days' journey into the wilderness of Etham, following the cloud. There they are at Marah, beginning their testings and the refining processes. They are forced to be subjected to the wilderness, and to all the designs which God had built into it. No longer are they in the comfort and food supply of Egypt. They are now subjected to the wilderness conditions, to all their trials, temptations, and testings.

What are you going to do when you get into the wilderness?

REMEMBER

If you have the four anchors you will meet your trials and testings with success. God is there. He is in the wilderness. He went there ahead of you. Knowing this, having the four points of truth He offers you, you become willing to follow God through the difficult places. You know that "God is faithful, who will not suffer you to be tempted above that ye are able; but will with the temptation also make a way to escape, that ye may be able to bear it." It is given to you to be able to walk through the testings, the difficulties, the trials. You can know that God is faithful, and that He is there. You can know that He will provide a light. You can know that He is leading.

It is very comforting to have God with you in the wilderness.

MUCH MORE AHEAD

The Wilderness of Etham was just the beginning point for the children of Israel. There are other wildernesses which they would experience. The sooner we can adjust and move properly in our first wilderness experience, the sooner we discover its benefits. Then the rest of our wilderness experiences become easier.

There is so very much in the wildernesses. Abundant wealth! Not only is God in the wilderness, but there are many other beneficial factors (in addition to those covered in this book) moving for you and me in the wildernesses.

Do not ever turn away from God Who is in the wilderness. Do not turn away from your testings and your trials. You must meet them squarely, but meet them with God, for He is there with you to cause you to prosper in the wilderness.

Chapter Four
Actions for Victory
in the Wilderness of the Red Sea

———∞∞∞———

"But God led the people about, through the way of the Wilderness of the Red Sea: and the children of Israel went up out of the land of Egypt armed for battle" (Exodus 13:18).

Where are the Wilderness of the Red Sea, the Wilderness of Shur, the Wilderness of Etham, and the Wilderness of Sin? Some of the wildernesses in the experiences of the children of Israel will be located for you on Bible maps, and some will not. There is little profit in seeking the physical and the geographical locations. The Wilderness of Etham and the Wilderness of Shur are believed to be the same location. The pinpointed locations of other wildernesses are simply unknown. The important thing is not the location, but the name and the events associated with the name. This will get us to the core of God's intention: to communicate a message.

As we look first at the name "Red Sea," we discover a meaning which is going to be followed throughout the events. The word "Red" is translated from the Hebrew word "suf" (5486-5492, the numbers of *Strong's Concordance*, cover the use of this word in its various forms). The root meanings are, "to come to an end, to cease, perish, destroy."

The very first time the Red Sea is mentioned in Scripture, the meaning of the Hebrew word is seen in the event which took place, "And the LORD turned a mighty strong west wind, which took away the locusts, and cast them into the Red Sea; there remained not one locust in all the coasts of Egypt" (Exodus 10:19). These destroyers which wasted the land were finally dumped into the Red Sea and destroyed. But the locust is not the last destroyer God dumps into the Red Sea.

The Egyptian army pursued the Israelites. Its intention was not to kill them all. Although casualties could be expected, Egypt's intention was to reenslave them. What would have been destroyed, if Egypt was successful, was God's will for Israel. God delivered His people out of bondage. The enemy pursued.

In Christian living, there are at times an overtaking and a reenslaving by the enemy, "And that because of false brethren unawares brought in, who came in privily to spy out our liberty which we have in Christ Jesus, that they might bring us into bondage" (Galatians 2:4). These false brethren were not successful in their attempt to enslave Paul and his companions. Yet in the case with the Galatians themselves, there was some success. See Galatians 3:1 and 4:9: "O foolish Galatians, who hath bewitched you, that ye should not obey the truth, before whose eyes Jesus Christ hath been evidently set forth, crucified among you? But now, after ye have known God, or rather are known of God, how turn ye again to the weak and beggarly elements, unto which ye desire again to be in bondage?"

The apostle Paul calls upon the Galatians to "Stand fast, therefore, in the liberty wherewith Christ hath made us free, and be not entangled again with the yoke of bondage" (Galatians 5:1). Once we are in this liberty of which Paul speaks, people, places, popularity, pleasures, pride, worldliness, wealth, worry, words, strife, self-seeking, sex, storms, shadows, slop, smoke, snares, spirits (and on and on until the list looks like the roster of a great army, and indeed it is), march against us in an effort to bring us into bondage once again. Our safety and defense are found in obedience to that which God has spoken to us.

THE ENEMY PURSUES; WE WIN

"But the Egyptians pursued after them, all the horses and chariots of Pharaoh, and his horsemen, and his army, and overtook them encamping by the sea, beside Pihahiroth, before Baalzephon. And the LORD said to Moses, 'Lift thou up thy rod, and stretch out thine hand over the sea, and divide it; and the children of

Israel shall go on dry ground through the midst of the sea.' And the Egyptians pursued and went in after them to the midst of the sea, even all Pharaoh's horses, his chariots, and his horsemen. And the LORD said unto Moses, 'Stretch out thine hand over the sea, that the waters may come again upon the Egyptians, upon their chariots, and upon their horsemen.' And Moses stretched forth his hand over the sea, and the sea returned to his strength when the morning appeared; and the Egyptians fled against it; and the LORD overthrew the Egyptians in the midst of the sea" (Exodus 14:9, 16, 23, 26, 27). Obedience brought deliverance.

A young lion roared against Samson. The lion was not saying, "Hello there, Samson. I want to be your friend." The lion did not come to Samson wagging his tail and licking Samson's hand. The lion was going to do Samson damage, if not kill him. But something happens to prevent the lion's fulfillment of intention. The Spirit of the LORD came upon Samson. He tears the lion apart with his bare hands. He returns to the carcass of the lion and finds honey therein. After this he puts forth a riddle, "From the eater there came forth meat."

We are often overtaken by that with which the enemy has designed to kill us, or to bring us into bondage. When we face such a threat, we often tremble with fear, "And when Pharaoh drew nigh, the children of Israel lifted up their eyes, and, behold, the Egyptians marched after them, and they were in great fear" (Exodus 14:10). When being overtaken by the enemy, don't stop halfway in the action of lifting up your eyes. Continue to lift them up, up past the enemy, up into the realm of the LORD of hosts. This will allow you to see the enemy through Samson's eyes. Then you can lick your chops and say, "Here comes my food." For God will take the very thing designed for your harm, and nourish and strengthen you with it. God sees Pharaoh and his army move against His children. "Goody goody," He says, "I can use these to nourish faith in My children."

You do not have to be afraid of the eater, for greater is He Who is in you. You can eat the eater. Actually, this is how God has arranged it. How did the children of Israel get in this confrontation with the army of Egypt? By following God! Yes, it is God's arrangement! He is collecting your enemies to put through His meat grinder in order that you may have a big juicy hamburger. "Thus the LORD saved Israel that day out of the hand of the Egyptians; and Israel saw the Egyptians dead upon the seashore" (Exodus 14:30).

The destroyer was dead, and the ones he meant to capture were very much alive and free. These living ones were walking around looking at the dead ones. God hoped that this would help their vision in the future. Are you going to see the bull goring you, or are you going to see ground meat? Are you going to see the enemy's victory or his defeat? How far up are you going to lift your eyes? God has not designed defeat and death for you. He has designed victory and life for you. He has designed death for the destroyer. This is God's order, His arrangement. We can always move with confidence in God's arrangements. In any situation, in any temptation, in any trial we can look up and see the victory.

The enemies surrounded Elisha and his servant. His servant saw the enemies and feared (II Kings 6:16). But Elisha saw beyond the Syrians to the army of the LORD and its victory. Fear, disturbance, unbelief come from lack of vision. The servant feared; Elisha was undisturbed. These two men had two different visions and two different inner states of being. In the servant's vision, the Syrians were coming to kill them. In Elisha's vision, God had everything under control. Elisha did not say, "Oh me, oh my, what are we going to do?"

That was the servant's testimony (II Kings 6:15). The servant doesn't know what his master knows, due to lack of vision. Elisha was aware of God's provisions; the servant was not. Only Elisha could look in the faces of the Syrians and see the real truth of the matter. Most of us have to wait till the game is over before we know the score. But those with sufficient vision will know the outcome before the game begins.

Before David encounters Goliath, he knows the outcome. Goliath moves to kill David, but David kills him. All of those witnessing this event had no vision, thus, had no prior knowledge of the outcome. How few have vision! Only David saw Goliath as his sandwich. But look, everybody, open your eyes and see, for

God has designed us to be the victors! Can we dare to be a David or a Daniel? We can if we can see.

The enemy has no real advantage. If we live in God, he is up against staggering odds. The enemy is defeated. He plans death, and God works life out from it. The power of God doesn't give him a fighting chance. The real battle, the real contest, is fought within you to determine whether or not you are going to obey and move in the will of God with faith and vision. Samson tore up the lion, and he had nothing in his hands. This is not the difficult part. The difficult part is getting you to go to battle the lion with nothing in your hands.

We must win the battle concerning equipment. We must come to faith and vision which will, like the boy David, lay aside King Saul's armor and take simply that which God will supply. We must come to a place of victory where faith will meet the enemy with nothing but God. First the battle is for your *values*. In what are the power and victory? Is the value in man-made armor, or in God alone? Will the church program hold more value for you than the moving of the Spirit of God? Is your will more valuable than the will of God? God is the greatest!

Once the preliminary battle is fought and won in our own hearts, then we can go with God into any engagement with the enemy and come out winners. "For by thee I have run through a troop; by my God have I leaped over a wall," sings King David in II Samuel 22:30.

The children of Israel were saved from the forces of Pharaoh's army by means of the Red Sea. If there was anything in the hands of the Israelites, they did not use it. They moved in God's arrangement, as did Samson against the lion, as did David against Goliath. They did not move in the methods of man. I hope you can get that straight. They moved in God's divine order where there are methods to use, but the methods differ from one divine arrangement to another.

Because one method worked well in one case, does not mean that it will have success in another case. One method which produced amazing results in one set of circumstances may prove useless in the same circumstances at another time. We need to be saved from fleshly judgment as well as from fleshly methods.

Flesh is the greatest enemy we have. The flesh is more subtle than any other enemy, since it is more closely related to us than any other enemy. We are with it all the time. It is commonplace, and we take it for granted, ignoring its power and danger.

Israel escaped from her enemies; she is alive. This is the result of the leading of God. It is not because Israel did battle with Egypt. "For we wrestle not against flesh and blood," the apostle Paul writes in Ephesians 6:12. Therefore "the weapons of our warfare are not carnal" (II Corinthians 10:4). If, in our preliminary battle in our hearts, we choose carnal wrestling and carnal weapons and methods, we will lose. If such an approach is not corrected, the battles with all enemies will also be lost.

PRESUMPTION IS DANGEROUS! BEWARE!

"Speak unto the children of Israel, that they turn and encamp before Pihahiroth, between Migdol and the sea, over against Baalzephon: before it shall ye encamp by the sea" (Exodus 14:2). Why do the children of Israel camp by the sea? Because God told them to. They did not make the decision. They come to this place and camp due to the leading of their Shepherd. The leading of the Father is in stark contrast to presumption. In a true leading of the Lord there is the benefit which He has planned. In presumption there is danger, from insignificant danger to fatal danger, "And the Egyptians pursued, and went in after them to the midst of the sea, even all Pharaoh's horses, his chariots, and his horsemen" (Exodus 14:23).

The Egyptians presumed. The fatal result is stated in verse 28, "And the waters returned, and covered the chariots, and the horsemen, and all the host of Pharaoh that came into the sea after them; there remained not so much as one of them."

In the Old Testament, "presumption" and its related words are translated from four different Hebrew words meaning "pride, fill, strength, direction." All of these different meanings give us a good idea of what is producing presumption. The Bible mentions presumptuous sins. That must be sins coming out of a life filled with pride, moving in its own direction under its own strength.

Surely there must be a lack of wisdom, if not a complete leaving of the senses, in order to become a presumptuous person. Webster's definition of presumption is, "to take for granted." Taking for granted requires no wisdom or reason. The more one presumes, the greater he jeopardizes his own life.

Spiritual life is greatly jeopardized when the believer presumes to move in his own direction with the excuse that he is trusting God. Or he presumes to reach toward God to receive what he wants with the excuse that he is exercising his faith. Israel makes it through the Red Sea by believing what God has spoken, and then obeying it. Pharaoh's army enters the divided sea, but not by faith, but by presumption. One will make it (by faith); the other will not make it because there is no faith, only presumption.

In a certain Bible school which is no longer in operation, there was a student with sugar diabetes. There was much prayer and fasting for her healing. As time went on and no healing occurred, it seemed necessary to take a drastic step of "faith." She stopped her medication and, along with most of the student body, went to prayer. They intended to pray as long as necessary for her healing. She instructed that if she would go into a coma, no insulin was to be given her. After five hours she went into a coma and others gave her no insulin, but continued to pray and "believe" God. That day the girl died.

In another case of presumption, a man with a serious heart condition was told (after he had been prayed for at the front of the church) that he was healed, and to run to the rear of the church and run back to the front. He ran to the rear of the church, turned to run back to the front, and dropped dead.

Presumption will never bring life, but, in most cases, death. Presumption is birthed out from the flesh. "That which is born of the flesh is flesh," said Jesus in John 3:6. "*That* which is born" (not "who") refers to a thing, a something which comes out of the flesh. And flesh will produce death. The apostle Paul says, "If ye live after the flesh, ye shall die" (Romans 8:13).

Presumption is not all that easy to avoid. This is why King David prays, "Who can understand his errors? Cleanse thou me from secret faults. Keep back thy servant also from presumptuous sins; let them not have dominion over me. Then shall I be upright, and I shall be innocent from the great transgression" (Psalm 19:12-13). Flesh is a very presumptuous fellow. And we are so closely tied to our own flesh that it is very difficult to move and live apart from it. David, in his prayer, leans heavily upon God to help him in this area, and so must we. The Wilderness of the Red Sea is provided to take care of such matters, the sins of the flesh, the flesh's desires. So let us go through the Red Sea.

We may avoid presumptuous sins by not acting, but then we would miss real faith. The basic difference between the births of presumption and faith is that presumption comes out of our own *mind* (perhaps gathered from the Bible or past experience), while faith is birthed in our hearts as the result of a communication from the Holy Spirit.

LEARN WHERE GOD WORKS

Most of your life here on earth will be wilderness if you are going anywhere in God. If you are to survive the wilderness and prosper in it, you will have to learn to live by every word which is proceeding out of the mouth of God. It is the desires of the flesh which cause defeat and death in the wilderness. It is the flesh which murmurs and tempts God in the wilderness. Hopefully we will lose these fleshly enemies in the Red Sea. "But lift thou up thy rod, and stretch out thine hand over the sea, and divide it: and the children of Israel shall go on dry ground through the midst of the sea. And Moses stretched out his hand over the sea; and the LORD caused the sea to go back by a strong east wind all that night, and made the sea dry land, and the waters were divided" (Exodus 14:16,21).

God divided the Red Sea in the night. In the beginning when darkness was upon the face of the deep, the Spirit of God moved in this darkness (Genesis 1:1). He delivered the children of Israel from Egypt at night (Exodus 12:31). We prefer light. When it gets too dark, we cry for some light. We are not content to be with God in His work in the night. It is Pharaoh's army, it is the flesh that cannot see God working at night (Exodus 14:20). If there is to be the work done in us which God wants, we must be brought into the night.

Saul of Tarsus was brought into darkness (Acts 9:9) before he became the great apostle. These believers who see everything, hear everything, and know everything have never entered the darkness of God. And in these there will not be the work done that God desires. The actual crossing of the Red Sea was at night. During the crossing, Exodus 14:24 refers to the "morning watch," which was the last watch of the night or the third watch in those days.

Pharaoh's army is having a hard time pursuing the Israelites because God is making it difficult for them. It is the work of God which will ultimately be the downfall and death of the flesh. And finally, "Moses stretched forth his hand over the sea, and the sea returned to his strength when the morning appeared" (Exodus 14:27). In the light of the morning Israel stood on dry ground, the Red Sea had returned to normal, and the Egyptian army was dead. The division of the Red Sea is no longer manifested, but the results are evident.

The results of God's work at night will always be seen in the morning. There is joy in the camp. There is joy in Heaven and in the heart of the one delivered from the power of darkness. The one who sat in darkness saw a great light. Thus God must work in the dark in the blinded heart in order to set him at liberty in light. Morning appears in this soul, the enemy has been vanquished, and there is great joy.

THE WILDERNESS OF THE RED SEA IS TO DESTROY THE FLESH

When we come into a spiritual wilderness, we come into testings. The reason we come into testings is because there remain in us things of the flesh which are against the spiritual qualities which God wants us to have. If we have these qualities, and there is no longer any flesh set against them, there could be no test, even in the wilderness. Before a test can occur, there must be that element within which can be tested, or touched. For example, if there is nothing in a person to cause him to become angry, then there is nothing on the outside which can stir anger, and therefore there can be no test.

There are two reasons for a test: 1. There is something within which can be tested; 2. There is a need for change. A test is to correct, to teach that which is right, and to establish one in that which is right. Everything which was happening in the lives of the children of Israel in the wildernesses came to try or test them: the coming of Pharaoh's army, the hemming in with no way out, the opening of the Red Sea, Israel's safe passage, and Egypt's drowning.

After the Red Sea parted, Israel faced a test. The question of the bottom's condition would plague them. The unknown factor of such a path would frighten some. What ferocious sea monsters would be waiting to devour them? With Pharaoh's army behind them, they had little choice in the matter of direction. Often this is the only way God has in getting us to go in the right direction.

Even the passage through the Red Sea becomes a test, "The waters were a wall unto them on their right hand, and on their left" (Exodus 14:22). If there was not already in you a perfect trust, how could you peacefully and calmly walk for miles between two walls of water seemingly held up by nothing? Even after God does a miracle for you, the living in that miracle may in itself be a test.

Tests are not designed by God to destroy His children. The children of Israel will not drown nor bog down in the mud. "When you pass through the waters, I will be with you; And through the rivers, they will not overflow you. When you walk through the fire, you will not be scorched, Nor will the flame burn you" (Isaiah 43:2, NASB). Whatever we must go through in our walk with God, there should not be fear, unbelief, disobedience, murmuring, complaining, and other such nonsense. If there is, then the situations become tests.

In our wilderness testings God does not want to lose one soul through death, nor does He want failure in the soul. But both occur. They occur because the soul has made a choice to live in rebellion against the dealings of God. The Father is very wise and careful in His testings in order to prevent loss, "For dill is not threshed with a threshing sledge, Nor is the cartwheel driven over cummin; But dill is beaten out with a rod, and cummin with a club. Grain for bread is crushed, Indeed, he does not continue to thresh it forever. Because the wheel of his cart and his horses eventually damage it. He does not thresh it longer" (Isaiah 28:27-28, NASB). The Lord does not want to lose grain.

And so all these methods are designed to preserve and to bring to usefulness. They are designed to separate the undesirable elements from the grains. Therefore God does not move toward us, nor allow anything to move toward us which will in itself be too much for us and result in our destruction, "No temptation has overtaken you but such as is common to man; and God is faithful, who will not allow you to be tempted beyond what you are able; but with the temptation will provide the way of escape also, that you may be able to endure it" (I Corinthians 10:13, NASB).

The weakness of the flesh seems to be always apparent. The children of Israel did not have sufficient strength in the flesh to combat and overcome Pharaoh's army. The weakness of Israel is evident. On the other hand, Egypt's mighty host (the strongest nation at that time) lacks the might and ability to fight against and overcome the power of God. Thus the weakness of their flesh is very evident. All flesh is weak: mighty flesh, able flesh, proud flesh, religious flesh.

Flesh is corrupt. It dies, "All flesh is grass, and all its goodliness is like the flower of the field. The grass withereth, the flower fadeth" (Isaiah 40:7-8). Flesh is supposed to die. Let it die. God attempts to triumph over flesh, "Then Moses and the sons of Israel sang this song to the LORD, and said, 'I will sing to the LORD, for He is highly exalted; The horse and its rider He has hurled into the sea'" (Exodus 15:1, NASB). The might of flesh is destroyed.

How can the might of flesh surrender to the Almighty? It is very difficult, if not impossible. This is the reason why it must be destroyed, "Pharaoh's chariots and his host hath he cast into the sea; his chosen captains also are drowned in the Red Sea" (Exodus 15:4). Strength and might must drown.

The weakness of the flesh is another story. Weakness surrenders much easier than strength does. And in that surrender the Lord's strength can become what He intends it to be. "My (the Lord's) strength is made perfect in weakness" (II Corinthians 12:9). When mighty flesh cannot surrender, the Lord performs a mercy killing, "He overthrew Pharaoh and his host in the Red Sea: for his mercy endureth for ever" (Psalm 136:15).

EVER-INCREASING FAITH

"By faith they passed through the Red Sea as though they were passing through dry land" (Hebrews 11:29, NASB). Faith is a quality of vast variety. There is a weak faith (but nonetheless faith), and there is a strong faith. There is a self-centered faith, and there is a God-centered faith. There is the faith of a little child, and there is the faith of a father. There is a faith which gathers to one's self, and there is a faith which causes one to abandon all to God. "God hath dealt to every man the measure of faith" (Romans 12:3). This is true on a certain level. There is another level where the opposite is true, "All men have not faith" (II Thessalonians 3:2).

There is faith in every man which is enough to get him started toward God. There is greater faith in only some which allows them to carry and support those who are weak in faith. Whatever may be the variety, or the lack, or the fullness, or the personal distribution of the faith bringing the children of Israel through the Red Sea, the point is that there was a need to develop it further.

The Red Sea experience was designed to strengthen faith. Just seeing the mighty power of God at work should have been sufficient to produce a faith in the children of Israel which would have carried them through all other difficulties. But that was not to be. The Red Sea crossing did not fully develop faith; it did not fully develop a complete trust in God; it did not develop full obedience; it did not drown all the flesh. The flesh will live and rise up in its murmuring and rebellion against the LORD.

The Wilderness of the Red Sea has been designed for us. That is, we are brought into impossible situations and delivered by the power of God. We experience victory out of certain defeat in order that our flesh might perish, and that we might gain a faith and a trust in God which will result in obedience.

I Corinthians 10:1-15 (NASB)

"For I do not want you to be unaware, brethren, that our fathers were all under the cloud, and that all passed through the sea; and all were baptized into Moses in the cloud and in the sea; and all ate the same spiritual food; and all drank the same spiritual drink, for they were drinking from a spiritual rock which followed them; and the rock was Christ. Nevertheless, with most of them God was not well pleased; for they were laid low in the wilderness. Now these things happened as examples for us, that we should not crave evil things, as they also craved. And do not be idolaters, as some of them were; as it is written, 'THE PEOPLE SAT DOWN TO EAT AND DRINK, AND STOOD UP TO PLAY.' Nor let us act immorally, as some of them did, and 23,000 fell in one day. Nor let us try the Lord, as some of them did, and were destroyed by the serpents. Nor grumble, as some of them did, and were destroyed by the destroyer. Now these things happened to them as an example, and they were written for our instruction."

We are given the lessons, but will we learn them? We are called by God to lead victorious lives in Him. The flesh does not bring us into such living. The flesh brings us into fear and concern. But God tries. The refining fire tests, and hopefully separates the dross from the gold.

When the blessings are not falling we become discouraged. All of our testings are blessings. The Wilderness of the Red Sea is a blessing. While we accept all blessings to the flesh, we fuss about blessings to the spirit. When we enter into the Wilderness of the Red Sea we enter into blessings for the spirit, but discomfort for the flesh. If we are willing to lay aside the desires of the flesh in order to follow after the things of the Spirit, God will be able to bring us into the victory He has for us.

Chapter Five
Limitations
in the Wilderness of Shur

—⚬⚬⚬—

The Wilderness of Shur was a very distressful situation for the children of Israel, who just came out of Egyptian bondage. A particularly difficult occasion is clearly expressed in Exodus 15:22, "Then Moses led Israel from the Red Sea, and they went out into the wilderness of Shur; and they went three days in the wilderness and found no water" (NASB). Finding no water is not only distressful; it is also a matter of life or death.

The Hebrew word "shur" means "wall." The situation conveyed by this meaning is "walled up" or "hemmed in" or "shut in." This is the condition of the Wilderness of Shur, and can be true of any wilderness. In Exodus 14:3, it is in reference to the wilderness in general, "For Pharaoh will say of the sons of Israel, 'They are wandering aimlessly (entangled) in the land; the wilderness has shut them in'" (NASB). Pharaoh understood the natural conditions of the wilderness. He understood that the Israelites were pressed into a death-threatening situation. But he did not understand the purposes, work, and provisions of God, which are to be important factors in the wildernesses, even when applied to today's believer.

LIMITATIONS

The walling up brings a severe restriction, or limitation, to the children of Israel. In every wilderness there are restrictions. God brought His people into the Wilderness of Shur and its severely limiting conditions. The Israelites followed divine guidance, the cloud, which appeared in the beginning of their flight out of Egypt and led them (Exodus 13:21). They did not come to this place of limitation because of disobedience and rebellion. God had definite reasons and purposes in bringing them to the Wilderness of Shur. One reason was to press God's people into limitations.

Limitations are needed in order to realize the fulfillments God is seeking in the lives of His chosen people, even the Gentile Christians. People often complain of their personal limitations when they should be thanking God for them. Limitations are of God; they are His provisions. Fulfillment cannot be attained outside of limitation. There is only failure outside of God's confining boundaries. *All* (spiritual and natural) fulfillment takes place inside limitations. Fulfillment is impossible without limitations.

The sooner your heart is gripped with this truth, "Fulfillment is impossible without limitations," the sooner you will find ease in limitations, and move toward the fulfillments God yet has for you. The farmer is not overly distressed because he is saddled with limitations necessary for a harvest. He is not disturbed because he cannot sow his wheat on the highway. He is not frustrated because he must prepare plowed ground in which to sow. He does not tear out his hair because he cannot harvest his wheat in April instead of having to wait until July.

The only way an apple can realize the fulfillment which God intended is to limit itself to the apple tree for as long as is necessary. Like the apple, you may be limited in a certain condition for a short period. Some, perhaps most, limitations are only for a season. These temporary limitations are designed to bring the believer into a richer and more rewarding role.

If we suffer with Christ, we shall rule with Him. Suffering is very restricting, but it is temporary. It serves the purpose of building into the life of the believer the quality of kingship. Those with that quality will rule. Those willing to accept severe limitation will gain the quality. It is like becoming empty in order that you might experience the fullness of God. It is like becoming poor in order that you might experience the richness of God. It is like dying in order that you might live. Limitation can launch you into the unwalled glory of God. Thank your Master for the walls He now provides for you.

If you accept your present walled-up condition, and if that limitation is strictly maintained for its duration, it brings you into abundant areas. Even in a relatively great freedom you will discover that you have been (and will always continue to be) under limitations. The angels who serve God do so under limitations. The angels who fell and now serve Satan were unwilling to continue under the limitations of God. Your ruling with Christ will always be limited to the will of God. The truth that fulfillment is realized only in limitation is an eternal truth.

The young and immature do not readily accept this doctrine of limitation. This was expressed by the children of Israel to Moses in Exodus 14:11-12, "Is it because there were no graves in Egypt that you have taken us away to die in the wilderness? Why have you dealt with us in this way, bringing us out of Egypt? Is this not the word that we spoke to you in Egypt, saying, 'Leave us alone that we may serve the Egyptians'? For it would have been better for us to serve the Egyptians than to die in the wilderness" (NASB). Without spiritual awareness, these people desired the limitations under the Egyptians rather than the limitations under God. It does not matter which way one goes, he will never escape limitations. One may be the slave of sin or the slave of righteousness. One may escape the limitations of sin, but not of righteousness. One may escape the limitations of righteousness, but not of sin.

Romans 6:17-20 (NASB)

> But thanks be to God that though you were slaves to sin, you became obedient from the heart to that form of teaching to which you were committed, and having been freed from sin, you became slaves of righteousness. ...For just as you presented your members as slaves to impurity and to lawlessness, ...so now present your members as slaves to righteousness.... For when you were slaves of sin, you were free in regard to righteousness.

The children of Israel could not properly evaluate the limitations in their bondage to the Egyptians as opposed to the limitations of bondage to God. They were too carnal and immature to recognize value. Some Christians will live their whole lives not knowing values because of permanent immaturity. God cannot communicate higher spiritual values to them. The apostle Paul learned this from experience, and records it in I Corinthians 3:1-2, "And I, brethren, could not speak unto you as unto spiritual, but as unto carnal, even as unto babes in Christ. I have fed you with milk, and not with meat: for hitherto ye were not able to bear it, neither yet now are ye able." The immature, the youth, the babes, the carnal believers cannot eat limitation.

Jesus said to Peter, "When you were young, you went where you wanted to go. But when you become old, another will gird you and carry you where you would not go" (See the Gospel of John 21:18). In his youth Peter was his own man going his own way and even urging Jesus along that way, "And Peter took Him aside and began to rebuke Him, saying, 'God forbid it, Lord! This shall never happen to You'" (Matthew 16:22, NASB). As Jesus walked the path which the needs of men demanded, so would Peter. In the mature believer, man's needs carry him where he might not want to go. But he goes anyway, wanting to fulfill the will of God.

Willingness to take the yoke of limitation is a sign of maturity. The sooner one can take on limitation, the better. This is why Jeremiah writes, "It is good for a man that he should bear the yoke in his youth" (Lamentations 3:27, NASB). Some believers will live for fifty years in childhood. Others will show signs of maturity in five years or less. Lack of maturity is reflected in the murmuring of the children of Israel. They looked at their plight in a childish way, with limited vision and without a proper perspective. As children they were willing to move in a detrimental limitation, under the Egyptians, while refusing to move in a beneficial limitation under God. They saw death, but they could not see life, although the Life followed them through all their wildernesses. They could not see God because their vision was restricted to circumstances. In their childhood they feared personal suffering and limitations.

WITHHOLDING AND GIVING

The children of Israel feared for their very lives. The danger to life was not imagined, but real. People have died in the wilderness. Bishop James Pike went into the wilderness alone and was never seen again. I also took a walk into the wilderness. I planned to be gone one hour, two at the most. In my ignorance I took no water. After an hour and a half, on my way back to the house, I thought I would drop of thirst. The dangers of spiritual wildernesses are as real as those in the physical wildernesses. The children of Israel failed to see the provisions and purposes of God. Today's vision in many believers is not any better than that of the people under Moses.

God provides for life while He seeks a certain death for the Christian. The purpose of God is to bring the individual into a death to self. This is the only way He can bring His fullness of life into that individual. Death is sought. Thus God brought the Israelites to a place where there was no water. They traveled three days into the Wilderness of Shur and still found no water. "This is a death trap!" they screamed. Indeed it is death (the cross) to the carnal man, in order that the spiritual man may find his release in God.

Water is good. It is necessary. What's wrong with having water? Yet God brought His people to no water. Why does God often withhold the good? Because many believers have never seen God as the Good, the only Good. Many believers see that which they want or need as the good. Believers will see that which God provides and does as the good. That which pleasantly affects the believer's life is good. It is impossible for God to fulfill Himself in an individual who has filled himself with these good things. James must have understood this. He writes, "You ask and do not receive, because you ask with wrong motives, so that you may spend it on your pleasures" (James 4:3, NASB). It is often necessary for God to remove everything from a believer in order that *He* may become everything to the believer.

As long as there is water, we do not mind serving God. As long as our carnal nature is pampered with material blessings, we will serve God willingly. As long as God showers us with obvious spiritual blessings, we are zealous to serve Him. We love the water. We love to feel personal pleasure and satisfaction. "As the deer thirsts for the water, so do I." From this animal instinct we determine our direction in life. Many will attend a certain church as long as the pastor feeds their carnal nature. "As long as the blessings of God and the kindness of the people cater to my lower nature, I will be happy to attend your church."

I personally know what this is; I have lived there. Years ago when I was single, away from home and alone, I sought a church whose people would lift my blues, love me, and keep me company. I was not interested in a church in which the Spirit of God moved. I was not interested in having my spiritual needs met. I wanted human arms around my shoulders. I went from church to church. When one church was not friendly toward me, I went to another. Thus I continued my search until I found that which I sought. There at last my lower nature was fed. Yes, God will feed your lower nature. He finally supplied water to the children of Israel. After the attempt to bring them into greater faith and fullness fails, God must provide that which keeps His children alive for the next attempt.

There is one thing you must always remember, whether you are a babe, or dealing with babes. The *needs* of a babe in Christ are one thing, while the *needs* of mature believers are another thing. Do not cut off someone's water supply by withholding your friendship and care. God may provide you to keep him alive. If you, as a mature saint, are dealing with babes, be careful to give them what they need. You must provide them with the grace and pleasantries which they desire. When Jesus was feeding the five thousand, who basically were babes, He said to His disciples, "Cause them to sit down in fifties." Then we read, "For there was much grass in that place" (John 6:10). Provide the babes with grass in order to induce them to sit down for feeding. Grace comes before truth in Christ Jesus (John 1:17). That which is pleasing to the external becomes the forerunner of an inner spiritual work.

I was sustained by those dear people in that church catering to my lower nature. That preserved me and gave God further opportunity with me. How I thank God today for those people and that pastor. Because of them a further work of God was completed in my life. They gave to me on a natural plane in order that God could bring me into spiritual wealth.

God knows whether or not you are mature. He knows what you need at any given time in your life, "Feed me with the food that is my portion" (Proverbs 30:8, NASB). If immaturity is your present condition, remember, you will not starve to death. Eat your portion and pray that you grow.

HIGHER APPETITES

As we mature, this aspect of lower nature appetites will be displaced by higher spiritual appetites. At this point we are able to move above the lower natural desires. Now, after some maturing, when I am ignored at a new church, I do not respond, "I'm not going back to that church again." It's not that I no longer desire attention and friendliness; I do. The fact is that I am no longer a babe dependent upon such feeding, and seeking such satisfaction. Now God is my portion. He is the Good.

In the stage of maturity, external pleasantries and unpleasantries are not our standards of what is good and what is not good. We learn those words of Jesus, "Only God is Good." After this is learned, then everything else is good only in proper relationship to God. The standards of good and not good will no longer be hinged to our personal desires. In our growth into God we bow less and less to our natural assumptions and desires.

As we grow spiritually we cater less and less to our emotional and social structures, and more and more to God and His spiritual arrangements. Emotion, society, desire, and flesh will all be a part of us as long as we live in our mortal bodies. But we must be aware of the dangers in making these things centers in our spiritual walk with God. They are not to become the core of our spiritual life. If they continue to gain in their dominance in the spiritual life, spiritual death will be close on their heels.

No one can avoid the emotional life and displace it with a spiritual life. We all must live in our physical and natural compositions while at the same time living in the spiritual realm and pleasing God. The point is, in which of the two areas, spiritual or natural, do we place the more value? God wants our focus of living to gradually and continually shift from the temporal to the eternal.

In this shifting in our lives, in the changing of our values, in our growth into maturity, if there is no water, we become less and less concerned about it. If someone does not give us a pat on the back when we are needing it, that's all right; we won't worry about it, and we will get along without it. We cannot afford to make that pat on the back the core of our lives for as long as we live. In our maturing we learn to get along without that which we formerly needed.

You are brought into the wilderness to be weaned. God will see to it sooner or later that you are neglected by others. He will bring you to where there is no water. He will withhold that which is good. When this happens, do not let it gnaw at you and eat the spiritual life out of you. Do not make that hurt and disappointment your daily diet. As it is, we have too many Christians running from church to church because of hurt feelings. Do not you do that and add yourself to that great number.

Can you daily remember, "This is the day that the Lord has made; we will be glad and rejoice in it"? The hurt feelings, the neglect, the insults, all make up the day which the Lord has put together *for you*. Do not run away from that which the Lord has made for you. Do not choose your own directions simply upon the basis of your own hurt feelings. Your carnal and emotional feelings are not structured to lead aright along God's pathway. There is a way which seems (feels) right to man, but the end of it is death (Proverbs 14:12, NASB). Instead of reacting according to your emotions, allow the Word and the Spirit to fulfill the functions of divine guidance.

In maturing, we move more and more away from touch and feel, and more into faith. This allows for greater stability in our spiritual walk. We become less and less affected by highs and lows in our lives. And this saying becomes fulfilled in us, "Every valley shall be filled, and every mountain and hill shall be brought low; and the crooked shall be made straight, and the rough ways shall be made smooth" (Luke 3:5).

GOD IS LEADING

In Exodus 15:23 Israel comes to the bitter water. How do they get there? God is leading, and they are following. Do you mean to say that God is leading them into bitterness? That's not a proper place for God to lead anyone! That's what you think! Israel is led into bitterness. The bitterness is not simply the bitter water, but their whole experience. They have been traveling three days without finding water (v. 22). Now they come to this unfit water. And all of this is according to the will of God. Can you imagine that! But that could not be the will of God.

But it is. The only reason, *the only reason* they arrive at the bitter waters is that they are following the cloud. They find themselves with bitter waters only because of the leading of God. Today sinners repent, surrender their lives to God, and dedicate themselves to follow Him. They have a song of victory and joy (Exodus 15:20-21); everything is super good and they are riding high. Then three days later, or three months later (however long it takes), we hear a different song from them. What went wrong? How did I get in this mess? Surely I am backslidden. The causes of the different tune and words are God's leading and their following. Nothing went wrong; they simply followed the cloud.

A friend of mine was asked, "What is the evidence of being filled with the Spirit?" He answered, "Trouble!" Eventually, if we follow our Shepherd, we are brought into bitter experiences. This is okay. Notice Revelation 10:10, "And I took the little book out of the angel's hand, and ate it up; and it was in my mouth sweet as honey (our first days with the Lord): and as soon as I had eaten it, my belly was bitter."

Why did he eat something which was going to cause bitterness? Because the angel told him to do so. Why does John experience bitterness? Because of his obedience. He followed the will of God. Why do we come to such things as this? Because we are following God, and He leads us into them. Why the bitter experiences? They are going to bring to surface bad attitudes and other undesirable traits dwelling deep within us.

"And the people murmured against Moses" (Exodus 15:24). They have the capacity, the audacity, and the willingness to disagree with God. They said to Moses, "Hey, Man! This surely is not the day that the Lord has made. This is your doings! It's your fault we have to face this miserable situation. Blah blah blah, murmur murmur murmur." They are disagreeing with the arrangements which God has made for them for that day. So they murmur against Moses because of their own disagreeing attitudes. God is moving one way; they are moving in another direction. God is saying one thing, and they are disagreeing with it. How could this situation be of God? Look at it!

Look at it with what? Look at it with your carnal eyes and fleshly desires and feelings. Our physical vision will not bring us very far into God and His ways. Why the bitter experiences? Hopefully for the destruction of anti-Christ attitudes, attitudes contrary to the life and person of Jesus. God leads us into situations in which we have the opportunity to see our ugliness and deal with it. He expects us to look, to see, and to understand our contrariness to Him. He expects us to repent and seek the victory which is in Christ Jesus. He wants us to leave our ways, attitudes, and desires which are not pleasing to Him. He wants us to see and to understand His ways and to walk in them. He desires to rid us of our ugliness and beautify our lives with His Son, and increase our faith in Him and in His leadings. He wants to bring our hearts into harmony with His, that we may walk with Him in agreement. He yearns to bring to our hearts a delight in doing His will.

Why the bitter experiences? They are used by God in an attempt to bring us out of unbelief and into perfect trust and rest. Unbelief will do you in. Referring to the children of Israel in the wilderness, the writer of the epistle to the Hebrews, in 3:19, states, "They could not enter in because of unbelief." Their cry in Exodus 15:24, "What shall we drink?" manifests their unbelief. This is a cry of hopelessness. They are expressing their belief that there is nothing to drink and death is certain. They certainly are not believing and resting upon the fact that God can provide water in the wilderness. A bitter experience can reveal your true state to you (and to others).

How many of today's believers can believe and rest upon the truth, "The Lord is my Shepherd, I shall not lack"? There is provision. Often it is not seen. But through a certain bitter experience it will be seen, and hopefully faith will be instilled in the heart.

REVELATION

Even Moses could not see God's provision. But he had sense enough to take the situation to the Lord instead of murmuring about it. In Exodus 15:25, "Then Moses cried out to the LORD, and the LORD showed him a piece of wood. He threw it into the water, and the water became sweet." The main differences between Moses and most of the other Israelites were in attitude and faith.

Because of the faith and proper attitude in Moses, he became the salvation of the children of Israel on many occasions.

God is in the habit of seeking vessels through which He may pour out His mercy and grace upon the less fortunate. To find such a vessel He may overlook its shortcomings, murmurings, and unbelief. He will work these undesirable traits (at least most of them) out of that vessel. Then through that vessel He will be very gracious, not only to those who fall far short of the glory of God, but even to those who resist Him. Thus, in the midst of man's failures God-ward, God bends over backwards to be good to man and to help him. God approaches the ungrateful with His mercy and love.

No man can say that he deserves God's favors. God's goodness should cause man to feel ashamed of his own lack of godliness. But in some there is no shame. Murmuring and unbelief may continue. Yet God repeatedly appears in His goodness and mercy. He comes to us in our failings. That is a marvelous thought! In all this mess in the hearts of the children of Israel God arrives. God comes to their unbelief and murmuring. God comes to the situation of murmuring, and shows Moses a tree. This is God's goodness to the murmurers. This is revelation. God brought needed revelation to the situation in the Wilderness of Shur. He brought to the murmuring and unbelieving people that which they needed. Time after time we see revelation in the wilderness. There is more revelation given in the wilderness than in any other place upon earth.

Through revelation there is provision. The needed tree is revealed (how that speaks of Jesus, the Tree of Life) and becomes the healing element which turns bitterness into sweetness, so much like Jesus. There is healing for bitterness. There is a balm (a small evergreen tree of the myrrh family) in Gilead. How delightful, that God would bring us into bitterness to introduce us to the One who sweetens! There is no better place for this particular revelation. Indeed, it is the only place for such a revelation. And the bitterness in heart is dispelled. Not only was the water of Marah bitter, but bitterness also resided in the ones who were murmuring. For those willing to receive the balm flowing from the throne of grace, their lives can be sweetened. Your embittered life can be made sweet. Isn't that nice?

Have you ever known a person whose life and character reeked of bitterness? Then you do not see him for a number of years. Now you meet again. But instead of bitterness there is sweetness; something drastic has happened. What made such a turnabout? The Tree touched him! Saul, on his way to Damascus, was filled with hate and murder. But on the road the Tree touched his life, and he became another person, the apostle Paul.

"Bitter" is the meaning of the Hebrew word "marah." But it also carries other meanings. Checking number 4784 (marah) in *Strong's Concordance* you will discover that "marah" also means "rebel" and is so translated in its various forms about twenty-five times in the King James Bible. Just as God provides healing for bitterness, there is also healing for rebellion. "Marah" is also translated "provoke." God was provoked by the murmuring and complaining of the children of Israel against His arrangements. But there is healing for this also. A life can be changed from provoking God to pleasing Him. There is healing for unbelief. There is healing for all the inner disturbances and unrest. God desires to come to these conditions with His balm. He wants to come with revelation to reveal His glory and His sweet Son.

This rebellion found in the hearts of the children of Israel was not found in the heart of Moses, nor in Joshua, nor in Caleb. The revelation these three men had of God must have been much fuller and effective than the revelation the others had. Every person following Moses out of Egypt was thrown into the very same experiences in which all the others were involved. Yet we see altogether different responses to the identical experience. The same experience may affect two hearts entirely differently.

EXPOSURE

These experiences in the Wilderness of Shur will bring to the surface different things from different hearts. Here comes a situation and—POP! Something hidden in the heart jumps out for all to see. God has ways of letting the cat out of the bag in front of an audience. That is, He will expose your hidden faults for others to see. The wilderness will bring things to the surface. They murmured—in the hearing of all. He complained—in the ears of others. She found fault—openly. Unbelief is exposed. The cat is out of the bag.

It may have been in the bag for many years. That is, it may have been out of sight, hidden from all, even hidden from self.

Take Moses' sister Miriam for an example. She came through the Red Sea and witnessed God's victory over her enemies. She played her tambourine and sang and danced so wonderfully. She rejoiced and praised the LORD. Later we see what else was in her, later, in the wilderness where revelation can be distressing as well as encouraging. Later we see her as a murmurer, finding fault, setting herself against God's arrangement (Numbers 12:1-10). She didn't pick up these cats two days ago. These faults had been hiding in her for years. They came out of Egypt with her and survived the Red Sea with her. The Red Sea had been designed to kill the cats, that is the flesh (see the chapter on "The Wilderness of the Red Sea"). But cats have nine lives, they say; flesh seems to have just as many, if not more.

Miriam was so beautiful in her playing and singing and dancing. But she wasn't perfect. There were yet things in her heart which God needed to touch and correct. But before correction can be possible, these things must be brought to the surface in order to bring about awareness of need. God must "discover" things in you. He must unearth them, bring them to the surface. He must plow, as He plowed rebellious Israel with the plow of affliction.

Psalm 129:1-3

"Many a time have they afflicted me from my youth, may Israel now say: Many a time have they afflicted me from my youth: yet they have not prevailed against me. The plowers plowed upon my back: they made long their furrows."

Jeremiah 26:18

"Thus saith the LORD of hosts; 'Zion shall be plowed like a field, and Jerusalem shall become heaps, and the mountain of the house as the high places of a forest.'"

THE PLOWERS PLOWED
Psalm 29

The plowers plowed upon my back;
The painful plow struck roots of pride,
Tore loose from darkness hidden faults
Exposing them to eyes of men.

I also saw to my surprise
Ugly things come to light;
I did not know within me hid
So much of death and unbelief.

All of this I give to Him,
In confession of sinful wrong,
With a prayer that He will work
His purpose and pureness in my heart.

—*Charles Haun*

AWARENESS

Your progress in God will only be to the extent of your spiritual awareness. This is not to say that you must be aware of your spiritual progress. Before there can even be an approach made to God there must be some kind of an awareness of His existence, "Anyone who comes to Him must believe that He exists and that He rewards those who earnestly seek Him" (Hebrews 11:6, NIV). After your initial approach, and as you continue to come to God, more awareness is developed in you. You cannot ascend into God beyond your awareness. That does not mean you must be aware of the degree of your ascent. It means that your ascent will be directly affected by your awareness of God's character and ways, and your proper responses to such awareness.

Why is there earnest effort to seek God? Because of an awareness of reward. How does a person move toward Christ for salvation? Not without awareness. There must be an awareness of a particular person who is the Savior, and an awareness of the need to be saved. The Pharisees are a good negative example of this. They were not aware that they were blind. They were not aware that Jesus was the Son of God. The lack of awareness was so great in most of them that they never took the first step toward correction. Miriam was not aware of her own potential for murmuring and complaining when she sang and danced in her joy of victory.

In the absence of awareness of need, our salvation will lie in the fact that we move God-ward. That is, we, having a beginning awareness and a desire for God, retain hope in the face of hopelessness. There was hope for Miriam, even in the face of leprosy. Because of her desire for God, the time came when God exposed her waywardness and dealt with it. God's time to deal with Miriam was not in her victory celebration.

We also will carry many unhealthy tendencies with us through our times of victory. We will be aware only of our victory. Your awareness of one thing may hinder God's attempt to make you aware of another thing. Look at the parable of the sower and watch for awareness in it. In Matthew 13:20 there is a great awareness of joy, "But he that received the seed into stony places, the same is he that heareth the word, and anon with joy receiveth it...." This awareness blocks out the awareness of the need to be rooted deeply in the Word in order to endure tribulation and persecution. Verse 21: "Yet hath he not root in himself, but dureth for a while: for when tribulation or persecution ariseth because of the word, by and by he is offended."

The person in verse 22 is very much aware of his cares in this world and his riches (or lack of them); this choked the Word, and there is no further progression, "He also that received seed among the thorns is he that heareth the word; and the care of this world, and the deceitfulness of riches, choke the word, and he becometh unfruitful."

This same truth can be seen elsewhere. In the days of Noah the people were so intent in their awareness of the natural realm that they were unaware of God's doing:

Matthew 24:38-39

"For as in the days that were before the flood they were eating and drinking, marrying and giving in marriage, until the day that Noah entered into the ark, And knew not until the flood came, and took them all away; so shall also the coming of the Son of man be."

Luke 17:27-29

"They did eat, they drank, they married wives, they were given in marriage, until the day that Noah entered into the ark, and the flood came, and destroyed them all. Likewise also as it was in the days of Lot; they did eat, they drank, they bought, they sold, they planted, they builded; But the same day that Lot went out of Sodom it rained fire and brimstone from heaven, and destroyed them all."

Thus, Jesus warns us that our intensive awareness of this present life will hinder our awareness in the spiritual realm. For many years we may not be aware that we keep a cat or two in the bag, faults hidden away even from our own sight. Because of the extent of our unwillingness and lack of surrender (about which we know nothing in our victory), God cannot get at some of our nasty cats in their bags. But let them alone; in the course of God's work in us, we are brought to places in Him where these cats can be exposed one by one, and dealt with.

The psalmist helps us on our journey. He urges us to meditate day and night on the Word (Psalm 1:2). The apostle Paul also helps us into greater awareness. He urges us to think on the things which are good, honest, and honorable, "And the peace of God, which passeth all understanding, shall keep your hearts and minds through Christ Jesus. Finally, brethren, whatsoever things are true, whatsoever things are honest, whatsoever things are just, whatsoever things are pure, whatsoever things are lovely, whatsoever things are of good report; if there be any virtue, and if there be any praise, think on these things" (Philippians 4:7-8).

We must become more and more aware of the things of God. As our hearts are desiring God, personal awareness of Him comes into the picture more and more. This hope and assurance are expressed in a prayer of Paul's:

Ephesians 1:17-19 (NASB)

"That the God of our Lord Jesus Christ, the Father of glory, may give to you a spirit of wisdom and of revelation in the knowledge of Him. I pray that the eyes of your heart may be enlightened, so that you may know what is the hope of His calling, what are the riches of the glory of His inheritance in the saints, and what is the surpassing greatness of His power toward us who believe."

The extensiveness of awareness for which Paul prays is seen in the above verses. If we are ever to arrive at such a fullness of awareness to which Paul refers, we must first become aware of the waywardness and sin within ourselves. If we really and truly want God above all else, we will take care of personal problems as we become aware of them. God will certainly bring the ones hungry for Him into the higher realm of spiritual awareness and understanding. But He can work toward such heights only in proper conditions of heart, or good soil ("a good and honest heart," in the words of the parable of the sower).

The good seed is sown; this is the Word of God. But it falls into various soil conditions. In some individuals there is no growth at all. In other hearts there is a little growth, but no harvest. In yet others there is a harvest of good ripe fruit. Since good soil is needed for a good harvest, God must work upon the soil to get it in good condition. This is the reason for the plowman, or exposure; the cat must be left out of the bag. Thus, we are brought into the wilderness, like Miriam, in order that God can accomplish His necessary work in our hearts.

HE WILL GET YOUR GOAT

We are brought into the wilderness because it is a very distressing and disturbing place, the very best place for exposure of hidden traits. When I am disturbed because of some circumstance and reacting improperly in it, that should be to me a revelation of incorrectness in my heart. But my heart then should be surrendered to God in order that He might correct it.

The work of God is not going to eliminate outward *reasons* for the inner disturbance, but will eliminate the inner *cause*. If people and conditions "get your goat," do not eliminate the people and conditions, but eliminate the goat. Unhealthy awareness, undue care, and self-centeredness are among the goats God desires to eliminate. Once there is no goat, there can be no disturbance. It is a great help when God shows you your goat; then you can lead it to its slaughter; then there can be the victory God has planned for you.

The wilderness is an ideal place to bring our weaknesses under the light of His judgment in order for us to be brought into victory. For it is the wilderness which will allow us to see personal defects which we could not see in our joy and gladness. The Lord has patience with our shortcomings while we rejoice before Him, "A bruised reed shall he not break, and smoking flax shall he not quench, till he send forth judgment unto victory" (Matthew 12:20). He will not destroy the reed because it is cracked, and thus its notes are out of tune. He is not going to give up on the wick because it is not properly trimmed, and thus gives off smoke. He will bring it all to the light of His judgment. "But when we are judged, we are chastened of the Lord, that we should not be condemned with the world" (I Corinthians 11:32). He will bring the flute into proper tune. He will trim the wick.

How do you know your flute is cracked? When you make a joyful noise unto the Lord, you do not consider it noise. God will hear a cracked flute's off tune, as He did Miriam's. But He will give His attention, for the time being, to the joy in the heart. Later He will deal with the crack in the flute. He will test it in the wilderness. "There (in the wilderness) he proved them," Exodus 15:25. There in the wilderness you will hear your cracked flute produce off-key squeaks. NOW you know your flute is cracked.

Will you turn it over to the Master for repairs? "He can make a perfect heart." Will you surrender to His work? Will you take the yoke of Jesus upon you and learn of Him, of His humility and meekness? Will you walk with Him in order to walk like Him? In our hearts of malice, dishonesty, hatred, bitterness, and unbelief His light shines; there is an unsightly revelation. Do not gaze at the awful revelation and get stuck in your own pitiful condition. Allow the revelation of your pitiful condition to direct your gaze into His glory; beholding His glory you will be changed into the image of Jesus (II Corinthians 3:18).

GOD'S PROMISES

A careful look throughout the Bible will show that most of the work of God is done in the wilderness, that is, at difficult times or in difficult places. Notice also that most of God's promises are given in the same situations. If you want a wealth of promises, go to the hard times of King David, and look among the seventy-three psalms ascribed to him. Or look through the Scriptures dealing with the wildernesses. Here, in the Wilderness of Shur, in Exodus 15:26, we read of one great promise, "If thou wilt diligently hearken to the voice of the LORD thy God, and wilt do that which is right in his sight, and wilt give ear to his commandments, and keep all his statutes, I will put none of these diseases upon thee, which I have brought upon the Egyptians: for I am the LORD that healeth thee." If you want personal promises from God, you may have to go to the wilderness for them.

The promises given under adverse situations are for the purposes of encouraging and directing. The encouragement is in the promise itself. The direction is in the conditions attached to the promise. Most promises are given with certain conditions or requirements, which should help the believer to take proper direction. But in most cases this direction is ignored in favor of the promise itself. Promise boxes should contain cards with the promise on one side and its conditions on the other side. The believer has a tendency to focus upon the promise, as if his mentality has some power to cause that promise to be fulfilled in his life. It will never happen. "Claiming" the promises is found nowhere in the Word, and will not work. Even if you claimed a promise, and it was fulfilled in you, the claiming did not cause the fulfillment. Instead of focusing upon the promises, we should focus upon those conditions which bring the fulfillments. Obedience, in Exodus 15:26, is the condition from which health springs.

Although Moses, in Exodus 15:26, is addressing the entire congregation, he uses a singular pronoun in the second person, "I am the LORD that healeth *thee* (singular)." In the wilderness the disobedient experienced the plagues of God. Notice the words,

"I will put ... upon you" (singular in the Hebrew text). Because of disobedience, all that generation died in the wilderness, except Caleb and Joshua whose state before the Lord was not affected by the disobedience of the majority. While the wilderness meant death to some, it meant life and inheritance to Caleb and Joshua. The wilderness is a place of death for some. But from a place of death, life springs forth for those who meet the conditions of the promise. Except a grain of wheat fall into the ground and die it will not bring forth life. It must meet the condition for life. Life comes out of Jesus' death on the cross. All life comes out of death. The more complete the death, the fuller the life. The apostle Paul testified that he met the condition of life when he said, "I die daily."

Whatever the type of death, it brings with it the limitations mentioned earlier in this chapter. In the spiritual realm, the greater the limitation, the fuller the life. This also applies to fulfillment of promises. The Wilderness of Shur ("Shur" means "wall"— hemmed in) is limitation. Limitation will bring you to fulfillment relating to the promises of God as well as to the purposes He has for your life.

Many are brought to the Wilderness of Shur, to limitations. But not all respond properly to God while in these limitations, and thus some never realize that which God had promised them. But Caleb and Joshua, who "wholly followed the LORD," realized the possession of the Promised Land. Some will fall short of the promises of God due to unbelief (disobedience), while the faith of others will bring the promises to them.

Many fail to realize what God has promised. But God will still deal with a single individual when He cannot accomplish His purpose in the rest of the group. Many are thrown together in the same experiences of bitterness, rough times, or whatever form the testings take. In these group situations God will move and work in your life according to your individual responses to Him, and not according to the responses of the others in the same situation.

GOD'S PROVISIONS

The wilderness situation seems to be left behind in Exodus 15:27 when the children of Israel come to Elim. What a setup! There are twelve wells of water and seventy palm trees. This is a good and pleasant place to camp. But they are still in the wilderness. There are oases in the wilderness. It is not a total waste, totally deprived of provisions. If it were, no one would ever make it through the wilderness. There is much in the wilderness. True, you have the bitter water, but you also have the tree which sweetens. True, you have waterless stretches, but you also have oases. True, you have very rough paths, but you also have the opportunity to develop hinds' feet.

This oasis becomes a refreshing station for the children of Israel. There is an Old Testament word ("nahal" 5095 in *Strong's Concordance*) used ten times and translated with various words. It is found in Psalm 23:2, "He leadeth me beside the still waters." It means "to bring from one refreshing station to another." The purpose of this particular kind of God's leading is to be refreshed, to rest, to be nourished in travel. In the Gospel of John 14:2 Jesus said, "In my Father's household are many mansions."

"Mansions" is transliterated from the old Roman word "mansiones" in the Latin Vulgate Bible (fourth century). These "mansiones" in the Roman empire were inns along the roads in which one could find shelter, rest, food, and other services and supplies. They were built to aid the traveler in his journey. Thus in our journeys God has provided the stations we need. There are many mansions. God doesn't put one gasoline station here, and the next one five hundred miles down the road when your car can go only four hundred miles on its maximum gasoline supply. God is wise enough to properly space the oases in your wilderness. Of course, you may not agree with His wisdom, but it is better than yours.

At your oasis you are refreshed and nourished. Drink deeply, eat heartily; you have many a weary mile to travel before the next watering hole. You are on a journey. You are on your way to the Promised Land. What is the Promised Land, Heaven? No, not Heaven. The Promised Land is the place of battles and conquest. It is a place of your possessions, held in another's power.

In the wilderness the Israelites moved for forty years. In these forty years they encountered in battle about a half dozen kings with their armies. In one year in the conquest of the Promised Land Joshua subdued thirty-one kings. The wilderness is not the place of battle. It is only the training ground. Manna is the training diet. Manna is no diet for battle.

After the wilderness, after the training, the manna ceased; the diet switched to meat. "Prepare victuals ("venison" in the Hebrew, and applied to the flesh of any game animal used as food)," said Joshua (1:11). You cannot go to war on manna. You must go on a fighting diet. All the provisions and diet in the wilderness are in preparation for the time when you will gear up for battle and possession.

In your walk with God, He will prepare you for greater things. So do not ever disagree with Him, no matter when He leads you. Watch out for the bitter waters. Be careful when you encounter dryness. If you discover you have a complaining heart, surrender it to Him for repairs. Walk softly and tenderly before the Lord in the wilderness. You are in the wilderness for specific purposes. Be more concerned about the purposes than you are about the wilderness. God will take care of you very well, wherever you may be. Cast all your care upon the One who cares for you (I Peter 5:7, "Casting all your care upon him; for he careth for you").

Even in the wilderness His love and care are ever with you, though most of the time unseen and not felt. But in His manifestations in the wilderness, you will see and know Him in a way which cannot be accomplished in any other place. So learn well in the wilderness. There are lessons taught there which are taught nowhere else. Do not seek to learn that which He is not teaching you. But concentrate upon that which He is showing you, and learn it well. It will pay big dividends tomorrow. Rest in Him, relax in faith, and let Him do his work in you in the wilderness.

Chapter Six
Moving Forward
in the Wilderness of Kedemoth

—⚬≈⚬—

This particular wilderness is a wilderness where the focus is on progression. Forward progression is to be the characteristic of the child of God in the Wilderness of Kedemoth. Progression should be present in the believer's life in whatever wilderness or other place he is found. Kedemoth simply brings progression into the spotlight. The Hebrew word "kedemoth" means "to go forward" or "to go eastward." It also means "beginning," but in relationship to past time rather than a future beginning.

Yet another meaning is "to comfort," whether referring to a friend or an enemy. A trace of this meaning colors Deuteronomy 2:26, "And I sent messengers out of the wilderness of Kedemoth unto Sihon king of Heshbon with words of peace."

REST IN PEACE

There was a peaceful relationship Israel had with the descendants of Esau and with the Moabites. These people helped the Israelites. This same peace and help is requested at Heshbon. Moses does not instigate antagonism; he does not send a well-equipped army. His message to the king is not, "Like it or not, we are marching through your land." Moses' message is "words of peace." This is a peaceful confrontation. The request from Moses is, "Let me pass through your land; I will travel only on the highway; I will not turn aside to the right or to the left. You will sell me food for money so that I may eat, and give me water for money so that I may drink, only let me pass through on foot, just as the sons of Esau who live in Seir and the Moabites who live in Ar did for me, until I cross over the Jordan into the land which the LORD our God is giving to us" (Deuteronomy 2:27-29, NASB).

Moses is moving forward. The meaning "forward" also colors the Deuteronomy 2:26 text quoted on page 115. The direction is forward, being from the wilderness to the Promised Land. The direction is also eastward (due eastward if the Israelites' camp was at the northern end of the Wilderness of Kedemoth).

There was one objective before Moses, even before leaving Egypt: the Promised Land. He wanted to move toward it in peace. When he first approached the Pharaoh of Egypt, he came to him in peace with the request, "Let my people go." No fuss, no muss, just a simple nonbelligerent request.

The believer's forward progress should always be characterized with peace. Always! There are believers who are, in spirit, antagonistic. This type of spirit is often demonstrated through public prayer in some churches. It seems that there are quite a number of believers living with an antagonistic spirit against a spiritual enemy. The reason for this, in most cases, if not in all cases, is that the believer himself has strife characterizing his life. If you do not believe this, watch such believers at home and on the job. Even in church in prayer at the "altar" you can witness some striving with unbelief. Have you ever seen them strive? I have. "Lord, I believe, I believe. O God, I believe, I believe." On and on some go with this, striving with their lack of faith. Have you? If only our dear, beloved, striving brother realized how much such striving hinders, what a difference it would make in his life. If he could only know what he should be doing instead of striving, he could walk God's way more perfectly.

Rest and Peace should characterize the believer's life. Your approach to God and your forward progression into faith, or into whatever, are to be without that strife in your heart. Your heart should be a heart without antagonism. It should be without that great effort of thrust which threatens to force everything out of the way.

DON'T BE PUSHY

A pushy spirit is sometimes manifested by a preacher ministering the Word. I have seen young preachers ministering a pushy spirit instead of "ministering the Spirit," as the apostle Paul mentions in Galatians 3:5. They are wanting to thrust something upon you by force. They cannot rest in the Spirit's work. They are sincerely desirous and anxious that you receive it, and they are furiously attempting to get it in you. But that is not God's way.

Let us join these messengers of Moses to appear before the king of Heshbon. Just wait till we see this heathen king. If he doesn't receive our message and honor our request, bless God, we'll pound him into the ground.

But that is not our joining the messengers of Moses. To really join them, we must be as they are. We must come to this king in and with peace, not simply with words of peace which may be covering up a striving heart. We are not supposed to be like those who say with their mouths, "I forgive," but never have such worthy words in their hearts. Don't put up a front. Your forward progression in God will depend upon a "frontless" life. It will do you ill to live a life in a disguise. This habit will eventually bring you before God in a disguise. You will wear your disguise when you read the Bible and when you pray.

Disguises are fabricated for self-preservation and personal gain. Quit catering to the self-life. Leave off your disguises. Let God into your weakness, your ugliness, your short temper. His strength and work of grace are waiting and ready for you. Let Him provide that which you need.

Once you make the discovery of His work of grace (the rest, peace, and the ease of which Jesus speaks in Matthew 11:29-30), His qualities will begin to become part of your character. They will become your true character.

You don't even have to be antagonistic against the devil. That, in most cases, is simply a cover-up for spiritual weakness and lack of confidence, faith, authority, and power. Satan knows what that type of a person is doing better than the person himself knows. The enemy is not frightened by such threats.

In a summer camp meeting a twenty-year-young man was walking back and forth on the seat of the front bench while the preacher was preaching from the platform. The Lord spoke to this preacher, who was small in stature, "Go down there and cast that demon out of that fellow." So the preacher stopped preaching, left the platform, went over to the youth, and with a wee voice, without antagonism, said, "I cast you out in Jesus' name." Immediately that demon-possessed person fell in the straw, gathered himself up, and sat quietly on the bench, completely and forever delivered. Complete victory! No striving!

HUMAN ENERGY

Many times there is displayed by believers a greatly intense and lengthy struggle with satanic forces. It is almost as if the expenditure of huge amounts of human energy is necessary to get the job done. The casting out of demons is not through human energy or human antagonism. Faith does not need these items. They do not fool the enemy. With true authority and power one word can defeat him. A struggle upon your part will not defeat him. Prayer and fasting will not defeat him (it will nurture faith). With a true word the enemy is given no choice. There is no reason to argue with him. The saints are in a conflict. "We wrestle" (Ephesians 6:12). Our enemy may be mighty, mighty as compared to us. But he is nothing as compared to God. When the power of God is involved, there is no contest with the enemy; God wins, hands down. There is no possible way to defeat and overcome God.

In any battle, and in any conflict, I am on His side. I can rest in that, and in the battle I can have God's character in me: rest, peace, faith, love. I can do without antagonism.

The one who has learned to cease from his own labor can rest in God. He has no task to accomplish. It is God's task and He is at work. We are to join Him, working at His tasks with His character filling our being. Jesus said, "I have completed the task which You gave me to do," in John 17:4 (Phillips). The task came from the Father. It was not the work of Jesus, but the work of God. If we are involved in what God is involved in, then the victory is guaranteed.

DON'T BE CONTENTIOUS

A contentious man will be contentious. Avoid this plane of life. The apostle Paul wrote, "But avoid foolish questions, and genealogies, and contentions, and strivings about the law; for they are unprofitable and vain" (Titus 3:9).

Your life is not to take root in such characteristics and find its activities there. Your life is not to be motivated by that which you want to accomplish, but by God. At all costs avoid antagonism and contention, which are most costly to life.

The contentious heart is made manifest toward the enemy, toward a brother, and in the verse in Titus quoted above, toward God's Word. Believers argue and contend over the Word. Contention jumps out of the contentious heart in almost every circumstance and situation. Believers reveal their hearts to others. They are "known and read of all men." That which is characteristically manifested in one area is generally moving in the whole of that person's life.

Jesus said that if one is unjust in a small thing, he will be unjust in greater matters (Luke 16:10). The truth of His statement rests upon the fact that you are what you are, regardless of the circumstances in which you are operating. In the church, in the home, on the job, your character remains basically the same, with differences in the wrappings. Some wrappings are designed to hide the real character, which may fool some people. But many folks see through the coverings to see the character for what it really is.

A contentious heart can be seen even in prayer, and in reading and discussing the Word. The-real-you can be nothing more nor less than the-real-you. There is no helping that. "For the mouth speaks out of that which fills the heart" (Matthew 12:34, NASB).

WHAT ARE YOU?

Do not be dissatisfied and disgruntled in what you do in this present life. Be dissatisfied and disgruntled in what you are. If there is a real dissatisfaction in what you really are, that is the beginning of change. Only God can change the leopard's spots. He can correct a malignant heart. You cannot affect the change simply by acting differently. It takes the creative powers of God, "Create in me a clean heart, O God; and renew a right spirit within me" (Psalm 51:10). A life surrendered to the burning coals of God's altar will be purified, as was Isaiah's life (Isaiah 6:7). But there must be a willingness for the fire to burn your dross, a willingness to let go of your malignancy for the sanctification and purity God desires to establish in you.

The peaceful approach to Sihon by Moses is rebuffed, and the king sets himself against the children of God. His heart is contrary to the character of God, and becomes more cemented in its malignancy by a continuous refusal of God's dealings. Thus he becomes the enemy to this peculiarly peaceful people. "But Sihon king of Heshbon was not willing for us to pass through his land; for the LORD your God hardened his spirit and made his heart obstinate, in order to deliver him into your hand, as he is today. Then Sihon with all his people came out to meet us in battle at Jahaz" (Deuteronomy 2:30,32, NASB).

VICTORY

As an enemy against the children of God, Sihon became God's enemy. It is not up to the children of God to conquer this enemy by their own strength alone. But as an enemy, judged and defeated by God, he is delivered into the hands of the children of God for the execution of God's will. We may have a will, as Moses once did, zealous to get our hands upon "enemies" to give them several stinging swats, sending them sprawling to the sand. That is not what God had in mind for Moses, or for us today.

It is God who delivers your enemy into your hands. It is then they become powerless in your grip. Watch this carefully in the Bible. You can see this in the case of Samson (Judges 14:5-6). A young lion roars against him, and the Spirit of God comes upon him. Samson is not characterized by a spirit which says, "I'll show you that I've got the power!" This is not an antagonistic spirit which comes upon him, making him so mad that he tore the lion to pieces. In the Bible, "wrath" is only appropriate in God; it does not belong in the heart of man.

When the Spirit of God rose up in me to jump into the water to grab a 15-foot water boa with my bare hands, I was not angry. It was simply a matter of fact, executing the will of God by the power invested in me, to kill the snake and free the children from its danger.

Samson "had nothing in his hand." This refers to no natural faculty to execute his feat. I do not have the natural strength to handle a 15-foot boa constrictor in the water. "Without me ye can do nothing" (John 15:5). With Him (in the full sense of the meaning) we have in our hands all that is necessary to execute His will. In the final analysis He gives the victory which we think we have won.

If there is to be a forward moving on in our victorious Christian living, we must deliver ourselves into God's hands, and take our orders from Him. It is not for us to move in our own intentions, fulfilling our own wills. It is not for us to execute our decisions upon the enemy. Watch this in the Bible. Read the Bible. Do not spend more time listening to preachers and reading books than you spend in the Bible. The Bible is your place of anchorage in truth. In the Bible watch the prerogatives of God versus the prerogatives of man. And learn!

Moses does not have to change his spirit of peace to one of antagonism simply because the king of Heshbon is moving against him. Moses had never thought that he had to knock over every king in his path. His basic concern is the will of God. God delivers kings into the hands of the children of Israel, who receive the victory God gives. Later, out of the will of God, Israel herself is defeated upon a number of occasions. This whole thing of victory moves upon God's prerogative, His intentions, His direction, His purposes. "Not by might nor by power, but by My Spirit" (Zechariah 4:6, NASB).

Moses does not move against Sihon, "Then Sihon with all his people came out to meet us in battle at Jahaz" (Deuteronomy 2:32, NASB). David does not move against Goliath. Sihon and Goliath move against the children of God, and thus against God. In Moses and David there is a response from God.

I am never disturbed by enemies outside my soul. If any enemy sets his power and forces against me, that is his problem, not mine. I have a strong high tower, "For thou hast been a shelter for me, and a strong tower from the enemy" (Psalm 61:3). I have no need to set myself against the enemy. It is not in my heart to strive with the enemy. If it were, it would distract me from my focal point upon God and His will. I am not against anyone. I am for God. If God is against someone, that is His business, not mine. My business is to serve God, doing what He wants me to do. If He wants me to confront a hostile enemy and defeat him, fine; that is what I will do.

GOD'S WILL

Confronting a hostile enemy in or out of the will of God makes a heap of difference. Joshua faced the children of Ai both out of and in the will of God. The different results were opposites: one of defeat, one of victory. So you must be careful as to how you face the enemy. One of the reasons why most Christians live in defeat today is that they face the enemy contrary to the intentions of God. Of course, they face the world and life itself the same way. They have much in their hearts which is contrary to God, and thus they are defeated, as was Joshua at Ai.

The only place of victory is in harmony with God. I cannot depend upon my own spirit, my own thoughts, my own faith, or my own strength for victory, "'For My thoughts are not your thoughts, Neither are your ways My ways,' declares the LORD. 'For as the heavens are higher than the earth, So are My ways higher than your ways, And My thoughts than your thoughts'" (Isaiah 55:8-9, NASB).

Instead of moving in line with God, many work up an emotional stir against the enemy. This seems to fortify them. It certainly deludes them. But when you are moving with God against an enemy, the battle is not yours in the first place; and, in the second place, the victory is certain. You can't get a better deal, no matter how hard you try. We are not to engage in a struggle with the enemy; we are to engage in a lopsided battle; we are to win the victory.

Since the battle is not ours, but God's, we can afford to stand still and see the salvation of the Lord. Even while moving, one can stand still in God. Even while engaged in battle, one can rest. In God one can do nothing and at the same time accomplish mighty deeds. The mind cannot understand this. Only experience can, "For it is God who is at work in you, both to will and to work for His good pleasure" (Philippians 2:13, NASB); "For he that is entered into his rest, he also hath ceased from his own works, as God did from his" (Hebrews 4:10). If we can surrender our own works and our own strength, and rest in God, He can give us, from Himself, all that we need; He can accomplish His will in and through us.

We can meet the enemy, or the problem, or the storm, or the difficulty in the power of God. That is victory. Catastrophe and defeat occur when we attempt to face and overcome such things in our own strength, the reason why some Christians do not progress.

And that also is the reason why some Christians never possess that which God has for them. Let all life's confrontations take place in God. It is not healthy to confront the enemy outside of God. That would frighten me. Almost anything outside of God frightens me. It would frighten me to choose a mate outside of God (not a mate outside of God, but to choose outside of God). It is rather restful to let God handle things. Then it really doesn't matter what path your life takes, or what you confront. With God you could meet a wild lion and be at rest.

A notice arrived in the mail. I was being sued for $40,000 because of an auto accident in which the fault was not entirely mine. I had absolutely no insurance. I smiled. It would have been difficult for me to come up with $400 at that time. I rested. It went to a hearing. I stayed home. A judgment of $4,000 was recorded against me. Then the Lord sent me and my family to Israel for two years. Shortly after returning, the Lord provided $1,000 which I felt was to be offered as settlement of the judgment. The offer was accepted. At no point did I presume. The rest was real, not simply a mental exercise to delude myself.

BATTLES BRING BENEFITS

Battles bring spoil which enrich our lives, "And the LORD said unto me, Behold, I have begun to give Sihon and his land before thee: begin to possess, that thou mayest inherit his land" (Deuteronomy 2:31). The territory of Sihon became part of the inheritance of Israel because this king made himself Israel's enemy. The conquest of this portion of the land did not result from Moses' decision and strength. Don't get the idea that you are going to jump on the enemy and beat him to the ground just because he is there. Moses moved under the commandments of God, and we should do likewise.

"At that time" may be the most important element in every victory God gives, "And we took all his cities *at that time*, and utterly destroyed the men, and the women, and the little ones, of every city, we left none to remain" (Deuteronomy 2:34, emphasis added). There is a time for judgment (such as the Flood); there is a time for mercy. There is a time for all things (see Ecclesiastes 3:1-8). Out of God's time will spell unfulfillment and defeat. If you so focus upon the mighty works of God that you lose sight of important details and ramifications, it may send you to your defeat.

Did you miss the details in Deuteronomy 2 which led to the powerful actions of God? We tend to overlook many things. Why does Israel work such havoc and destruction? Because they were angry? No! They are moving under the commandment of God. If you move on the basis of your anger, you sin. "Be angry and sin not," Paul writes in Ephesians 2:26. Do not allow anger to be your directive force and the basis of your actions. Direction should come from God.

Some confrontations are pleasant while some are unpleasant. The character of the confrontation should not alter our sense of our needing our Shepherd. He is with you in all your situations. There, He wants to help you.

It is very dangerous, or at least useless, to attempt to defeat an enemy which the Lord has not delivered into your hands, "And the LORD our God delivered him before us; and we smote him, and his sons, and all his people" (Deuteronomy 2:33). Receive that which the Lord gives you, but allow to go by that which the Lord is not giving you.

VICTORY TO VICTORY

One victory may lead you into another victory, "From Aroer, which is by the brink of the river of Arnon, and from the city that is by the river, even unto Gilead, there was not one city too strong for us: the LORD our God delivered all unto us" (Deuteronomy 2:36). One victory may actually be a foundation for a future victory. This is our forward thrust in God. We experience victory after victory, taking city after city, in the will of God. For there is no victory out of the will of God. The fullness of victorious Christian living is found in a limitation bounded by the will of the Father.

It would be well if you learned the secrets of the battle and victory early in your Christian life. As long as you live here in the flesh, it seems that the enemy and the battle are ever present. But you may have the victory, always, if you learn the secrets.

LIMITATIONS

A secret: The greater your personal liberty, the greater God's limitation in you. The greater your personal limitation, the greater the freedom that God has in you. Moses could not capture just any city he chose. Israel was limited to that which God was giving them, "Only unto the land of the children of Ammon thou camest not, nor unto any place of the river Jabbok, nor unto the cities in the mountains, nor unto whatsoever the LORD our God forbad us" (Deuteronomy 2:37). Don't take! That will get you into trouble. Receive! That is the healthy, scriptural way. Most difficulties that believers have are of their own creation. "Take" is the world's philosophy. It has invaded the Church, and has caused many personal problems. It sets believers on the roads of their own choosing.

A secret, perhaps the greatest secret, to constant victorious living is, "Seek not your own will, but the will of the Father." This was the path of Jesus, who could do nothing on His own (John 5:30). But many of today's Christians believe and feel that they are able to operate for God on their own. If they do not admit this with their mouths, they do with their lives.

Once you move out on your own, in a direction or action of your own choosing, you lose correctness. The reason for the accuracy of Jesus is very clearly stated in John 5:30, "My judgment is just because I seek not mine own will, but the will of the Father who has sent me."

STAY ON TRACK

In this Wilderness of Kedemoth the main theme is forward progression. But in such a progression there should be a concern for accuracy. Otherwise there may be regression rather than progression. Otherwise your spiritual life may be more unhealthy than healthy. Otherwise you may have spiritual poverty rather than spiritual riches. Thus, it is imperative that you take His yoke upon you, coming under His limiting factors. All fulfillment is bound by limitations.

This applies in the natural realm as well as in the spiritual realm. Fulfillment in the marital relationship is bound by limitations. Fulfillment in agriculture is bound by limitations. Fulfillment in transportation is bound by limitations. And in our textual subject, Moses must move in the limitations imposed by God in order to come to fulfillment. He moved out of that upon one occasion. It was when he struck the rock for water when God told him to speak to it. He moved apart from God, taking his own direction in striking the rock instead of speaking to it, as God directed. As a result Moses was not permitted to lead the people into the Promised Land.

If the Kedemoth in our lives is to be that which God intends it to be, there must be progression; forward, healthy, prosperous progression. In order for this to be so there must be vision, "Where there is no vision, the people are unrestrained" (Proverbs 29:18, NASB). There can be no limitation without a vision. How could we be limited to God's ways if they do not come into our view? Because many do not have a vision, there is little or no progression in their Christian living. Our own ways often fill our visions. We must be willing to lay aside our own wills and seek the will of our Father.

If we have a desire to clobber the enemy, we might first consider the will of the Father. He may not be moving in certain desires of ours. He may want us to wait for His timing. When Satan came to Jesus in Matthew 4, Jesus did not immediately bounce on him. Jesus stayed under the temptation until it was the Father's time for Him to say to Satan, "Get thee hence." The Father can bring us into immediate action in some situations. Or it could be a situation in which we must wait until the Father's time arrives. Or it could be that the Father does not want us ever to mess with a certain situation. We must have vision.

VISION

Vision is not difficult to obtain. Many believers try to obtain vision. That effort does make it difficult. There should be no effort made to obtain vision. The easy way to obtain vision is to stop focusing upon your own will. Erase! Then the Father can fill in the blanks.

My own words may hinder forward progression. Jesus did not speak His own words, but those of the Father, "The words that I say to you I do not speak on My own initiative," said Jesus in John 14:10 (NASB). The "piece of my mind" which I give away may be to my spiritual detriment. The more prerogatives of my own I use, the less chance I have for spiritual progression.

If all of your confrontations in life could be as much under God as it was with Moses in our text, you would discover a wondrous state of daily victory. You would discover an ever-increasing fulfillment in life. If you could refrain yourself from moving against things, and move in God, you would discover an ever-abiding deep and satisfying peace. Stand still and take to yourself the whole armor of God, "Stand" (Ephesians 6:14). Do not decide where you are going to go. Do not begin to move in your own determined direction. Stand. Wait for your orders.

In the U. S. Air Force I could not move anywhere without orders. If I changed locations, I had to do so under written orders. Be ready to move, but wait for your orders. If I heard that we were moving to another location, and I eagerly went on my own, not waiting for my orders, I would be in serious trouble with the Air Force. Do not be that eager to do the Father's will. This is one reason why most do not know the Father's will in advance. They would jump the gun, and be out of God's timing. And that's bad.

Off timing of aerial acrobats has meant untimely deaths. There have been spiritual and physical deaths due to missing God's timing. Eager missionaries have been involved in this. Young people in relating to marriage have been involved. The prophet who came from Judah to Bethel was involved. When he should have been back in Judah, his untimely delay in Bethel cost him his life (I Kings 13:1-24). Walk obediently with God, keeping in step.

PRAYER

Our Father, we are grateful to Thee. Thy mercy, which has endured forever, has come to us. Your love and Your Spirit, which have always wooed men, woo us today. With these tools of Yours, help us to cease from our own efforts and strivings in order to come into the rest which You have provided for us. Help us to live more fully in Thee, to move and have our being in You. Help us to take our directions from You instead of out from our own self-seeking. May we look to Thee for our orders. May our going and coming be under You. May we live a life surrendered and committed to You, for all authority is in Thee. Jesus, teach us the life that You lived. Teach us, Lord, the limitations under which You lived. May we be willing to follow in Your footsteps, to do what we see the Father do, and to say what we hear the Father say.

Jesus, teach us Your way. Oh, that we may learn of You, so meek and lowly, so submitted to the Father, so limited in Yourself. Oh Lord, that we may see You and follow You in Your path, becoming like You. Our cry is that we might be shaped into the image of God's dear Son. May we, in that image, become the expression of the Father, as You did, dear Jesus.

Father, be in us; fill us with Thy fullness; flow out from us. Oh, that You may have the glory and the honor that You seek in and through us, both now and throughout the ages to come. Amen.

Chapter Seven
Critical Turning Points
in the Wilderness of Zin

I have traveled Israel from Dan to Beersheba. Southwest of the Dead Sea, I stood on the northern edge of the Wilderness of Zin. This area bordering the Promised Land would logically be the place for the children of Israel to launch their first search of the land, "So they went up and searched the land from the Wilderness of Zin" (Numbers 13:21). They were camping in the Wilderness of Zin when they went up to spy out the land, "Then came the children of Israel, even the whole congregation, into the desert of Zin in the first month: and the people abode in Kadesh; and Miriam died there, and was buried there" (Numbers 20:1).

There are two sets of meanings which the word "zin" has. The first set is "prick," "barb," "hook," "something that is quite unpleasant or quite painful." The other set of meanings is quite different; it is "preserve," "keep," "protect." So in one meaning you are torn to pieces in the brier patch (a loved one dies), and in the other meaning you are kept by God and can rest in His protection. As strange as it may seem, the very incidents occurring in the Wilderness of Zin work in parallel with these meanings of this Hebrew word "zin."

The place in which the children of Israel lived while in the Wilderness of Zin, Kadesh, is a focal point, and plays prominently in the message of this wilderness. "Kadesh" also carries two different meanings, much wider apart than the two sets of meanings for "zin." "Kadesh" means "holy" and its related words. "Kadesh" also means "prostitute" and its related words. The very ones God called to holiness, a dedication to Himself, became spiritual prostitutes, dedicated to other gods.

This place, the Wilderness of Zin with Kadesh as its capital, so to speak, is a place of crises. For the children of Israel it is a very critical place and time. We all have points of crises in our lives, turning points—perhaps. For a decade I have watched Bible school students go through their years of training. For most, the critical point is during their second year in school. That seems to be the point in which their direction is determined. That is, they will either begin to move more away from truth, or move closer to it. The student's second year seems to be his Wilderness of Zin. Whatever your Wilderness of Zin may be, it is the place and time when your die is cast (your mold is made), and you will set yourself in a certain direction until you come to the end of the road, the end of your earthly life. The only thing which will change such a determined course is another Wilderness of Zin with a crisis greater than the previous one. The Wilderness of Zin is a very critical place.

It would make it a lot easier for us if we were able to recognize the Wilderness of Zin when we come to it. When I stood in the physical Wilderness of Zin there was no sign or markings to let me know where I was. Someone had to clue me in as to my location. There is no spiritual wilderness which is so marked that when we come to it we immediately know where we are. It seems that God at least should mark the Wilderness of Zin since it is such a critical place. It is the point where you either go forward in God or begin to regress away from God. But the response necessary to carry us forward in God is not a response which God wants to see *only* in the Wilderness of Zin.

The decision to move in the will of God and to obey the commands of God is ours to make, not only in the Wilderness of Zin, but every day of our lives. When God calls us on into progression and into a greatness in Him which we have not yet known, it is our prerogative to heed or not to heed the call. Thus, what happens to us in the Wilderness of Zin is not because we are there; it is because of our decisions. The decision which you will make will be based upon what you know or what you do not know, upon what you believe or don't believe, upon what you desire or don't desire.

Your decision may be based upon the facts that God is wise and has your interest at heart. Or these facts may escape you and a different decision is made. Each, the knowing and the not knowing, will have a great effect on the way you respond to God and make your choices. If you do not believe that God loves you, you may choose differently than you would if you believed that God loves you.

God may be calling you into a certain direction concerning His will for you. But a great desire for a different path may cause you to refuse His calling. A lack of a certain desire may make easy obedience to His calling. Or a strong desire to do His will may cause you to be obedient. These three elements, knowing, believing, desiring, are not the only elements influencing our decisions. There are many elements playing their parts in our lives which help to bring us to certain decisions, and thus help to mold us.

FOR BETTER OR FOR WORSE

Because the Wilderness of Zin is a critical point, it can be a turning point, for better or for worse. Thus it can be a point of a new beginning. This is the place from which God calls the children of Israel to go up and to possess the land. That indeed would be a new beginning for them. But the choice of these people is going to determine whether they have a new beginning and a better life, or a dead-end course and a worse life. And so the choice itself becomes critical.

Jesus says to the rich young ruler in Mark 10:21, "Sell all that you have and follow me." The rich young ruler is forced to make a decision. Will he or won't he follow? One way or the other he will make a decision which will set his course for life, and then some. Just that one decision will carry unimaginable implications. "Come," Rich Young Ruler, "take Judas' throne." Judas, called by Jesus to be one of the twelve chosen disciples, desired money, and so made material gain his objective in life. He made the greatest decision of his life, which cost him his life and his eternal position. Saul of Tarsus, on the road to Damascus, met this same person who crossed the lives of the rich young ruler and Judas. Saul responded in Acts 9:6, "What will you have me to do?" That resulted in monumental implications not only in the life of Saul himself (later to be known as the great apostle Paul), but in the whole of the Body of Christ. That was just one decision.

God doesn't say to you, "Now watch out; this is your critical decision." How often is the right decision missed? We may never know. We are to be ready at all times to give the Lord the answer, the response, the decision which He seeks. *Always* give God what He wants. That way you will not have to be concerned about when the critical decision may occur. Your safety in this matter is to lay aside your own will and do the will of your heavenly Father. Ananias and Sapphira made their most critical decision when they decided to lie to the Holy Spirit and to God (Acts 5:1-10). There are many, many incidents which cross our lives, determining whether we go up to possess the lands which God has for us, or die in the wilderness.

The Wilderness of Zin, and especially the specific place of the encampment of the children of Israel, Kadesh, are very critical. "Kadesh" means "to consecrate," "to cleanse," "holy." These meanings play an important role in our choices. If these meanings are part of our lives and desires, they guarantee that we will make the correct decisions. This life which is consecrated to God, this heart which is daily cleansed from sin, this walk of holiness and pureness before God, the desire to obey God at all costs, become the elements in our lives which will take us in God's direction and to His conclusions.

It was at Kadesh that Moses gathered the people to the rock and failed to sanctify or consecrate the Lord God in the eyes of the people when he smote the rock instead of speaking to it (Numbers 20:9-13). God told Moses to speak to the rock in the presence of the people. Moses chose to disobey and it cost him; he was not allowed to go into the Promised Land; he died.

A life in God must be maintained through daily rededication. God brought Moses and the people to a place of rededication, or renewed separation and consecration and cleansing. This was done at Kadesh. On the basis of this renewal they would go up to possess the Promised Land. But if they failed in the time of renewal, they would fail in their choice, and they would fail in their forward spiritual progression, and they would fail to go up to possess the land, failing to inherit that which God called them to inherit.

If there is to be any degree of success in God, there must be a constant renewing of our separation and consecration, our separation from the flesh and our consecration unto God. Just as the mercies of God are new every morning, so must our spirit, strength, inner man and mind be constantly renewed. See II Chronicles 15:8; Psalm 51:10; 103:5; Isaiah 40:31; Romans 12:2; II Corinthians 4:16; Ephesians 4:23.

There was so much of the flesh moving in the children of Israel that possessing the land would be impossible for that particular generation. They saw the giants in the land; they saw this mighty flesh. When the Israeli spies (sent out from Kadesh) saw these giants, most of them brought back the report that Israel was not able to fight against such great flesh. At that time Israel failed to separate herself from the flesh.

Kadesh, this place of holiness, was to be for Israel the place of final separation from the flesh. The finality of it is seen in "and Miriam died there, and was buried there." Who is Miriam? She is the one who carried leprosy with her through the Red Sea. That is, she carried her faultfinding and murmuring within herself, only to be manifested later. There is to be death to all this; sin shall not rule. Sin and flesh are not to have the victory.

EITHER DIE OR DIE

All Israel should have joined Miriam in death, death to self and the flesh. The apostle Paul died daily. You are brought into the Wilderness of Zin to die a death to self so that there is no more crying for water. The Israelites were very concerned about their fleshly needs. They did not want physical death. They never were able to die to the flesh. Jesus said that if you attempt to preserve your life, you will die. And He said that if you want to live, you must die (Matthew 10:39).

When God brought Israel into the Wilderness of Zin, He brought them to the opportunity to die and live. This was to be their place of renewal where their finality of death to the flesh and unbelief was expected. Unbelief is very fleshly. Yet they continually moved in that. This prevented them from possessing the Promised Land, "They were not able to enter, because of their unbelief" (Hebrews 3:19, NIV).

The Wilderness of Zin has been designed for perhaps the greatest victories of life. But the place which has been designed for victory can actually become the place of defeat and death. This is a very sad note because that which God has designed for life and victory (as also was the case of the Law [Romans 7:16; Deuteronomy 4:1]) often becomes the very thing in which death and defeat occur. Man has this dubiously wonderful talent of turning life into death, "And there was no water for the congregation: and they gathered themselves together against Moses and against Aaron" (Numbers 20:2). They lost no time in turning life into death. It doesn't sound like dedication or consecration to the LORD. Sounds like rebellion and complaint. Sounds like death.

The Wilderness of Zin becomes a place for a refresher course. This is not the first time these people were without water. Previously they had failed the test in waterless places. Now they have another chance. Have they learned anything from their previous experiences? The test is given again to find out. It is the same test they already had, word for word, question for question. Can they pass it this time? The conquest of the land depends upon their passing this repeated examination. How can God graduate anyone if he does not pass the final examination? God is not going to excuse you from testings. After three failures He is not going to say, "That's okay; we'll forget it and move you on anyway." But He will keep bringing you back to the same test as long as there is opportunity for Him to do so.

Now behold their stupidity! They answer the questions exactly the same way they did the first and second times they took this test. This is after God provides them with the right answers twice before, once at the bitter waters and once when water was produced from the rock. It must take great effort to be so stupid.

"And the people strove with Moses, and spoke saying, 'Would God that we had died when our brethren died before the LORD'" (Numbers 20:3). And the LORD says, "That's the wrong answer; that's not the right answer to this examination!" That was the answer they had given on the occasion to which they refer ("when our brethren died before the LORD," when the earth swallowed the rebels). That occasion goes back to Numbers 16:41, "The children of Israel murmured against Moses and against Aaron." At that time the LORD told them that this was the wrong answer, "Get you up from among this congregation, that I may consume them as in a moment."

"Those who died were 14,700" (verse 49). How smart or spiritual do they have to be to be able to know what's going on? These people are difficult to understand. We wouldn't be so stupid, would we? Well, I don't know. I certainly would not want to guarantee that we all are smarter than they were. It all boils down to unbelief and a desire to have the flesh comfortable.

BELIEF IS CORRECT

The refresher course is given. The final exam is taken. All but two failed. The underlying factor causing failure was unbelief, as was faith the underlying reason for Caleb and Joshua's passing the test. Two years ago this same unbelief was in them when they were delivered out of Egypt. They came out of Egypt, went into the wilderness, and found bitter water. Did they believe God would provide sweet water for them? Noooo! Instead they "murmured against Moses, saying, What shall we drink?" (Exodus 15:24). "That's the wrong answer," the LORD expressed by pointing out the tree which made the bitter water sweet.

About a month and a half later they came to the Wilderness of Sin, and there was nothing to eat. Did they believe God would provide them food? Noooo! They believed that they were going to die in the wilderness. They murmured and strove with Moses, "And the whole congregation of the children of Israel murmured against Moses and Aaron in the wilderness. And the children of Israel said unto them, Would that we had died by the hand of the LORD in the land of Egypt, when we sat by the flesh pots, and when we did eat bread to the full; for ye have brought us forth into this wilderness, to kill this whole assembly with hunger" (Exodus 16:2-3). "That's not the right answer," God expresses by sending manna.

Next they encamped in Rephidim where there was no water. Again they give the wrong answer, "The people did strive with Moses, and said, Give us water that we may drink. And Moses said unto them, Why strive ye with me? Wherefore do ye put the LORD to the test? And the people thirsted there for water; and the people murmured against Moses, and said, Why hast thou brought us up out of Egypt, to kill us and our children and our cattle with thirst?" (Exodus 17:2-3). "That's the wrong answer," the LORD expressed by bringing water out of the rock.

Two years go by, almost to the day. Now they are in the Wilderness of Zin under the same situation which they had experienced upon a number of other occasions. In spite of the demonstrations of God's provisions upon those other occasions, these people still move in unbelief. It must take a great effort of stubbornness to move against such demonstrations of God. God's faithfulness is seen, yet there is unbelief.

"And why have ye brought up the congregation of the LORD into this wilderness, that we and our cattle should die there?" is a familiar refrain repeated in Numbers 20:4. They had just expressed a desire for death in verse 3, "Would God that we had died when our brethren died before the LORD." The problem with their death wish is that they always wanted to die in another place in another time, rather than in the here and now. But eventually their fake death wish will be fulfilled. Actually they wanted to keep their murmuring flesh alive as long as possible.

Is today's Christian much better than the murmuring and complaining Israelite in the Wilderness of Zin? Has not God also called the Christian to a death of the flesh? Does not the Christian come into situations where his comfortable flesh is disturbed? Does not he complain and murmur because the flesh has been agitated? Does your flesh ever get agitated? If it does, it is very much alive. What are we going to do when we make the discovery (hopefully) that our flesh is very much alive? We must come to rededication and reconsecration. We must come to Him for renewal or further cleansing and separation.

When you discover your flesh is still alive, do not continue to feed it. Do not continue to give the same wrong answers to God. Change your song. Do not sing the tune of flesh's desires and life. Rather, sing of flesh's death, of the altar of God upon which the flesh is consumed. Bring the flesh to the altar of dedication and consecration. Offer it. Allow God to consume it. In that way your answers can become correct. You can pass the test. You can graduate and go on to possess that which God has for you.

Has your Miriam died? Is she still buried? Or is she up, moving around? The Wilderness of Zin is the last place where you have opportunity to deal with her. Better stay there until you get your Miriam dead and buried. If need be, go back to the altar of consecration again and again and again, as often as you must. There are some folks who must "get saved" every week or so. They seem to live a life of repeated dedications and consecrations. If that's what it takes to keep you going, then follow that route. It's better to do that for four years than to be turned back into wilderness wanderings for forty years, and final death without victory.

Only if your Miriam is dead can you move out of the Wilderness of Zin into conquest and possession. The only other alternative is to die in the wilderness. But that is not God's intention for you. His intention, and the purpose of the wilderness, is a healthy spiritual overcoming life, "And wherefore have ye made us to come up out of Egypt, to bring us in unto this evil place?" (Numbers 20:5). As this demonstrates, there was more than one live Miriam still operating.

BLIND FLESH

The more that fleshly desires and comforts are pushed forward for fulfillment, the less understanding there is in the ways of God. To the Corinthians the apostle Paul wrote, "I cannot teach you properly and feed you meat because you are carnal. You cannot understand further spiritual truth" (I Corinthians 3:1-3). The place described as evil by the children of Israel is a place appointed by God for their good. The flesh is in such prominent activity that it impedes spiritual understanding. Thus God cannot take you on, up and up into the heavenly places, as long as the flesh remains so active.

The question, "Why did you bring us to such an evil place?" cannot be answered. No answer will satisfy them. They could not understand the real reason. Today people ask questions for which there is no satisfying answer, and the correct answer cannot be understood nor received by them. The very questions they ask tell me all about them. That is, the questions tell me of their lack of understanding, that there is little foundation for revelation, that there is little vision.

"This is no place of seed, or of figs, or of vines, or of pomegranates; neither is there any water to drink" (Numbers 20:5). This is their vision. Their vision is focused upon the natural, that which is earthly, the physical. "I don't see any fig trees here. I don't see any water here. There are no pleasant things here with which to satisfy my flesh. I don't belong here. Who needs this?" We who are so dependent upon these things need to be weaned as was Habakkuk, "Although the fig tree shall not blossom, neither shall fruit be in the vines; the labor of the olive shall fail, and the fields shall yield no food; the flock shall be cut off from the fold, and there shall be no herd in the stalls; yet I will rejoice in the LORD, I will joy in the God of my salvation. The LORD God is my strength, and he will make my feet like hinds' feet, and he will make me walk upon mine high places" (Habakkuk 3:17-19).

Is your flesh supposed to like the Wilderness of Zin? No, in no way. The wilderness has not been designed for fleshly comfort. The wilderness is supposed to bug your flesh. As long as your impatience prevails you will continue to be bugged. We must allow God so to work in us as to bring us to wait for Him *patiently*, to trust Him completely in all types of situations. We must be brought to inner peace where there is no more agitation. We must let go the provisions for the flesh. We must be weaned. If not, there is a tremendous failure.

FIRST THINGS FIRST

Prevent failure by a rededication, by a reconsecration, again and again, as often as is necessary. Remember the returning to the altar in the Wilderness of Beersheba (see chapter 2). If you do not have a proper foundation, return to the basics. Otherwise you will always be in trouble. If you continue to build and build on a faulty foundation you will lose a great deal. There are no shortcuts in this. Certain issues and testings cannot be avoided if there is to be spiritual gain and health. We cannot leave out one-fourth of our foundation and expect spiritual prosperity. Not too many Christians seem to be interested in the ABCs. More seem to be interested in the XYZs. But God wants us to fulfill the ABCs.

Many times when someone is initiated into the Kingdom of God, they soon think that they should be operating in the PQRs. This is why there are so many problems in the churches today. There is lack of proper foundations. Let us fulfill the basics before wanting to go on to something greater. Even if God has called us or is leading us into greater things, let us make sure of our foundation before we go on into them. This was necessary in the life of Moses. Even the will and leading of God had to be delayed in his case until the foundational work was completed. At age forty Moses knew of his calling. But the foundational work was not completed until he was eighty. Remember that there are basic obligations you have under God which hold priority to other obligations, even those which God is laying on you.

When I was a missionary in Peru, I met another missionary who left his wife in the United States in order to fulfill his calling to Peru. I do not doubt his calling to Peru. But there is a more basic calling whose fulfillment takes precedence over his calling to Peru. His first obligation is to fulfill the scriptural requirements toward his wife. Likewise I know women who insist upon moving in the leading of the Spirit in spiritual ministry when it disrupts and worsens their relationships with their husbands. The universal excuse which covers it all is, "We must obey God rather than man." Then do it. Obey God. But do not obey God in the matters you like and allow the other areas to rest in disobedience.

In obeying God, be sure of the order. Obedience to the basics must take precedence over obedience to the other types of God's leadings. The basics are found in the Bible. This will bring you to a choice, a multiple-choice test. Which of the following is your first and most important obligation: (a) being dedicated to your wife; being submitted to your husband; (b) laying hands on the sick; (c) prophesying; (d) following a specific directive from God; (e) obeying the call to preach? God gives tests. Tests can be so simple and easy that they serve no purpose. So God gives difficult tests. The difficulty does not lie in the fact that we cannot know the answers, for we can. The difficulty lies in the individual's unwillingness to follow God's correct path. The difficulty lies in the individual's lack of faith to believe God's correct path once it is pointed out to him.

I cannot understand how some can fulfill spiritual ministries while their households are not provided for, and are in great need due to lack of attention and provisions. I do not know how anyone can skip fulfilling ABC and move on up to PQR without creating plenty of serious personal problems. If this is your case, you will have to back down to ABC if you ever expect to solve your personal problems. Always return to the basics if they yet need fulfillment.

"When therefore the Lord knew how the Pharisees had heard that Jesus made and baptized more disciples than John, he left Judea, and departed again into Galilee" (John 4:1,3). All the works and words of Jesus come from His Father (John 10:32; 12:50; etc.). Thus, in making disciples and baptizing, Jesus was doing the will of His Father. But another principle enters the picture, and it takes precedence over the present leading of God in the life of Jesus.

The ministries of John the Baptist and Jesus were to be in a certain arrangement, according to prophecy. Thus, Jesus had to back down from making disciples in order to fulfill something more basic. Not until John was off the scene did Jesus come preaching, "Now after that John was put in prison, Jesus came into Galilee, preaching the gospel of the kingdom of God" (Mark 1:14). At age twelve Jesus said, "Knew ye not that I must be about my Father's business?" (Luke 2:49). But what He knew to be the will of His Father had to be laid aside for eighteen years while the basics were being fulfilled, "Though he were a Son, yet learned he obedience by the things which he suffered" (Hebrews 5:8). First things first.

During my eleven-year missionary career, I met missionaries who had problems in raising financial support. I was curious enough to want to know why. So I started observing and asking questions of those who were having this problem. In almost every case I found that they never bothered to tithe faithfully or to give generously. No wonder they had problems. They better go back to the basics. Get the foundations laid correctly. Otherwise your building will be out of line and not truly functional. Do not fail in the basic matters, in the ABCs.

"And when thou (Moses) hast seen it (the Promised Land), thou also shalt be gathered unto thy people, as Aaron thy brother was gathered," said God in Numbers 27:13. Moses could only see, not enter, the Promised Land because thirty-eight years ago he failed in the basic matter of consecration at Kadesh. Moses died without victory and conquest, "For ye rebelled against my commandment in the desert of Zin, in the strife of the congregation, to sanctify me at the water before their eyes: that is the water of Meribah in Kadesh in the wilderness of Zin." Do not fail at your Kadesh, that is, in this matter of personal consecration. Failure in the ABCs means failure in the XYZs. Do not avoid a "foundation" walk with God; it must be a constant factor in your Christian life.

MAKE A CHANGE

We are brought to the same situations as the children of Israel for the same tests over and over again. In this way, we have ample opportunities to correct our errors, then change our attitudes. Take advantage of these testings. Repent, make your renewed dedication, and avoid permanent failure.

The Wilderness of Zin is the most critical and serious of all the wildernesses in the Bible. Rebellion persists right up to the last minute of opportunity; that's serious, "For you (plural) rebelled against my commandment in the desert of Zin" (Numbers 27:14). There was no submission to God in the situations and conditions in which they lived. The attitude of knowing more than God persisted, "Why did you ever take us out of Egypt and bring us here? Don't you know any better than that?" Thus they bring an indictment against God at Kadesh, the place for their renewed dedication (Numbers 20:4-5).

Are we much smarter than these people? Have you ever heard or said words something like these? "Why am I in this situation?" "Why is it so dry, so waterless?" "Why am I without the blessings of God?" "What did I do wrong to be brought to such a desolate place?" "What's going to happen?" "I don't understand any of this." "I'm going to die here, I just know it." Indictments against God. This is a manifestation of a heart in disagreement with God's divine arrangements. At this point there is only one element into which this heart can enter, and that is failure. Prevailing impatience, murmuring, and rebellion mean failure. There can be no further progress in God until these matters are out of the way, "Wherefore, laying aside all malice, and all guile, and hypocrisies, and envies, and all evil speakings (take care of the basics), as newborn babes, desire the pure milk of the word, that ye may grow by it" (I Peter 2:1-2).

To follow the correct course is not a matter which is so mystical, so high above us that we cannot come to it. It is a simple matter of obedience. It all boils down to a heart desiring to be submitted to God and all His appointed situations. It is not something which is so far above our understanding that it is difficult to comprehend and obtain. It is simply doing that which we know God wants done. It is not even doing that which God wants done. It is doing what we *know* God wants done. It is a matter of reading the Bible over and over to become familiar with God's priorities in relation to His will.

The problem with most intelligent people is that they always must stop to analyze everything. There is no matter they can allow to rest in simplicity, "See, the LORD your God has given you the land. Go up and take possession of it as the LORD, the God of your father, told you. Do not be afraid; do not be discouraged. Then all of you came to me and said, 'Let us send men ahead to spy out the land for us and bring back a report about the route we are to take and the towns we will come to'" (Deuteronomy 1:21-22). Let us analyze this situation. It is difficult for some to obey without analyzing. As a result, paralysis of analysis sets in. Instead of a simple obedience to the word, their feet are stuck in the analytical quagmire. They are attempting to understand, rather than obeying, "How can we obey an order we do not understand? We must first see what it is; we must tear it apart and examine it." Instead of moving on in obedience, they piddle around in some curious investigation. Thus a substitute for obedience and dedication stops them cold.

So when you come to your Wilderness of Zin, the very first thing you must do before you start looking around is to make sure your dedication is up-to-date. If need be, again come to your Father in complete surrender so that you can follow Him in obedience. This will assure your success in going up to possess that which He has set before you. He has set before you the great unknown. Do you have the courage and faith to move toward it?

THE UNKNOWN
Charles A. Haun

There is a light
which seems to beckon me,
to where, I do not know.

There is a call
(it seems to come from God)
to what, I do not know.

It is tugging;
my heart now answers it;
I race to open arms.

There is a work,
a mysterious kind
I do not understand.

There is a hand
(of nature rough and soft)
I cannot understand.

There is a heart
which beats for me with love
and beckons enter in.

There is a path
(the way it turns is strange);
it leads to realms unknown.

There is a door.
Open? I do not know.
One day He'll bring me there.

There is a place
of grace beyond the known
which now I cannot see.

There is a faith
which yet I do not have;
I pray it grips my heart.

There is a love.
It's His. I wish it mine,
that I may know His way.

There is a light
I need that I may see
the One who calls to me.

Chapter Eight
Making of a Soldier
in the Wilderness of Sin (Part One)

The Wilderness of Sin is the making of soldiers, or the attempt to do so. A hint of this purpose is seen in the meaning of the Hebrew word "sin" (5512), which is "clay."[4] The hand of God is continually attempting to mold His children. We particularly are going to look in the Wilderness of Sin for details of this, and from that point move out into further Scriptures.

The children of Israel had camped in an oasis at Elim, and from there journeyed to the Wilderness of Sin:

Exodus 16:1-3

And they took their journey from Elim, and all the congregation of the children of Israel came unto the wilderness of Sin, which is between Elim and Sinai, on the fifteenth day of the second month after their departing out of the land of Egypt. And the whole congregation of the children of Israel murmured against Moses and Aaron in the wilderness: And the children of Israel said unto them, Would to God we had died by the hand of the LORD in the land of Egypt, when we sat by the flesh pots, and when we did eat bread to the full; for ye have brought us forth into this wilderness, to kill this whole assembly with hunger.

These people were exposed to hardships. Hardships are necessary in a soldier's life because of battle conditions. Therefore, in training, God brings His people into difficult conditions in order to

---

[4] *A Hebrew and English Lexicon of the Old Testament*, Brown/Driver/Briggs, Oxford, 1959 edition, page 695 b.

train them for battle. It was God's purpose for the children of Israel to learn to endure hardships without grumbling and complaining about the situations.

There are hardships today which the believer must endure if he is to live victoriously. The apostle Paul urges Timothy to "endure hardness, as a good soldier of Jesus Christ" (II Timothy 2:3). Still the intention of God is to raise up an army, against which the gates of Hell will not prevail (Matthew 16:18).

There are conquests to be made today in the spiritual realm:

II Corinthians 10:3-6

For though we walk in the flesh, we do not war after the flesh: (For the weapons of our warfare are not carnal, but mighty through God to the pulling down of strong holds;) casting down imaginations, and every high thing that exalteth itself against the knowledge of God, and bringing into captivity every thought to the obedience of Christ; and having in a readiness to revenge all disobedience, when your obedience is fulfilled.

Ephesians 6:12

For we wrestle not against flesh and blood, but against principalities, against powers, against the rulers of the darkness of this world, against spiritual wickedness in high places.

WILL THERE BE SUCCESS?

The attempt by God to mold an individual into the character and condition necessary for his fulfilling God's will is not always successful. In the Bible and in our present surroundings we see many failures in this area. Even though this first generation of the children of Israel, fresh out from Egypt, failed to be molded by God, it was nevertheless God's purpose to do so. God intended to train them for battle, for the conquest of the Promised Land. He did succeed with the second generation.

Notice in verses 2 and 3 of Exodus 16, "And the whole congregation of the children of Israel murmured against Moses and Aaron in the wilderness (this Wilderness of Sin): And the children of

Israel said unto them, Would to God we had died by the hand of the LORD in the land of Egypt, when we sat by the flesh pots, and when we did eat bread to the full; for ye have brought us forth into this wilderness, to kill this whole assembly with hunger." God brought the Israelites into hard places. In these hard places they were to endure patiently without murmuring and complaining. They did not do this.

In these wildernesses God worked almost daily to bring about in His people the faith and stamina that He wanted. They must be trained for battle. They were brought into the Wilderness of Sin for that very purpose. There were to be many battles fought in the conquest of the Promised Land. "And it came to pass the selfsame day, that the Lord did bring the children of Israel out of the land of Egypt by their armies" (Exodus 12:51). "By their armies" hints of the intention of God in His delivering program: to call forth armies from the children of Israel in order to serve the purposes which He had in mind. The purposes for the Israelite army were twofold: they were to possess the Promised Land through conquest, and they were to execute the judgment of God upon the godless (the Canaanites), whose cup of iniquity was full. Thus, the first order of business was to train the delivered people.

"And it came to pass, when Pharaoh had let the people go, that God led them not the way of the land of the Philistines, although that was near; for God said, Lest peradventure the people repent when they see war, and they return to Egypt" (Exodus 13:17). The idea was not to lead them too quickly into the Promised Land through a route that would take them only a matter of a week or two. God had to train them for war. If He did not, they would see war, repent, and return to Egypt. "But God led the people about, through the way of the wilderness of the Red Sea: and the children of Israel went up harnessed (or armed) out of the land of Egypt" (Exodus 13:18).

God led an army out of Egypt, armed. He led them out of Egypt in order to train them to endure hardships. The strong soldier will not faint when he sees war; he will not become afraid; he will not repent and return to Egypt. God must lead His children into a training program. And so we are brought into the Wilderness of Sin—to be trained to endure war.

"Then came Amalek, and fought with Israel in Rephidim" (Exodus 17:8). There they were being trained under actual battle conditions. These first battles which they fought were training battles; they were not conquest battles. They were not wars fought to conquer and possess any land; they were simply training battles. There were only a very few training battles. In the forty years that Israel wandered in the wilderness they fought five armies in their training battles. Once they moved into the conquest of the Promised Land, within one year thirty-one kings were fought and defeated. Joshua 12:24—thirty-one kings in the space of one year, compared to five in the space of forty years, "The king of Tirzah, one: all the kings thirty and one" (Joshua 12:24).

OUR TRAINING GROUND

The wilderness is a place of training for conquest. The wilderness is not the end, rather, the wilderness is a means to an end. In the Wilderness of Sin there were difficulties and pressures due to circumstances and Egyptian blood, called the mixed multitude, "And a mixed multitude went up also with them" (Exodus 12:38). At times there was no water. At other times there was bitter water. The children of Israel experienced all of these pressures, these sufferings, these afflictions, and trials—God's training tools.

These experiences of the Israelites become our lessons, "Take, my brethren, the prophets, (that is consider them) who have spoken in the name of the Lord, for an example of suffering affliction, and of patience" (James 5:10). Watch these for an example. As we look at those who have passed on before us, we can see them in the light of the experiences into which God brought them. Some of them we can scrutinize through many years of their lives and all the way to the end of their lives. We can see that some failed. Others, we see, succeeded. Hopefully, through their experiences, we can see and understand certain vital spiritual lessons that God is attempting to teach us in similar circumstances.

The results we see in the successful lives become our encouragement, "Behold, we count those blessed who endured. You have heard of the endurance of Job and have seen the outcome of the

Lord's dealings, that the Lord is full of compassion and is merciful" (James 5:11, NASB). Looking back to the lives of others, we do not see only the beginning or the middle of certain experiences, but at times we can see the whole, from the beginning to the end, including the results. We have the privilege of watching individuals and groups in the Bible as they are brought through their difficulties and pressures. We can look upon the end results; we can see who succeeded and who failed, and often, the reason why. The ones that go through the testings victoriously, patiently enduring, plodding on, we count blessed. We do not count blessed those who perished in the wilderness. We count blessed those who entered into the Promised Land to possess it.

You can fail in the midst of the evil which comes against you. If you fail in this, you can destroy yourself. The only reason the children of Israel died in the wilderness is because they destroyed themselves. It wasn't the wilderness that killed them. It didn't kill Joshua and Caleb. It wasn't the circumstances. It wasn't anything except their own fault that they fell in the wilderness. The direction of man into his eternal damnation results only from his own will. That thing was never caused by God. That thing was the result of the will of man, his destructive ways, his perverted ways, and his decision to move contrary to God's will. Peter wrote that men die in their own corruption. They bring about that result themselves.

God does not count failure as failure until you are stuck in it. Just because you fail, God doesn't say, "Well that's the end of that. I'm going to haul him out to the city dump and leave him there." No way! However, a continuation of being stuck in failure, habitual unbelief, and disobedience results in bringing you to a dead end.

The only way that man ever came to death was through his own fault. He made death for himself and for all who followed. When Adam was created there was nothing of death about that man. The element of death did not exist in Adam when God created him. The only reason death came to Adam was that he was the maker of it. Adam made it. Death does not come from God. Satan was not allowed to make it.

Don't fear them that are able to kill the body; fear yourself who is able to both kill the body and cast the soul into hell. You fear the element that is able to put you into the eternal place of destruction. Your failure never comes from without; it comes from within. We come under horrible situations and circumstances. We are ready to scream and tear out our hair. The only way we can collapse under such pressure is through our own unbelief and disobedience. There is no possible way that anyone else can bring you to destruction.

If your life is hidden with Christ in God, no one can do you harm. You can harm yourself. All that Satan brings against you for harm, designed to destroy you, can only do you good. Remember when Jesus was talking with His disciples and He said that they were going to be delivered into prison and beaten and killed. Then, right after that, He said that not a hair of their head shall perish. That is quite an arrangement of statements. It doesn't matter what they do against you. They can crucify you, they can burn your body, they can defame you in every newspaper in the country. They are unable to touch you. They cannot touch you. The only thing they can do is do you good.

The enemy will render evil for good. No matter how good you may be toward the enemy, he will return evil for that good. But remember: Evil is not of a destroying nature to you. The only one who is destroyed is the one from whom it originates. That is why Paul instructed Timothy to speak evil of no man. Paul wasn't concerned about the man's welfare; he was concerned about Timothy's welfare. Destruction is from within.

The person ruled by the Spirit is under pressure from the person ruled by the flesh. Always. This is a law. The Spirit and the flesh are contrary one to another, "But as then he that was born after the flesh persecuted him that was born after the Spirit, even so it is now" (Galatians 4:29). This pattern continues today. The malicious piercing, the attempt to damage and destroy, the attempt to defame and to dishonor, the attempt to insult and wound, are found in today's world. These things are the necessary elements in the believer's boot camp. They are being used to train him for greater battles.

Perhaps the closer you get to your conquest, the rougher the training becomes. More than one modern soldier died in training. They did not endure it, "But watch thou in all things, endure afflictions, do the work of an evangelist, make full proof of thy ministry" (II Timothy 4:5). If there is to be the fulfillment that God is after, there must then be the enduring. This is necessary and an absolutely vital part of the Christian life. Look at the words of Jesus in Matthew 10. Jesus is telling His disciples exactly what they might expect on their Christian walk:

Matthew 10:16-31 (emphasis added)

Behold, I send you forth [they're not going on their own] as sheep in the midst of wolves: be ye therefore wise as serpents, and harmless as doves. But beware of men: for they will deliver you up to the councils, and they will scourge you in their synagogues; and ye shall be brought before governors and kings for my sake, for a testimony against them and the Gentiles. But when they deliver you up, take no thought how or what ye shall speak: for it shall be given you in that same hour what ye shall speak. For it is not ye that speak, but the Spirit of your Father which speaketh in you. And the brother shall deliver up the brother to death, and the father the child: and the children shall rise up against their parents, and cause them to be put to death. And ye shall be hated of all men for my name's sake: but he that endureth to the end shall be saved. But when they persecute you in this city, flee ye into another: for verily I say unto you, Ye shall not have gone over the cities of Israel, till the Son of man be come. The disciple is not above his master, nor the servant above his lord. It is enough for the disciple that he be as his master, and the servant as his lord. If they have called the master of the house Beelzebub, how much more shall they call them of his household? [They're not going to call you an angel of God.] Fear them not therefore: for there is nothing covered, that shall not be revealed; and hid, that shall not be known. What I tell you in darkness, that speak ye in light: and what ye hear in the ear, that preach ye upon the housetops. And fear not them which kill the body, but are not able to kill the soul: but rather fear him which is able to destroy both soul and body in hell.

OUR GREATEST ENEMY

There is only one person that can destroy both soul and body in hell—you. Satan cannot do it, God will not do it, no other man can do it, no other power can do it. There is only one person that can destroy you in hell, and that is yourself. You are your greatest enemy. I wouldn't trust me as far as I could throw myself. The Bible says that my heart is desperately wicked. Therefore how can I really and fully know such a heart? If I decide to walk the pernicious ways of my own heart, I know where that will lead. I can take myself to a place where no one else on earth, in hell, or in heaven could ever take me—eternal damnation. And that's the Gospel truth.

"Are not two sparrows sold for a farthing? One of them shall not fall on the ground without your heavenly Father. You are of more value than many sparrows." Your Father keeps track of the very hairs of your head. Your head may be cut off. Your hair may be burned. More realistically, you may grow bald. Still, not a hair on your head shall perish. Even your body shall be raised in health and perfection. To add to that, nothing of your spiritual life and character shall perish. Not a speck.

The enemy designs to destroy us. When the lion roared against Samson, it was for the sole purpose of destroying him. Samson slew the lion. Later he found honey in the carcass of the lion. He put forth a riddle about it, "From the eater [from the enemy that wanted to eat me], there came forth meat." And so you say, "Come on lion, come on lion, give it your best shot." You know that your meat is on the way. You have no fear. You move under the impact of revelation, not under the impact of the enemy.

There comes forth from the enemy a type of meat which you do not find in other sources. There are different aspects of your spiritual diet. There are all kinds of things on the menu. The honey in the lion is on the menu. That particular dish is not served in another area. In the Scriptures you will find a different kind of feeding. In waiting upon God there will be yet another dish, unlike the others. On the mountaintop there is food served in its own uniqueness. In the valley the table is spread with valley food. God comes and reveals Himself to you and feeds you in different ways, needing different circumstance and situations in order to prepare and serve the different dishes to you.

How do you know that He is the One that supplies all your needs? You first have to be in need. In that situation He comes. Then you know Him as Supplier. That is part of your feeding.

ENDURE HARDSHIPS

Hopefully we learn to endure all that God has for us. Hopefully we learn to pray in affliction and trouble, "Is any among you afflicted? let him pray" (James 5:13). The children of Israel murmured in their affliction. Let others murmur. Let us pray. Learn to pray in affliction rather than practice murmuring. Murmuring won't do you any good; it will do you damage.

"A good man out of the good treasure of the heart bringeth forth good things [Murmuring?—No, Prayer]: and an evil man out of the evil treasure bringeth forth evil things [murmuring, unbelief, disobedience]. But I say unto you, That every idle word that men shall speak, they shall give account thereof in the day of judgment [These are words that destroy. The destruction is from within, never from without. If it came from without we wouldn't stand a chance]. For by thy words thou shalt be justified, and by thy words thou shalt be condemned" (Matthew 12:35-37). "Out from the heart"—that's where it is. Jesus said that it is not what enters into the stomach that defiles a man; it is what comes out from his heart that defiles the man. There is where your destruction is. In affliction we learn to endure and to give the expression which God desires—out from the good heart.

Paul wrote to Timothy, "Endure hardness." Paul was telling Timothy that there is a difference between a good soldier and a poor soldier, "Thou therefore endure hardness, as a good soldier of Jesus Christ" (II Timothy 2:3). There is a good soldier, and there is a poor soldier. A good soldier will endure the pressures, the hardships, the afflictions, and bear up under all difficulties. A poor soldier will not. A good soldier will maintain his faith in God, always believing in Him and continuing in obedience to Him. A poor soldier will not. Keep your eyes open and you can tell the quality of a soldier.

GOD WILL PROVIDE

God will provide everything that is needed for His soldiers, "Then said the LORD unto Moses, Behold, I will rain bread from heaven for you; and the people shall go out and gather a certain rate every day..." (Exodus 16:4). This was the provision for the time that they were in training as soldiers.

God will provide for you as a soldier, whether you are simply in training or in exhausting conquest. When you enlist in the army you do not go through basic training at your own expense. Everything is provided. What is provided? Your transportation to basic camp is provided. Once in camp, you decide you need a car. They decide you don't. You think you have to have a candy bar before you go to bed. They think you don't. You don't see the necessity for immunization shots. They see it. You do not understand why you need to rise from bed at 4:00 a.m. They understand. They decide what you need in your training program. You don't.

God's sense of the trainee's needs may differ from the trainee's sense of need. God provides the soldier in training with the things which are necessary in his training. The soldier in conquest will have different needs. But whatever the needs are, God will provide for His soldiers. The soldier does not provide for himself, "Who goeth to warfare any time at his own charges?" (I Corinthians 9:7). God is training His soldiers how to survive, how to live, "And he humbled thee, and suffered thee to hunger, and fed thee with manna, which thou knewest not, neither did thy fathers know; that he might make thee know that man doth not live by bread only, but by every word that proceedeth out of the mouth of the LORD doth man live" (Deuteronomy 8:3).

God planted eternal life in the first man, but man brought himself into eternal death. God remedied that situation by providing for every man the wherewithal that can bring him out of death and into eternal life. "Man doth not live...." He's dead; all died in Adam. But man shall live by every word that is proceeding out of the mouth of the Lord. That's tremendous. There's a lot of stuff in there. These are the rations of God; He provides that. If a man eats, he shall live. This is Old Testament. The same truth is in the New Testament, "Then Jesus said unto them, Verily, verily, I say unto you, Moses gave you not that bread from heaven; but my Father giveth you the true bread from heaven. For the bread of God is he [He—the logos, the expression of God, in the beginning was the Word] which cometh down from heaven, and giveth life unto the world" (John 6:32,33). He comes to give life to those who are dead. He becomes the living Word, the Word that imparts life to the dead. That is the true bread. Whenever John uses this word "true," he is referring to that which is real in an eternal sense—the real, the spiritual, the eternal bread.

"As newborn babes, desire the sincere milk of the word, that ye may grow thereby" (I Peter 2:2). This is for growth. Pollutants will hinder or prevent growth. If you drink the milk of the Word and also take into yourself guile, malice, hypocrisy, envies, evil speaking, there will be no growth, there will be no strength. Some Christians are weak and defeated because they have mixed pollutants with God's Word. "And did all eat the same spiritual meat" (I Corinthians 10:3). All those in the wilderness ate of the provisions of God. They also ate pollutants.

"But he said unto them, I have meat to eat that ye know not of" (John 4:32). Jesus was fed. God provided for Him as He lived and ministered. As Jesus was provided for, so are we, "For my flesh is meat indeed, and my blood is drink indeed. He that eateth my flesh, and drinketh my blood, dwelleth in me, and I in him. As the living Father hath sent me, and I live by the Father: so he that eateth me, even he shall live by me" (John 6:55-57). This is the provision of life; otherwise, man shall not live. Eat and live.

Drink and live. "And did all drink the same spiritual drink: for they drank of that spiritual Rock that followed them: and that Rock was Christ" (I Corinthians 10:4). "Jesus answered and said unto her, If thou knewest the gift of God, and who it is that saith to thee, 'Give me to drink;' thou wouldest have asked of him, and he would have given thee living water" (John 4:10). "...and my blood is drink indeed. He that...drinketh my blood, dwelleth in me, and I in him" (John 6:55,56). That's your life—drinking and eating. You are to ingest and digest that which God gives you for food.

"But strong meat belongeth to them that are of full age, even those who by reason of use have their senses exercised to discern both good and evil" (Hebrews 5:14). This is productive training—having their senses exercised, through use. "For when for the time ye ought to be teachers, ye have need that one teach you again which be the first principles of the oracles of God; and are become such as have need of milk, and not of strong meat" (Hebrews 5:12). This is a lack of success in their training. There was time and training enough to bring about the ability to eat strong meat. But they were still on the milk, still unskillful in the Word of righteousness. Why? Lack of proper response to God's training program, and messing up the diet by mixing pollutants with it.

A *PROPER* DIET

God provides the proper diet. The diet is greatly varied. The diet in the Old Testament is very revealing. The diet in the New Testament gives much instruction. God gives you through the Holy Spirit the spiritual food necessary for a specific time and occasion. When God wants to give you manna, don't cry for meat. Gladly take that which He is feeding you. Very specific feedings are necessary in order to become what God wants you to be. If you are willing to eat from God's hand and leave other things alone, you will succeed in being a good soldier rather than a poor one. There's a difference between a good soldier and a poor soldier. For one thing a good soldier will live longer than a poor one, and be more productive while he lives. By faith and trust and desire, we reach out to God to receive from Him the rations that He gives us.

PROPER EQUIPMENT

"For whatsoever is born of God overcometh the world: and this is the victory that overcometh the world, even our faith" (I John 5:4). John is not talking about "whosoever." He is talking about "whatsoever." (There is a "whosoever" as well as a "whatsoever;" don't get the two confused.) Our faith has been born of God. Jesus is the author and finisher of your faith which overcomes the world. We were born of God too; don't forget that. We are overcomers. As we overcome, the Lord grants us to sit with Him in His throne as He overcame and is now set down with His Father in His throne.

But overcoming is not limited to the "who," it also includes the "what." "Whatsoever is born of God overcometh the world."

Anything that is born of God can overcome anything of the world. God translates us into His Kingdom. There we come under many things which are born of God. They all are designed to overcome, or bring the victory. (The Greek word translated "victory" and the Greek word translated "overcome" are the same word. One is a verb and one is a noun). "Whatsoever is born of God gets the victory over the world."

It is encouraging to know that we are moving under that which is born of God. There is no defeat in God. Defeat exists, but not in God. No Christian needs to be defeated at any time. There is a permanent victory in God. "Whatsoever is born of God"—that's part of the soldier's equipment. It is for the battle. It is provided in order to win victory and to conquer. Satan has no power over man except what man gives him. He cannot, of his own volition, do evil to man, or harm him. Only with the authority which has been delivered to him can he hurt man. Satan has no authority in any realm except that which has been delivered to him, either by God or by man. We can live apart from those elements of Satan which conquer. In the words of Paul, "Let not sin therefore have dominion over you." Your faith is born of God. Birthing by God is not limited to your faith. The Bible says, "whatsoever."

"Whatever is born of God overcomes." A prayer that is born of God overcomes. It will overcome in the area to which it is directed. A burden of prayer means victory. God birthed that burden. The victory is obvious; it is something that is sure; there is no doubt. There couldn't be anything but victory. To even imagine that there could be failure and defeat is absolutely ridiculous. Whatever it is that God gives birth to overcomes the world. The overcoming aspect comes out from God. That is part of your heritage in God. The provision of God is that which He brings to us—that which He births in us.

"For the weapons of our warfare are not carnal, but mighty through God to the pulling down of strong holds" (II Corinthians 10:4). "That which is born of the flesh, is flesh; and that which is born of the Spirit, is spirit" (John 3:6). "Whatsoever is born of God overcometh the world." Our weapons are not carnal. Why? Because they are not birthed by the flesh. That's why they are not carnal. They could be carnal. We could possess weapons that our flesh birthed. Some people pray out from a fleshly desire. If a believer does not have a power birthed by God, he may attempt to use a power birthed by his flesh. That which is born of the flesh is flesh.

You may be very well equipped with weapons and yet not be conscious of their effectiveness. You may not even be conscious that you have weapons. Yet, while you are not conscious of your weapons, God can do with them what may not even cross your mind. There can be great victories won while the believer knows nothing about them. It may be in your life; it may be in the life of a friend; it may be in the lives of folks you do not even know.

I, and others, have effected victories in lives which we knew nothing about until they came and told us. If they didn't tell it, we would go the rest of our lives not knowing it. You may come across a person who is under tremendous attack by the enemy. That which God has birthed in your heart may be drawn out and offered to that person in that situation. It would then bring victory to that person. Perhaps you did not know that the person was under attack by the enemy. You may have been unaware that there was a battle or a struggle going on in that life. The soldiers that were fighting for Israel against Amalek were not aware that Moses had his hands raised to God. There are many things that we are not aware of. There are weapons, mighty through God. These are birthed of God to the pulling down of strongholds.

CARNALITY IS FAILURE

Carnality is a failure in the Kingdom of God. To be carnally minded is death. The carnal mind is enmity against God. If we attempt to have carnal weapons in the Kingdom of God, we are not fighting for God; we are fighting against God. Saul of Tarsus (the apostle Paul) was using carnal weapons to fight for God; thus, he was fighting against God. He was not fighting for God. God had to arrest Saul on his way to Damascus to arrest Christians and haul them off to prison. He thought he was doing God a favor. He was zealous for God. He would have done anything for God—carnally. But God has had more than His share of that kind of work. He is not asking you to put in your two cents worth of that type of weaponry. He is wanting that which is born of Him, that which is surrendered to Him, that which moves with Him and not against Him. All that we are and possess, our character, our physical body, our mind, we are to yield to God.

"The night is far spent, the day is at hand: let us therefore cast off the works of darkness, and let us put on the armor of light" (Romans 13:12). The works of darkness can be very shiny. The works of darkness can look like the works of light. Satan can look like an angel of light. Satan has most Christians bound in some form or another. A believer cannot get along with his brother. What is that? That is the work of darkness. You cannot call that the work of light. A Christian is troubled by a nagging recurring fear. What's that? Is it the love of God that brings fear? No! It is the work of darkness. It is not the work of God. Satan moves in. He is most clever. He takes and maintains a foothold in the lives of many Christians, and binds them in specific areas. Paul was not writing to the sinner when he wrote, "Let us cast off the works of darkness." He was addressing Christians in the church at Rome. He included himself, "Let us...."

"Let us walk honestly, as in the day; not in rioting and drunkenness, not in chambering and wantonness, not in strife and envying. But put ye on the Lord Jesus Christ, and make not provision for the flesh, to fulfill the lusts thereof" (Romans 13:13,14). Do not fabricate your own provisions for the battle to which God has called you. Be satisfied with the provisions that God provides. Do not worry about getting the spiritual provisions that you think you need. God will provide for you in every way. God provided manna for the children of Israel. They were dissatisfied with that; they wanted their own thing. They manifested the works of the flesh, the desires of the flesh. The works of darkness were in them. They wanted provisions which would fulfill the desires of the flesh. Let us be willing to put off the hindering factors, the works of darkness, and gladly accept the provisions of God.

"Wherefore seeing we also are compassed about with so great a cloud of witnesses, let us lay aside every weight, and the sin which doth so easily beset us, and let us run with patience the race that is set before us" (Hebrews 12:1). Believers are more apt at taking on hindering weights than they are at laying them aside. They look at pleasant and harmless-looking things of the world. They desire, and reach out and take. It would be to our advantage to look away from such things, and take a longer and more intense look at Jesus, "Looking unto Jesus the author and finisher of our faith; who for the joy that was set before him endured the cross, despising the shame, and is set down at the right hand of the throne of God. For consider him that endured such contradiction of sinners against himself, lest ye be wearied and faint in your minds" (Hebrews 12:2,3).

What believer wants to be defeated? No Christian wants to live a defeated life. There really should not be defeat for the believer. There is no way to be defeated in God. Does the believer have the willingness to take the correct direction? "Neither yield ye your members as instruments of unrighteousness unto sin" (Romans 6:13). We have many members. Not all members are apparent. We have members which cannot be seen. We have abilities. We are partly composed of abstracts: desire, ambition, mind, etc. They are as much a part of us as our hands. We can yield the abstract qualities. There are entertainers who yield their talents in very questionable areas. There are others with the same talents who yield them as instruments of righteousness. It is a matter of direction. Are we willing to take the proper direction? In God's training program He has provided for us specific direction.

Chapter Nine
Being a Soldier
in the Wilderness of Sin (Part Two)

———∞∞———

THE MANUAL

The Manual is available. Many believers do not use the Manual. Without following the Manual's instructions they go in the wrong direction and get in a mess of trouble. "When all else fails, read the instructions." After a believer messes up his life, then he decides to read carefully the instructions. We should read the instructions before we are in trouble, and stick to them. A lot of Christians are in trouble because they do not take the directives that God gives them. Paul says to think on these things:

Whatsoever things are true,
Whatsoever things are honest,
Whatsoever things are just,
Whatsoever things are pure,
Whatsoever things are lovely,
Whatsoever things are of good report.
Philippians 4:8

There are believers who think on everything but "these things." That is one reason why they are in trouble. They do not follow the Manual.

If we are to share with Christ in the ministry of the Gospel, we must be trained and approved. Our training takes place in various situations and circumstances, not just in a classroom. Paul listed some of them:

In much patience,
In afflictions,
In necessities,
In distresses,
In stripes,
In imprisonments,
In tumults,
In labours,
In watchings,
In fastings.
II Corinthians 6:4,5

Our college degrees will not be the evidence of approval. The apostle Paul had it right when he wrote, "But in all things approving ourselves as the ministers of God:

By pureness,
By knowledge,
By longsuffering,
By kindness,
By the Holy Ghost,
By love unfeigned,
By the word of truth,
By the power of God,
By the armour of righteousness
By honour and dishonour,
By evil report and good report."
II Corinthians 6:4-8

These things are the evidence of the approval of God. These are the parts necessary to function as a true servant of God. The list reads somewhat like the parts of a rifle in the manual. The soldier learns the manual and his rifle. Every part must be clean, in proper working order, and in its place. If a part is missing, out of place, or gummed up, the rifle will not work properly. It may not fire at all. Or it may misfire and hurt or kill the innocent. There are ministers of God who have parts missing. Through them many innocent people are hurt or killed. Every part Paul listed is vital, and should be in the life of the messenger of the Gospel.

Paul wrote, "I thank my God that He has put me into the ministry, counting me faithful...." God found faithfulness in Paul. This was the quality which God thought necessary and proper for putting him into the ministry. We must be faithful in following the Manual. We must be faithful in following the Master. We must be faithful in following God's will and direction.

In our training, we become qualified soldiers that will get the victory, moving into the areas which God intends us to conquer. In our training, we are exercised and we become strengthened. We grow in strength. "Finally, my brethren, be strong in the Lord, and in the power of his might" (Ephesians 6:10). How? It is by training, exercising, doing, obeying. "Put on the whole armor of God, that ye may be able to stand against the wiles of the devil" (Ephesians 6:11). Who is to put on the whole armor of God? Those who are strong. Don't insist that a babe puts on the armor of God. Don't insist upon that, please. David can tell you about that. He experienced that. Remember when he put on Saul's armor? God delivered the Israelites from Egypt. He prevented Israel's confrontation with Pharaoh's army. Before battle, the Israelites were to be tried and strengthened, "lest they see war and they become frightened and they repent and want to return to Egypt."

NOVICES DO NOT WAR

Paul said, "Not a novice, lest he be puffed up." In other words, not one who is newly planted. The Greek word translated "novice" means "newly planted." Why not a novice? Because he is not yet strong enough for the tasks. How would he be sustained in the particular spiritual battles found in the work of a bishop? And if he did experience success, he would become puffed up, proud, and therefore defeated. That's war. Paul was not talking about being puffed up in failure. Who is ever puffed up in failure? Paul was talking about being puffed up in success. Acclaim may come; compliments may be given. Because they are there does not mean that one must be puffed up over them. But a novice is very likely to be puffed up over success and that which it brings.

There is a novice in the church. What shall be done with him? He has ability. He can well fill the office of a bishop. He has qualifications. But we will not put him into that office. Why? Because he will fail? No, because he will succeed. Somehow the church has not gotten the message that people are the work of God. The more glory that you are called upon to hold and to carry, the stronger your structure and supports must be. The meat and muscles of a twenty-year-old cannot go on the bone frame of a four-year-old. That frame is not large enough to hold all that weight. The four-year-old must grow. As he grows, his structure, his bracing, the thing that holds everything together and enables him to carry more weight, grows along with the weight.

We grow in God. More and more of His glory comes to us (II Corinthians 3:18). More and more of His grace is given to us. More and more persecution comes our way. For everything God adds to us, we need strength enough to carry the load. As we are moving on in God, we must move on in strength. We must gain in strength in order to be able to carry that which God puts upon us. We must be strengthened in order to sustain that which the enemy hurls at us. God may give us a burden. We may be brought into God's glory. Can we successfully support all things? We have honor and dishonor. Can we carry dishonor as well as we carry honor? It will depend upon the individual's degree of strength. God's provisions are growth and armor, the full armor:

Ephesians 6:12-18

For we wrestle not against flesh and blood, but against principalities, against powers, against the rulers of the darkness of this world, against spiritual wickedness in high places. Wherefore take unto you the whole armor of God, that ye may be able to withstand in the evil day, and having done all, to stand. Stand therefore, having your loins girt about with truth, and having on the breast plate of righteousness; and your feet shod with the preparation of the gospel of peace; above all, taking the shield of faith, wherewith ye shall be able to quench all the fiery darts of the wicked. And take the helmet of salvation, and the sword of the Spirit, which is the word of God: praying always with all prayer and supplication in the Spirit, and watching thereunto with all perseverance and supplication for all saints.

We wrestle. Be aware of who your opponent is. Do not wrestle with God. Never do that. Those who say that they wrestled with God do not know what they are talking about. "Well," they say, "Jacob did that." This they say because they do not know the Bible well enough. The Bible says that there wrestled with Jacob a man that night. What did Jacob do? Foolishly he returned that; foolishly he wrestled back. Oh, Jacob, what in the world are you doing? Don't wrestle with God when He comes to correct you, to change you, to bless you. Wrestle against the spiritual wickedness, the rulers of darkness; don't wrestle against God.

Let us move in harmony with God that He may strengthen us to wrestle against that which is His enemy. He is training us for the battle so that we may move contrary to Satan. "Resist the devil and he shall flee from you." "Resisting" means "to flow contrary to him"—it does not mean "to say, 'I resist you, I resist you,' and to be stubborn about it." Resisting the devil is the flow of a life absolutely contrary to him. He flows one way, we flow the other way. The verse before states, "Submit yourselves unto God." Flow with God. Resisting the devil will be a byproduct.

We cannot avoid resisting the enemy when we flow with God. Resisting the devil is automatic when we flow with God because the two are contrary. God flows one way and Satan flows the other way. We need strength to flow with God. God provides us with much equipment. It would take much too much of this book to explain in detail the aspects of each piece. There is the shield of faith. Many, many pages would be used for that one piece of equipment. The extent of the equipment that God provides for His children is unimaginable. There is more in God than we will ever use in our entire life.

"I can do all things through Christ which strengtheneth me" (Philippians 4:13). Ability is provided. Do not take "all things" and use that to attempt to fulfill your desires. The "all things" is put there by inspiration of God and relates to the text which had been written just before the "all things." In that text you see that Paul knew how to rejoice and live above difficult situations. He knew how to live when in abundance. He knew how to live a victorious life when in poverty. In all your difficulties, you can say, "I am able for all things through Christ Jesus who strengthens me. I can be abased; I can abound; I can have nothing; I can suffer need; I can be full; I can hunger—I can do all things." Keep truth in its context and perspective. "I can do all things" does not mean "I can fly to Castor." If God wanted you near Castor, He would certainly get you there. But just because you want a close-up view of that star, "I can do all things through Christ Jesus" will not make it happen.

Using verses out of the Bible to gain one's own desires is for people who do not know any better and cannot read. Learn how to read the Word correctly. Watch the Scripture! What is its context? How is it applied? To whom is it applied? Under what conditions is it imposed? It is not put there for your use; it is put there for your direction. "This is the way—walk ye in it." Walk in it. Do not use it to get what you want. Do not use it to escape your testings. To some Christians the Bible is nothing more than a department store—to shop around and see what is there that they like. Do not use the Bible as a Sears catalog.

"I can do all things" is a valid statement and a tremendous blessing in its reality. God can bring you through all kinds of situations, lending you the ability for each and every particular situation. You have all the "can do" (the Greek word is "dunimas") that is necessary. God gives you the power for the occasion.

"And it came to pass, when Moses held up his hand, that Israel prevailed: and when he let down his hand, Amalek prevailed. But Moses hands were heavy; and they took a stone, and put it under him, and he sat thereon; and Aaron and Hur stayed up his hands, the one on the one side, and the other on the other side; and his hands were steady [faithful] until the going down of the sun" (Exodus 17:11,12). This entire battle situation moved with and without intercession. When Moses' hands were up, what happened? When his hands were down, then what happened?

Prayer is one of the most effective elements that we have at our disposal. Its potency and potential are out of sight. Daniel prayed and the nation was liberated from their bondage—just because one man prayed. God heard the cry of the children of Israel and He brought them out of Egypt—just the cry, how amazing! God heard a call. The call can take any form, or no form. The call can be deep in the heart without a vocal expression, yet it can be heard by God. The call can be expressed in intercession, supplication, petition, or whatever. The sublime beauty about it is that the attentive ear of our heavenly Father easily picks up the sound. Moses expressed his call by lifting up his hands. This expression brought the ability needed to win the battle. One of the provisions of God is the arrangement of communication between Him and man.

The expression which moves correctly is the one moving in harmony with God, not contrary to God. There is expression which moves opposite to God. Moses' expression moved in perfect harmony with God. Moses and the people used the equipment at hand. Moses or anyone else did not pray for better equipment. The people went to fight the enemy with the weapons already available in the camp of the Israelites. Moses went up to the top of the mountain and used that which was available to him. The message today is the same. We are being taught and trained to move against the enemy with the equipment available to us. We are being taught and trained to live and act in harmony with God.

Jesus spoke to Peter, "And I say also unto thee, That thou art Peter, and upon this rock I will build my church; and the gates of hell shall not prevail against it" (Matthew 16:18). The intention of the Lord Jesus is "I will build my church." This is not the picture of hell coming against the church. This is the picture of the church coming against the gates of hell. The gates are at the wall. The church takes the fight to the walls of the enemy. The gates are attacked. Why? Because that is the weakest place in the city's defense system. To get to the gates of hell, the church must bring the battle into enemy territory. The gate of the city is the gate of the defender, not the gate of the one who is on the offensive. The gates of hell shall not prevail or shall not be able to hold out against the church. Therefore the church moves against the enemy. The church of Jesus Christ is not supposed to be on the defensive. His victorious church is on the offensive. It captures territory; it moves progressively against the enemy; it carries the fight to Him.

TRAINED TO OBEY

The Wilderness of Sin is a training ground, "Then said the Lord unto Moses, Behold, I will rain bread from heaven for you;

and the people shall go out and gather a certain rate every day, that I may prove them, whether they will walk in my law, or no" (Exodus 16:4). This was a particular provision and exercise in the people's training. It was their test of obedience, "And he took the book of the covenant, and read in the audience of the people: and they said, All that the Lord hath said will we do, and be obedient" (Exodus 24:7). Obedience does not come from the spoken conviction and intention. Obedience comes through testings—for *everybody*, "Though he were a Son, yet learned he obedience by the things which he suffered" (Hebrews 5:8).

One of the objects of the training program in the Wilderness of Sin was to train these people in obedience. This is the very basic element in the training for battle. If there is no obedience in battle, there will be no victory. Obedience is a must. It is one thing to say, "All that the Lord has said will we do and be obedient," and quite another thing to do it. Words are much cheaper than actions. Jesus talked about a father with a vineyard and two sons:

Matthew 21:28-31

"But what think ye? A certain man had two sons; and he came to the first, and said, Son, go work to day in my vineyard. He answered and said, I will not: but afterward he repented, and went. And he came to the second, and said likewise. And he answered and said, I go, sir: and went not. Whether of them twain did the will of his father? They say unto him, The first. Jesus saith unto them, Verily I say unto you, That the publicans and the harlots go into the kingdom of God before you."

God is not after lip service; He is after a life that will be willing to march to His tune. He is gathering together a people who will serve Him in reality. He wants people who will do His will, rather than those who simply talk about doing His will. There are people who pray about doing His will, and that's all they do, pray about it. That is not what God desires. He desires a people who will actually do what He says to do; who will, in fact, take upon themselves to obey the Word of God. That is what He is after. How does God get this arrangement? People are not born with it. They must be trained to obey. When you disobey God, do not collapse in discouragement and defeat, and give up. Obedience is not something that is automatic. There is the need of learning obedience. You have to *learn* to obey.

When one is born again of the Spirit of God, it would be just lovely if God somehow dumped into him that quality of total and unquestioning obedience. But that is not the way it happens, "Though he were a Son, yet learned he obedience by the things which he suffered" (Hebrews 5:8). This is talking about Jesus. Jesus was not born with perfect obedience. He was not born with perfect judgment in order to carry out perfect obedience. When he was twelve years old He asked, "Wist ye not that I must be about my Father's business?" Says who? That was His story at twelve years of age, but that was not His time to be about His Father's business. His time to be about His Father's business was when He was thirty years old. John the Baptist, according to the will of God, had to be the forerunner of Jesus. John was not "forerunning" when Jesus was twelve. And so, at twelve years of age we see Him laboring under an imperfect judgment. His misjudgment led Him out of his Father's will. Joseph and Mary found Him and brought Him back to the place which God had ordained for Him.

LEARNING

How did Jesus learn? Did God say to Him, "Let's sit down together and I'll tell You how to be always in complete obedience"? Oh, no. "He *learned* obedience by the things which He suffered." How does a child learn obedience to the laws of nature? Can one take a child and sit down with him and explain hot and cold to him? Can the child be potty-trained by definitions of his bodily functions? Does one elucidate to a child about all the laws of his digestive system and all the things that he can and cannot eat? Does explaining to a child the danger of traffic keep him from playing in the street? No one can perfect a child by that method. The child must learn.

How does he learn? How does he learn not to fall down the steps? A few falls will help him. How does he learn of dangers? A few experiences will be valuable for learning. Hopefully he will learn by the things which he suffers. How does he learn that a pin hurts him? Can you simply tell him that this is a pin and, if he jabs himself with it, it will hurt him? Will the child answer, "I understand perfectly. I will never jab myself with a pin"? You know that a child never gives that answer. He will learn the obedience to certain laws by the things which he suffers as he acts in violation of those laws.

How did Jesus learn? By the things which He suffered. How did that work? It did not involve sin. But there are many things in which to err that are not sin. "For all have sinned AND come short of the glory of God." The Bible doesn't say, "For all have sinned" period. It doesn't say, "All have come short of the glory of God" period. It says, all have sinned AND come short of the glory of God. "To him that knowest to do good and doeth it not, to him that is sin." What about the other? What about "Not doing good because he does not know it to be the good"?

There are such things as misjudgments, errors, coming short, not coming to the fullness, which would bring into the life of Jesus some difficulties and sufferings. We will never be able to understand the struggles and testings Jesus endured. We could never imagine the strain of His knowing all that He did at age twenty-five and having to keep the lid on it. No one knows the difficulty He faced in obeying Joseph and Mary while yearning to obey His Father. Yes, He suffered. We cannot imagine how much He suffered. He learned. To some degree we can see the extent of His learning by gazing upon His perfect life. He went to school, but not in Jerusalem. He did not sit in a classroom, but He went to school—His Father's school. He learned in the circumstances and situations. Jesus needed to learn because He wasn't born with it. He needed obedience to the extent that it became a perfected thing in His life before He began His public ministry.

God is always working on perfect obedience in our lives. There are particular purposes which God brings to pass through human instruments. Some of these purposes He cannot fulfill until the obedience comes to the maturity and perfection which is needed in the particular situation. What would it have been like in the ministry of Jesus Christ if He had not learned complete obedience? We know that He would not have willfully disobeyed. But He would not have fulfilled the Father's full intentions if He had not learned fullness in regards to obedience.

Which would be better, giving one dollar in the church offering or giving five dollars in the church offering? Five dollars appears to be a fuller offering. A very close friend of mine was visiting a church in Florida. It was a small church. As the offering was being taken, he took a five-dollar bill from his wallet to put in the offering. Immediately the Lord spoke to him, "No, put one dollar in the offering." Mystified, he nevertheless obeyed. The five was returned to his wallet, and a dollar bill replaced it. The offering was taken and promptly the pastor said, "I want the offering counted right now." He seemed a bit troubled. The offering was hastily counted, and the amount reported. When the total was announced, the pastor burst into tears. Then he told his story. He said, "I was so discouraged. I came here tonight intending to resign as pastor of this church. Yet, I didn't have a complete peace and liberty to do so. But I was so determined that I put out an impossible fleece as a sign I should stay. I told God that if such an amount, exactly, is in the offering tonight, that I would not resign. The offering tonight was exactly what I had stated in my fleece. I am staying, for the Lord still has a work for me to do here."

The difference between disobedience and obedience may be narrower than a frog's hair split in two. The results may be two worlds apart. At times God needs a perfection in obedience that can split a frog's hair in two. He needed that in the life of Jesus. He took thirty years to train Him in order to get that thing to operate. Jesus learned. It operated in His selection of Judas. At times He would move out of the grasp of the enemy. Then the time came when He deliberately moved into the hands of the enemy. Many, many times it would simply be a very fine line of obedience. Not even the disciples knew at the time the narrowness of Jesus' path of obedience. It seemed so natural that much of its supernaturalness went undetected. Perfect obedience is not understood by many, let alone known through experience.

God is training us in obedience. Our training begins on an elementary level—not too difficult. As we progress, we are brought to more difficult levels, and on to most difficult levels. He wants to get from us the greatest degree of fulfillment possible. Obedience is an extremely important area—very, very important.

During a chapel service at a Bible school, the Lord said to a student, "I want you to crawl down the aisle on your hands and knees." Brother! In front of all these students? Yes. Inside he said, "I don't know about that; it would make me look kind of silly." "I want you to crawl down the aisle on your hands and knees." After a fierce struggle he left his seat and crawled down the aisle on his hands and knees. When he got to the front, the glory of God fell on everyone and God ministered to that student body for six hours. God moved in their midst because one person obeyed.

Obedience is better than sacrifice. *Obedience!* It has such far-reaching implications that it defies the imagination. Obedience is certainly necessary in our lives in order to function properly in God. How can you function properly in God's intentions if you cannot and will not obey? You will function as properly as you obey. You cannot function properly in disobedience.

One of my teachers in Bible School, Walter Beuttler, told us of an experience he had while walking down a street in Algiers. The Holy Spirit said to him, "Step to the right quickly." He stepped to the right quickly, just as a fellow darted by with a knife extended. The fellow intended to cut open Beuttler's pants pocket to extract his wallet. That act of obedience caused the fellow to miss his target. Obedience pays off. But you cannot stand around and question God. If obedience comes too late you may lose your wallet, or something more serious. In certain cases you would be dead.

God attempts to bring us to an obedience which is immediate and without reservations. Hopefully it becomes automatic. It is not put into us automatically. In our training and learning it becomes so ingrained in us that we just do it without thinking. God is after perfect obedience, full complete, immediate obedience without taking the time to think about it. Perfect obedience is far reaching. It is necessary, among other reasons, for the purpose of functioning properly in the millennium. It is necessary to fulfill God's intentions in the ages to come.

"Seeing ye have purified your souls in obeying the truth through the Spirit unto unfeigned love of the brethren, see that ye love one another with a pure heart fervently" (I Peter 1:22). Obedience works purification into us. "If you walk in the light," is the obedience to the light. The result of that obedience is "the blood of Jesus Christ his Son cleanseth us from all sin." Obeying the truth which you have is quite important.

There are believers who do not walk in the light which they have. Some will neglect one area of light which God gave them, in order to fulfill a certain desire or ambition. You cannot do that and still come to the fullness which your Father has in mind for you. You have to obey that which He brings to you; you have to walk in the light which you have; you have to obey the truth which you know and understand. Some folks will worry so much about the truth which they do not know or understand. What they should be doing is being more concerned about the truth which they do know or understand. Walk in that truth, rather than neglect it.

Obedience to the truth is necessary for the work of God to continue in us. There are two directions we can follow. In obeying the truth, there is a growth in obedience. This means that one grows stronger and is more deeply rooted in God. His obedience becomes more habitual and complete. In disobeying the truth, there is a growth in disobedience. This means that there is a stronger inclination to follow one's own will, ever drifting further and further from living in the truth.

HOLY SPIRIT POWER

Obedience is in the power of the Holy Spirit. We are called upon by God to live and transcend above the carnal and the natural. We are brought into the Kingdom of God to operate beyond our ability. No one in their own ability can live a life for God and please God, "Without faith it is impossible to please God." No one can come to the Lord and fulfill the thought, "I'll live for You. You step aside and let me do it." God picks us up and sets us on a higher plane. He provides us with an ability beyond our own to operate and function on that plane which is higher than we. It is a level higher than our natural, human capabilities. God is after responses from us in the area of obedience. Our heavenly Father calls for obedience in a certain situation. He has given the ability to respond correctly. The bottom line is, are we going to use that which the Father has provided and obey, or are we going to turn from it and disobey?

I was caught in a certain situation where, as far as my natural ability was concerned, it would have been total disobedience. To move in obedience to God in that situation seemed to be completely out of my hands. But the Holy Spirit rushed in and lifted me up above my natural inability and into an ability I did not have. At that point I still had a decision to make; was I or was I not going to response correctly to the enabling of the Holy Spirit? Against my own natural desire, I chose to obey God. Only with the help of my heavenly Father was perfect obedience possible. Such a thing brings a tremendous sense of victory. You know that God won the battle; you did not. You simply surrendered to the mind of the Spirit.

If we walk according to the Holy Spirit, we shall not fulfill the lusts of the flesh. Why not? Because the Holy Spirit is actively engaged in leading and directing us. The Spirit is constantly bringing to us God's desires. We surrender to His direction, "walking according to the Holy Spirit." At that same time it is impossible to be fulfilling our own carnal desires, "We shall not fulfill the lusts of the flesh." Quite impossible. Obedience becomes the manifestation of love. Jesus said, "If you love me you will keep my commandments." The power of the Holy Spirit moves in us to bring us to obedience.

Here is another power which also moves in us to bring us to obedience. The power of love brings to us the "want to" in obedience. There are those who do not wish to obey God. Love comes in. There is a change. Now there is a desire to obey God, "And being found in fashion as a man, he humbled himself, and became obedient unto death, even the death of the cross" (Philippians 2:8).

Obedience begins in the small, easy things in our Christian walk. We are first brought into obedience in our basic and undemanding babyhood. That is just a beginning for us. As we follow in His path, obedience will grow in strength. In its development it will carry us through our life into the fulfillment of the most difficult requirements that God has for us. We grow into this; we learn. We are not born again with this. Wouldn't it be nice if we were? But we're not. We disobey, we make a mistake. Failure is not failure unless you get stuck in it. Failure is nothing but a stepping-stone from one classroom to another classroom, higher ground. Progress on failure? Yes, on failure. The Bible is full of it.

The faith of Abraham failed in his stay in Egypt and in regards to the son whom God promised him. But he went on and came to the complete faith which God intended for him. Jacob's life seemed hopeless in its beginning. He went on and came to greatness. Saul's life was a disaster. He fought against God, killing the Christians. He went on and became the great apostle Paul. We see them succeeding in God because they did not get stuck and swallowed up in their failures, in their sins, in their disobedience. They did not give up and sink deeply down into the thick mud and trapping mire. They did not forget about everything, thinking that God had forsaken them. They did not bog down over the question "What must God think of me now?" They fell. They learned. They got up and went on, "For a just man falleth seven times, and riseth up again" (Proverbs 24:16).

Rather than sinking further down into the hopeless mire of self-condemnation, we can learn. Let us step up on higher ground where it becomes more solid. Let us allow our experiences to become learning processes for ourselves. Sometimes our experiences are costly. Since we pay, we just as well ought to get some benefits in return.

The learning process is best found in humility and submission, "He humbled himself...." This is where the success of learning obedience is found. He became a servant. In Philippians 2:7 we read, "But made himself of no reputation, and took upon him the form of a servant, and was made in the likeness of men." He became obedient in humility and servitude. There will be success in humility and servitude. You cannot carry pride in your life and learn obedience. That is quite impossible. You may obey to a certain extent, as it pleases your whims and inclinations. The extent of your disobedience will be in direct proportion to the extent of the pride in your life.

SELF-WILL MUST GO

Obedience is found in denying self's will. In the garden of Gethsemane Jesus prayed, "O my Father, if it be possible, let this cup pass from me: nevertheless not as I will, but as thou wilt" (Matthew 26:39). He became obedient. He humbled himself. He was a servant. He laid aside His own will. Thus, we must suffer death to self before we can take up our cross and follow the wonderful man of Galilee. Jesus had to die to Himself before He could be brought to the cross. Many believers will fight the cross for the sake of their own self-existence. Once we become willing to die to self, then God can bring us into the sacrifices which lie along our paths of obedience.

Do not rush too far ahead of the Lord's will. Training and learning are first necessary before coming into some aspects of His will. There must be a denying of self before there even can be a learning. Jesus said, "You cannot be my disciple unless you deny yourself, take up your cross, and follow me." The denying of self is necessary for your learning. Taking up your cross is necessary for your learning. All three—denying, taking, following—are indispensable to fulfill the learning process. "Disciple" means "pupil"—one who is a learner.

After Elijah was taken up, the sons of the prophets, fifty of them, said, "We want to go out and search for Elijah." Elisha said, "No, that is not necessary." And they said, "We want to do this." Elisha said, "No, no, that's not the thing to do; you will not find him." "Oh, we'll find him, for sure. We have to do this; this is a serious matter." Elisha said, "He's ascended; you won't find him." "No," they said, "we can't take that chance. He's out there some-where needing our help." And they urged Elisha to the point that he acquiesced and stepped aside to allow them to move in self-will. Revelation had to move out of the way to allow ignorance to func-tion. *Insisting to push forward in self-will lowers the possibility of Holy Spirit revelation.* Self-will does not function in revelation whether it has it or not. So why should the Holy Spirit introduce revelation into such a condition?

There is a direct ratio between obedience and victory. The more there is the laying aside of self-will, the greater the learning of obedi-ence. The fuller the obedience, the more numerous are the victo-ries in Christian living. Obedience brings victory. There are many examples which reveal the truth that obedience brings victory. Joshua and the people marched around Jericho in obedience to the

Lord's directive. There are examples of Moses and Elijah and many others who moved in obedience which brought the victory.

Along with the many examples we have of obedience bringing victory, there are the injunctions of the Lord. There is one in Isaiah 1:19, "If ye be willing and obedient, ye shall eat the good of the land." Obedience carried to victory, and victory carried to fulfillment. Obedience must move with the cooperation of man's will, "*If* ye be willing...." In willing obedience there is an appetite being created, "Ye shall eat the good of the land." The appetite is for fulfillment. Therefore the extent of willingness is also being increased. Obedience keeps you on the road to greatness in God.

Why did not the children of Israel possess the Promised Land after two years in the wilderness? Why did they have to go back and die in the wilderness? Disobedience. By obedience, fulfillment and possession finally were achieved. After generations in the Promised Land, the Israelites went back into disobedience. The result of that is stated in Nehemiah 9:36, "Behold, we are servants this day, and for the land that thou gavest unto our fathers to eat the fruit thereof and the good thereof, behold, we are servants in it." *Obedience must be constant if victory is to be constant.*

"But if thou shalt indeed obey his voice, and do all that I speak; then I will be an enemy unto thine enemies, and an adversary unto thine adversaries" (Exodus 23:22). God will oppose those who oppose you. He will afflict those who afflict you. Obedience aligns you with God. In that relationship He will relate to others just as they relate to you. Jesus said to His disciples, "For the Father himself loveth you, because ye have loved me, and have believed that I came out from God" (John 16:27). The words "loveth" and "loved" are translated from the Greek verb "phileo." The meaning is, "The Father Himself is fond of you." Why? "Because you have been fond of Me." Jesus obeys the Father. He aligns Himself to the Father's Person and will. As a result, the Father's fondness flows to those who are fond of Jesus. God will always do that. He was the first to say, "Any friend of yours is a friend of Mine."

AWESOME RESPONSIBILITY

"For as by one man's disobedience many were made sinners, so by the obedience of one shall many be made righteous" (Romans

5:19). Obedience is far reaching. What is the extent of the results of your obedience? You will never know in this life on earth. The extent of the results of obedience becomes a very serious factor.

During my years in the Amazon as a missionary, I have had to stand beside many dying people. Most were darkened in spirit and understanding, not having the knowledge of Christ. Most had died minutes before my arrival, or were so far gone that they were beyond my reach. That may not appear so bad in itself, considering that most folks decide to go the way of damnation and hell anyway. However, in the outlying villages along the Amazon river and its tributaries, 50 percent of those to whom I preached were converted to Jesus. For every two that I had to see die, one would have been reached with the saving knowledge of Christ. Some people in some of these areas had never seen a missionary or a messenger of the Gospel.

Because of the disobedience of some, others will suffer. We attempt to gain some self-comfort by inventing some doctrine which relieves us of the responsibility. Nevertheless, the Word of God still speaks, "For as by one man's disobedience many were made sinners." More sobering than that are the words recorded in Ezekiel 3:18, "When I say unto the wicked, Thou shalt surely die; and thou givest him not warning, nor speakest to warn the wicked from his wicked way, to save his life; the same wicked man shall die in his iniquity; but his blood will I require at thine hand."

"By the obedience of one, many shall be made righteous." By the obedience of one, a person comes to Jesus. By that new convert's obedience, two persons discover the Christ who saves. Then four come. How far does it go? Quite a ways! Obedience is so very important that God will take us through extreme difficulties to instill it in us by hard knocks. Who can fathom the importance of the life of obedience to which God has called us? Training is to project us into awesome fulfillment. If we are to get there, we must learn obedience in our training program.

Do not despair in your rigorous training circumstances. Remember their purposes. Always keep in mind the goal, and press on. The race is not to the swift. Those who are faithful in obedience win the prize.

Chapter Ten

Fear and Unbelief

in the Wilderness of Moab

⸻ ∞∞∞ ⸻

The only reference to the Wilderness of Moab as such is Deuteronomy 2:8. This is one of two wildernesses which should not be part of the Christian's life. However, at times it does touch the Christian's experience. The reference in Deuteronomy 2:8 is, "So we passed beyond our brothers the sons of Esau, who live in Seir, away from the Arabah road, away from Elath and from Ezion-geber. And we turned and passed through by the way of the wilderness of Moab" (NASB).

When the word "Moab" first occurs in the Bible, it is in an incestuous situation. "Ab" is the word for "father," and "Mo" is the preposition meaning "from," and attached to "ab." Thus the translation of "moab" is "from father." When the elder daughter of Lot gave birth to her child which she had conceived by her own father, she named him Moab, or From Father (Genesis 19:36-37).

No part of Moab, wilderness or whatever, was to be part of Israel's possession. "I will not give you any of their land as a possession," said God in Deuteronomy 2:9 (NASB). As the children of Israel were to have nothing to do with this territory, so is the Christian to avoid it in its spiritual sense, which, in its first setting, is incest.

Genesis 36:35 is the second reference in which "Moab" occurs. This is a setting of defeat: Midian is smitten in the field of Moab. Defeat is not to become a possession of the believer; victory is; but so many believers seem to be living in defeat, living in the field of Moab. Their problem is the field in which they live. They live in the world's field, or the field of personal circumstances. They do not live in God. If your life is hidden with Christ in God, you will discover that there is no defeat in God.

"Moab was in great fear because of the people, for they were numerous; and Moab was in dread of the sons of Israel" (Numbers 22:3). This is also mentioned in Exodus 15:15 (NASB), "The leaders of Moab, trembling grips them." This is more than suggestive. It presents a type of fear and dread which should not be part of the Christian's life; this is not the believer's possession. King David pens, "I will fear no evil." A believer's life in God should reflect his faith in God's power and care. Some believers live a fearful life. This is unbelief. Furthermore, there is no vision in the soul. God's loving care cannot be seen. God's power, ability, and control cannot be seen; instead, enemies and adverse situations are seen. They are the focal point of some Christians. Come out of Moab and be healed! Come out of Moab for your peace and strength! The aspects of Moab should not be found in a believer's life.

How can one come out of Moab? The very fact that a Christian is in Moab indicates a lack of complete and unconditional surrender to God. One's own will and desires are followed and catered to. Thus, to come out of Moab requires a reversal of these detrimental trends. How does one suddenly reverse patterns followed for years? He doesn't. The solution is to continually and habitually bring oneself in helplessness and dependency before God, asking Him to accomplish the reverse in you. The solution is to continually and habitually be reading the Bible with a desire to conform to it.

DEATH LURKS IN MOAB

Relationships to the area of Moab breed death. A life lived in fear, unbelief, and defeat not only leads to death, but brings the shadow of death over everyone it touches. Such a life can drag others into the death stream. Death, in the context of Moab, is seen in Numbers 25:9, "And those who died in the plague were twenty and four thousand." This was the result of the people of Israel committing "whoredom with the daughters of Moab" (verse 1). In application to the spiritual life: one's giving oneself to the spirit of Moab, that is, to the spirits of fear and immorality, is an indication of unbelief which leads to defeat and death.

Beyond the area of Moab, any area of the enemies of the cross of Christ (Philippians 3:18) can be likewise applied. Certain religious factions are enemies of the cross. Certain "Spirit-filled" Christians are enemies of the cross, refusing and denying death to self. This is why you see individuals in the church living defeated lives.

This present world's system and philosophy are enemies of the cross. When a believer is influenced toward ungodliness through his relationships with the world, we see the results in his defeat; we see his spiritual life ebbing from him.

God has put fear and trembling upon His enemies. Fear and trembling have never been meant for the child of God in their negative sense. "There is no fear in love," writes John in his first epistle, 4:18. Fear is a horrible feeling. Developing a pure relationship with the Lord (in which Jesus is allowed to be Lord of the life) will do away with this awful fear.

There is a direct relationship between a person's lack of dedication to the Lord and the amount of fear moving in his life. In other words, your fear is in ratio to your lack of dedication. If dedication is 40 percent, fear is 60 percent. If dedication is 99 percent, fear is 1 percent, and so on. When the dedication is complete there is no more fear in the surrendered heart.

In God there is no horrifying fear. God has no sense of dread which causes Him a seizure of fearful trembling. God is afraid of nothing, for His power and control are over everything and everyone.

"And his disciples came to him, and awoke him, saying, 'Lord, save us; we perish.' And he says to them, 'Why are you fearful, O ye of little faith?' Then he arose and rebuked the winds and the sea. And there was a great calm," records St. Matthew in 8:25-26 of his gospel. Was Jesus afraid? The disciples were afraid. Yet both were in the same boat under the same set of circumstances. They were all in the same storm. This situation was common to Jesus and his disciples. In the same danger Jesus was not afraid, but his disciples were afraid. Why? Completeness! Complete love (agape = dedication)! Perfect love relates to perfect trust—complete, absolute trust! Why are believers afraid? Of what are they afraid? Would they be afraid if they were sitting in God's lap upon His throne?

Because of fear those men of war who left Egypt failed to possess the Promised Land. The giants in the Promised Land were huge and powerful. "We are not able to go up against the people, for they are stronger than we," these men of war said in Numbers 13:31. This was the vision of these soldiers. They did not see God's strength being greater than that of the giants. They saw the giants as having the ultimate power and control. Danger filled their vision, danger to them and their families. And if this is their vision's focal point, they will fear, and pass it on to others. Our fear is defeat. Our faith is the victory (I John 5:4).

Many times faith operates contrary to natural sight. Faith does not depend upon natural agents. Faith trusts God. That which God speaks must be mixed with faith (Hebrews 4:2). God told the Israelite soldiers to go up and to possess the Promised Land. They feared; they doubted; there was no faith; there was no trust; there was no proper vision; they died in the wilderness. "The fearful and unbelieving ... shall have their part in the lake which burneth with fire and brimstone, which is the second death" (Revelation 21:8).

"Where is your faith?" Jesus asks His disciples (Luke 8:25). The answer to this question reflects the disciples' character and contents of heart. "Why are you so fearful? How is it that you have no faith?" Jesus asks them in Mark 4:40. Fear eliminates faith.

FEAR LURKS IN MOAB

This Wilderness of Moab is the Wilderness of Fear. We all go through it. But let us pass through it quickly. Do not camp there. Do not become entrapped in this wilderness, living a life trembling like a leaf in fear of one thing after another. Fear will not allow you to come into the victory which God has promised for you.

The giants in Canaan did not cause the ten Israelite spies to fear. Lack of trust in God was in their hearts before they ever saw those giants. Fear was in their hearts before they left the camp to go to spy out the Promised Land. They were evil men, with a history of disobedience to God, and they brought back an evil report. Twelve spies saw the giants. Two of them trusted in God and were full of faith, wholly following the Lord. These two were good men, bringing back a good report.

Numbers 32:11-12

Surely none of the men that came up out of Egypt, from twenty years old and upward, shall see the land which I sware unto Abraham, unto Isaac, and unto Jacob, because they have not wholly followed the LORD, save Caleb, the son of Jephunneh the Kenezite, and Joshua the son of Nun, for they have wholly followed the LORD.

Caleb and Joshua went with the other ten spies. They all were in the same place. They all saw the same giants. They all were in the same boat. Ten brought back an evil report. Two brought back a good report. The difference in the reports did not lie in the circumstances the twelve spies encountered. The difference lay in their hearts. If you wholly follow the LORD you will never have to worry about being stuck in the Wilderness of Moab. You will have faith and trust. You will not be forever bogged down in fear.

Today, fear torments many believers. There is such a lack of trust that some will not drive their car out of its driveway without "pleading" the blood of Jesus. I personally know one such man whose wife was dead and he seriously injured twenty minutes after they "pleaded" the blood over their car before beginning a long trip. Ten years after the accident the man was still bogged down in personal defeat over his tragedy. Multitudes of believers are running scared these days. Why are you so fearful? Where, do you think, reside the supreme power and control?

Lack of spiritual character (the character of Jesus) and lack of obedience are the causes of fear and defeat. No one is born with character. Neither is fear inherent in the newborn. Fear is a foreign matter in man. Adam was not created with fear in him. Later it entered into him because of disobedience.

There is a life where all the pressure of fear and trembling are turned off. It is life in which abide a complete trust and love of our caring heavenly Father. There cannot be fear in that fullness of love.

The work of God is not based upon fear or defeat. God always works and moves toward victory. In the final analysis God triumphs over all. Even in the case of man's beginning, when death first entered, there will be ultimate victory. God will bring all humanity back to the point where there shall be no more death. God will definitely fulfill His purposes.

Why should the Christian tremble in fear and defeat? If there is any trembling to be done, the enemies of God should be at it.

The Church is supposed to be at the gates of Hell bashing them in. Hell shall not withstand the onslaughts of the Church. Satan and his camp should be trembling in fear and defeat. There should be no such trembling among the children of God. The spirit of fear comes from the enemy's camp; God has not given it. It should not be part of the believer's life. The believer should be walking with God toward glorious victory.

The Wilderness of Moab is the camp of fear and defeat. Do not live there. God's love, power, and might can deliver you forever from frightening fear and frustration. Cast **ALL** your care upon Him, for He cares for you (I Peter 5:7).

Chapter Eleven
Withdrawing
in the Wilderness of Bethaven

‎⸺☙⸺

The wilderness of Bethaven is the second wilderness which should be avoided by the believer. "Bethaven" is two names in the Hebrew text: "beth" ("house of," #1004 in *Strong's Concordance* and other works) and "aven" ("wickedness," #205). "Vanity" is also tucked into the meaning of "aven," giving this Hebrew word for "wickedness" a particular shade of significance.

THE HOUSE OF WICKEDNESS

The Wilderness of Bethaven is the opposite of the Wilderness of Kedemoth. Remember that the Wilderness of Kedemoth was "a continual forward progress, moving ahead to victory into fulfillment." The Wilderness of Bethaven is a moving in the opposite direction from that which God wants. In light of this, it is interesting to note that "aven" is translated "idol" in Isaiah 66:3.

Idolatry is moving or being away from God. In one part of its Scriptural context, the Wilderness of Bethaven is a moving away from the inheritance which God has given. The Wilderness of Kedemoth is just the opposite, a moving toward your inheritance. The obvious picture is that the Wilderness of Bethaven belongs to no Christian, to no child of God. Bethaven is a backsliding direction, a moving back, a withdrawing, a moving out from that which is promised. A picture of this is given in Joshua 18:12, "And their border on the north side was from Jordan; and the border went up to the side of Jericho on the north side, and went up through the mountains westward; and the goings out thereof were at the wilderness of Bethaven." In this description of the portion of land belonging to the tribe of Benjamin, the leaving, "the goings out," is at the Wilderness of Bethaven. This is the door through which a

Benjamite could leave his inheritance. That is, when a Benjamite came to Bethaven in his eastward travel, he was about to leave the area of his inheritance.

THE BASIC PRINCIPLE

This "leaving" is the basic principle found in Bethaven. In the above context the physical inheritance is the point of application. In the realm of the Spirit, "inheritance," seen or unseen, will always be somewhere in the picture in relationship to the believer.

In the meaning of "Bethaven," there is always wickedness involved: rebellion—walking contrary to the revelation of God, in the vanity of one's own mind. Whatever actions and causes are in the picture, physical or spiritual, it is leaving—one is on the way out.

Bethaven is the door through which you leave. The Bible does not say that it is the point through which you enter. We know that it's the point through which you can come into a geographic area. But the Bible does not say that, due to the fact that the Father is wanting us to focus upon a certain aspect by excluding another aspect. This is clearly portrayed by the prophet Hosea (4:15-16), "Though thou, Israel, play the harlot, yet let not Judah offend; and come not ye unto Gilgal, neither go you up to Bethaven, nor swear, The LORD liveth. For Israel slideth back as a backsliding heifer."

Hosea addressed the divided nation, Israel the northern kingdom, and Judah the southern kingdom. Israel was playing the harlot in the sight of Judah. God warns, "Don't you follow suit, Judah. Don't go in that direction which leads to Bethaven." Israel had backslidden, and continued in that direction. Bethaven is seen as Judah's point of leaving, her sliding back, moving away from God. Idolatry was the scene of Israel's activity of worship, while swearing "the LORD liveth." This wickedness was to be avoided by Judah.

Leaving God for idols is very dangerous. We are to avoid the Wilderness of Bethaven. Let us move forward rather than moving backwards, so that the Wilderness of Kedemoth becomes to us an experience, rather than the Wilderness of Bethaven.

The Wilderness of Bethaven is indicative of a condition portrayed by Israel. It was to be avoided by Judah. This historic situation is a lesson for us. "Now these things happened as examples for us, that we should not crave evil things, as they also craved.

Now these things happened to them as an example, and they were written for our instruction" (I Corinthians 10:6,11, NASB). History is supposed to be our teacher.

BACKSLIDING

Historically, Israel was withdrawing; she was sliding back; she was leaving her inheritance. She was leaving the LORD, Who was her inheritance, and she was sliding back from Him. "The LORD is the portion of mine inheritance" (Psalm 16:5). This is Whom Israel was leaving. Hopefully Israel was to be an example and a lesson to Judah. As God moved upon Israel to chastise her for backsliding, Judah was able to take note, to take a lesson from her sister. If Judah was willing to learn, she would have been able to correct her ways. In the recorded history it is seen that Judah did not learn and repent. She moved into Bethaven; she joined Israel to leave God, and backslid into wickedness and unbelief. Finally she went into bondage. Upon her part, as well as Israel's, there was the refusal to move forward in the revelation which God had given her. She went backwards into ignorance, the extent of which can be seen in the Gospels, where this very tribe (not the northern part of the nation) calls for and receives the crucifixion of Jesus. There was the refusal to move forward in true and sincere dedication to God.

Every day people decide to move backward into a dedication to idols and self. They come to and live in the "House of Vanity," a place of wickedness and idolatry in varying forms. Do not tarry in such a place. It is not for the faithful.

LOSS OF REVELATION

With a change of scenery, we will take a look at something else moving in connection with this word "Bethaven." This second scene is not so much different from the first. More or less it is the same story in I Samuel, with different characters, activities, and props. It is the story of Jonathan and the victory which he won, and the exceeding victory which followed. But we will watch his father. What did King Saul do in this thing?

The scene is set in I Samuel 14:1, "Now it came to pass upon a day, that Jonathan the son of Saul said unto the young man that bare his armour, 'Come, and let us go over to the Philistines' garrison, that is on the other side.' But he told not his father."

He told not his father. In regards to this escapade, remember that his father at that time was moving, not in revelation, but in ignorance. Do not focus overly much upon this occasion, but rather upon Saul himself. Some years before that time he began to move in revelation. "Then, Samuel called him aside and said, 'Say to the servant that he might go ahead of us and pass on, but you remain standing now, that I may proclaim the word of God to you'" (I Samuel 9:27, NASB). Thus, in the life of Saul, the revelation of God began to move. But as Saul failed in his responses to God, and became disobedient, he gradually moved into the Wilderness of Bethaven, so to speak. He began to backslide, to move away from God and, consequently, out of the revelation which God had given him. Saul seemed to forget. There was the possibility of Saul's kingdom being established forever (I Samuel 13:13). But he moved back and withdrew his soul from that possibility. He did not continue to move in the revelation which he had. Thus forward progression was lacking in the latter life of Saul. He did not move into further revelation and light. He moved backwards into ignorance, backsliding away from God, away from the things he knew.

Saul knew nothing of Jonathan's move against the Philistines. He (Saul) "was staying in the outskirts of Gibeah under the pomegranate tree which is in Migron. And the people who were with him were about six hundred men" (I Samuel 14:2, NASB). Jonathan routed the Philistines. "So the LORD delivered Israel that day, and the battle spread beyond Bethaven" (verse 23). Between "the LORD delivered Israel that day" and "the battle spread beyond Bethaven" Saul entered the picture (verse 24). In the LORD'S deliverance, the Philistines were hacking each other to death (verse 20). Then entered some Israelites, but not from Saul, to help the cause (verse 21). Saul intended to get involved after he saw what was happening. Saul wanted to press the battle for self-vengeance (verse 24). Saul was here involved "beyond Bethaven." At a surface glance this does not carry much meaning. But in the previous chapter (I Samuel 13), Saul's gravitation toward "Bethaven" (his leaving God) is seen. And now in chapter

14 he has arrived at "Bethaven," the point of a continual back-sliding and withdrawing from God. Watch the rest of his life. Watch it in the following few verses.

In a glance backwards into chapter 13, before going onward into Saul's life, we pick up evidence of a heart prone toward pride and thus prone to move away from God, "And Jonathan smote the garrison of the Philistines that was in Geba, and the Philistines heard of it. And Saul blew the trumpet throughout all the land, saying, Let the Hebrews hear. And all Israel heard say that Saul had smitten a garrison of the Philistines" (I Samuel 13:3-4).

Jonathan led a thousand men against the Philistines and won. This news came to the rest of the Philistines. As a result of this victory, Saul caused trumpets to sound and a proclamation to be made. But the news which reached the Philistines (they heard that Jonathan smote the garrison of the Philistines [verse 3]) was not the same news which reached the Hebrews. Saul caused it to be announced that Saul himself, not Jonathan, won the victory (verse 4). He attributed Jonathan's victory to himself because of his self-ishness. He was jealous of Jonathan. There was no correction in Saul of this form of idolatry (self-worship); it grew.

Self-worship is the core and fullness of Satan. Some time later in the life of Saul, it is seen in a much greater magnitude.

We have already noticed in I Samuel 14 how, for the second time, Saul became involved in a victory which Jonathan won. Without Saul and his men, Jonathan and others were routing the Philistines. Then Saul and his men joined the battle. "Now the men of Israel were hard pressed on that day, for Saul had put the people under oath, saying, 'Cursed be the man who eats food before evening, and until I have avenged myself on my enemies.' So none of the people tasted food" (I Samuel 14:24, NASB).

Saul did not tarry for revelation. "And it happened while Saul talked to the priest, that the commotion in the camp of the Philistines continued and increased; so Saul said to the priest, 'Withdraw your hand'" (I Samuel 14:19, NASB). He moved to fulfill his own will, laying aside all concern for the will of God. This was a growing problem with Saul. It began its manifestation in these accounts of Jonathan's victories, and in Saul's disobedience to God's word in chapter 13, verse 13. Saul was self-centered, as is evidenced by the record. Because of this he moved back from God and more into his self-centeredness, doing his own will, leaving God, pulling a "Bethaven."

SELF-CENTEREDNESS

Evidence of Saul's self-centeredness is more pronounced later, as seen in I Samuel 18:8, "And Saul was very wroth, and the saying displeased him; and he said, 'They have ascribed unto David ten thousands, and to me they have ascribed but thousands: and what can he have more but the kingdom?'" Saul's very same problem manifested in Jonathan's victories in chapters 13 and 14, surfaced in David's victory.

Saul's self-centeredness seen in relationship to the victories of Jonathan and David, certainly was in Saul during the time between the victories, as noted in I Samuel 13:13. It was his ever-present problem.

Being self-centered is unavoidably manifested in certain situations. The situations are not the cause, but simply the occasion for the problem's manifestation.

When Saul moved to avenge his enemies in I Samuel 14:24, as noted above, he did not move in divine direction. He moved in his own spirit, wanting to do his own thing for his own purpose, "That I may be avenged on my enemies." Doing his own thing brought trouble, "Then said Jonathan, 'My father hath troubled the land: see, I pray you, how mine eyes have been enlightened, because I tasted a little of this honey'" (I Samuel 14:29).

Jonathan moved in one direction (eating) while his father moved in another direction (fasting). Upon one (Jonathan) there was enlightenment; upon the other (Saul) there was darkness. Jonathan acted out of necessity; Saul acted out of self-honor and glory. Saul hindered or limited God. "How much better it would have been if the men had eaten today some of the plunder they took from their enemies. Would not the slaughter of the Philistines have been even greater?" (I Samuel 14:30, NIV).

Because of the direction in which Saul moved, there was a coming short of the fulfillment of the victory which God had intended here. Jonathan knew and understood the need for food for energy in the time of battle. (The manna ceased and the meat diet began for the Children of Israel just before the conquest of the Promised Land). If the people had followed Jonathan's example, there would have been a greater victory, and sin would have been prevented. Saul moved in ignorance, being self-centered and blind, which brought about unfavorable results, "And the people flew upon the spoil, and took sheep, and oxen, and calves, and slew them on the ground: and the people did eat them with the blood. Then they told Saul, saying, 'Behold, the people sin against the LORD, in that they eat with the blood'" (I Samuel 14:32-33a). The direction which Saul took moved the people into sin.

As Saul continued to withdraw from God, there was a response from God to that withdrawal. The response was silence (which is no response). Thus a breakdown in communications occurred, "And Saul asked counsel of God, 'Shall I go down after the Philistines? wilt thou deliver them into the hand of Israel?' But he answered him not that day" (I Samuel 14:37). The reason God did not answer Saul, and was silent, was because Saul had withdrawn himself from God. Saul rejected the commandments of God. Disobedience led to rebellion. Therefore, God rejected Saul. He had been living in the disastrous place of wickedness, and was spiritually in very bad shape. But he continued to move more and more in his backsliding direction.

Saul did not intend to take the blame for his condition and the pitiful situation. He sought a scapegoat upon which to lay the blame. Self must not look bad, nor take blame, which is the pride of life. First John 2:16, "For all that is in the world, the lust of the flesh, and the lust of the eyes, and the pride of life, is not of the Father, but is of the world." When sin gravitates from "the lust of the flesh" to "the lust of the eyes," repentance becomes more difficult. When service to sin by the flesh and by the mind moves into man's spirit, "the pride of life," hopelessness sets in. Certainly it is not absolute hopelessness, but recovery is extremely difficult and rare. Saul did not recover. He laid the blame upon Jonathan:

I Samuel 14:38-45

"And Saul said, 'Draw ye near hither, all the chief of the people: and know and see wherein this sin hath been this day. For, as the LORD liveth, which saveth Israel, though it be in Jonathan my son, he shall surely die.' But there was not a man among all the people that answered him. Then said he unto all Israel, 'Be ye on one side, and I and Jonathan my son will be on the other side.' And the people said unto Saul, 'Do what seemeth good unto thee.' Therefore Saul said unto the Lord God of Israel, 'Give a perfect lot.' And Saul and Jonathan were taken: but the people escaped. And Saul said, 'Cast lots between me and Jonathan my son.' And Jonathan was taken. Then Saul said to Jonathan, 'Tell me what thou hast done.' And Jonathan told him, and said, 'I did but taste a little honey with the end of the rod that was in mine hand, and, lo, I must die.' And Saul answered, 'God do so and more also: for thou shalt surely die, Jonathan.' And the people said unto Saul, 'Shall Jonathan die, who hath wrought this great salvation in Israel? God forbid: as the LORD liveth, there shall not one hair of his head fall to the ground; for he hath wrought with God this day.' So the people rescued Jonathan, that he died not."

Jonathan, the one who moved forward in revelation, the one who "wrought with God," escaped. Still, Saul saw to it that the blame was attached to Jonathan. However, Jonathan was not to blame at all. It was Saul's order to fast which caused the sin among the people. The casting of the lot did not indicate that God was saying that Jonathan was the cause of it. God was not saying any such thing! In fact, God was not on speaking terms with Saul. "He did not answer him on that day," is recorded in verse 37. This was Saul's program here; he took the initiative. He was the one, not God, who suggested that Jonathan die because of some guilt. Jonathan was guilty of nothing; Saul was the guilty one. Saul moved in ignorance; Jonathan moved in knowledge. Verse 29 records, "Then said Jonathan, 'My father has troubled the land. See, I pray you, how my eyes have been enlightened because I tasted a little of this honey.'" Saul could not see. He did not move in revelation. He moved in his own self-centeredness. Jonathan was the one who was moving in God, "And the men of the garrison answered

Jonathan and his armorbearer, and said, 'Come up to us, and we will show you a thing.' And Jonathan said unto his armorbearer, 'Come up after me: for the LORD hath delivered them into the hand of Israel.'" Saul did not know that the LORD'S intention was to bring a victory to Israel that day. He wasn't in on the revelation. He was sitting under a tree with six hundred of his men, afraid, trembling, s c a r e d t o d e a t h! Spiritually speaking, he was in the wildernesses of Moab and Bethaven, while Jonathan was moving forward as in the wilderness of Kedemoth. Saul was sitting under a tree, idle, while Jonathan was going up to victory.

DEFEAT

Saul defeated himself with his foolish self-centeredness. He lost that which he so desperately tried to preserve—his kingdom, "And Samuel said to Saul, 'You have acted foolishly; you have not kept the commandment of the LORD thy God, which He commanded you, for now the LORD would have established your kingdom over Israel forever. But now your kingdom shall not endure. The LORD has sought out for Himself a man after His own heart, and the LORD has appointed him as ruler over His people, because you have not kept what the Lord commanded you'" (I Samuel 13:13-14, NASB).

The reason or foundation for Saul's ignorance, and for God's silence, was his persistent disobedience in the face of clear revelation. Saul was putting a distance between himself and God. God "honored" that distance, and withdrew from Saul, as if by Saul's own desire or request. When this happened, that which God brought to Saul initially was also withdrawn. The kingdom, and finally life itself, were withdrawn from Saul; he lost both. He moved backward into the Wilderness of Bethaven, in its meaning and spiritual significance.

Saul's consequences cannot be avoided in a life which constantly, knowingly, and willingly moves in the direction away from God. The life is away from the Spirit of God, and His leading and conviction. There is no longer the touch of God upon that life. No longer is victory found in God. The revelation which is in God is no longer available. The inheritance belonging to that life is lost. The person loses everything that God has provided for him.

Bethaven is a point of focus in this scene of Saul and the Philistines, "And the Philistines gathered themselves together to fight with Israel, thirty thousand chariots, and six thousand horsemen, and people as the sand which is on the seashore in multitude: and they came up, and pitched in Michmash, eastward from Bethaven" (I Samuel 13:5). Bethaven's being in the picture helps us to see what is going on under the surface of things. There are many aspects to this story. To obtain one aspect, I have focused upon the Bethaven connection. Once the clue is found and understood, its thread can clearly be traced through the whole story. Then, it is easy to see Saul in his deteriorating direction. Then, understanding is clear as to how he got himself into the position where God did not answer him, and consequently, why he searched for and communicated with the witch of Endor. When you begin to see and understand such things in lives, then you can "read life." You can know what is really going on underneath the smoke screen. You can read heart conditions easily. We can see Saul's heart condition. It is not because the Bible states it, but because Saul's own words and actions display it. Often, things like the loss of the kingdom, the loss of life, are blamed upon some condition relating to God's doing. But we know that it is Saul's condition which causes the loss.

This one event, which covers chapters 13 and 14, is connected with Bethaven and with the disobedience and sin of Saul. Disobedience and sin are also related to Bethaven at Ai in Joshua, chapter 7. So, you see, this particular moving is not found only in one isolated story. You can read it in Saul; you can read it in Judas. You can read it in lives today. You can see it in Ai.

Joshua 7:2,4,11

"And Joshua sent men from Jericho to Ai, which is beside Bethaven on the east side of Bethel, and spake unto them saying, 'Go up and view the country.' And the men went up and viewed Ai. So there went up thither of the people about three thousand men: and they fled before the men of Ai. 'Israel hath sinned, and they have also transgressed my covenant which I commanded them: for they have even taken of the accursed thing, and have also stolen, and dissembled also, and they have put it even among their own stuff.'"

The reason for Israel's defeat by the men of Ai was disobedience and sin. God declared that Israel had moved contrary to His word. The sin was committed in the face of clear revelation, willingly and knowingly. There was no excuse for it. Joshua was very explicit in communicating to the people that nothing from Jericho was to be taken for personal possession (Joshua 6:18-19).

Any time you are disobedient to God, you are moving backwards. You are not moving forward, and you are not standing still. Any time you move in disharmony with God, in disobedience to what you know to be right, that is sin. That does not bring you into any forward progress; that brings you into regression. You are moving and living in the Wilderness of Bethaven. You are leaving; you are not going anywhere. And this, as it continues, brings you into what is called a backslidden state. And finally it brings you into death.

The prophet Hosea writes on this subject in 5:7-8 (NASB), "They have dealt treacherously against the LORD, for they have borne illegitimate children. Now the new moon will devour them with their land. Blow the horn in Gibeah, the trumpet in Ramah. Sound an alarm at Bethaven: 'Behind you, Benjamin!' Ephraim will become a desolation in the day of rebuke; among the tribes of Israel I declare what is sure."

Disobedience and sin produced strange children, or a harvest which must be reaped. They lived contrary to God. They left God. Trace their path: Gibeah, Ramah, Bethaven. Warnings were given as they journeyed away from God, as they journeyed toward Bethaven: a horn in Gibeah, a trumpet in Ramah, the alarm at Bethaven. Benjamin's attention was called to the area behind them, to the land which they were leaving. They were reminded of their sister Israel (Ephraim, the northern kingdom) and her plight as the result of her disobedience. But Benjamin (with Judah) continued in the walk away from God. They opened the door of Bethaven and went out into disobedience, into the Wilderness of Bethaven, away from God. These people mentioned by Hosea were actively set against God in faithlessness and deceit. This was the direction of their movement.

You refuse to act and live according to the integrity of your heart. You act and live against what you know to be correct and right. You are living in the wilderness of Bethaven. There is no progress there, only a backward direction. There are no benefits there, only loss. There is nothing there. Hosea, in 10:1,2,5, touches upon this emptiness and the reasons:

> "Israel is an empty vine, he bringeth forth fruit unto himself: according to the multitude of his fruit he hath increased the altars; according to the goodness of his land they have made goodly images. Their heart is divided; now shall they be found faulty: he shall break down their altars, he shall spoil their images. The inhabitants of Samaria [ISRAEL, THE NORTHERN KINGDOM] shall fear because of the calves [IDOLS] of Bethaven: for the people thereof shall mourn over it, and the priests thereof that rejoiced on it, for the glory thereof, because it is departed from it."

These people of the northern kingdom departed from God; they went backward. Therefore there was loss. No fruit was produced for God. They were at Bethaven, engaged in idolatry and disobedience. They turned their backs, not only upon God, but upon their inheritance as well. They went after substitutes for God. All was lost. And, sad to say, Benjamin and Judah did not learn from this. Sadder yet, many of today's Christians will not learn from history.

OUR SALVATION

We have enough written in the Bible, and particularly in the New Testament, to guide us away from loss and fruitlessness. Specifically, the apostle Paul writes, "You must put to death, then, the earthly desires at work in you, such as immorality, indecency, lust, evil passions, and greed (for greediness is a form of idol worship). Because of such things God's wrath will come upon those who do not obey him" (Colossians 3:5-6, Good News for Modern Man).

Today, man's substitutes for God take forms other than metal and wooden figures. Self can take God's place. We can go our own ways, wanting our own things. In this, we are moving and living in the wilderness of Bethaven, regressing further and further away from God, until our disobedience and sin result in death. "Then desire conceives and gives birth to sin, and when sin is mature, it brings forth death" (James 1:15, Goodspeed).

God has called us to move onward, ever onward, and into victory. He has never called us, directed us, nor led us to the Wilderness of Bethaven. But in spite of this, I do not know of a believer who has never had the Wilderness of Bethaven in his life. At one time or another in our Christian walk, most, if not all, have stepped back from God. The sooner one recovers from backward regression, the better. Then, he can begin to move forward once again. But he must not be returning again and again to Bethaven, the door leading away from his inheritance and into death. The more time one spends in the Wilderness of Bethaven, the greater the detriment to his life. He may die there.

Perhaps you have known workers in the Gospel, preachers and others, in their heyday. Then, something happened and they began to lose their relationship with God, and started to move backwards. This can be seen in the Bible, as well as on today's stage of life. Solomon, who loved the LORD, turned away from Him (I Kings 3:3; 11:9). This seems to be the disastrous pattern in some lives. The scenery may differ, but the root of the matter is always the same: turning from God.

FAITHFULNESS

There is another pattern in certain lives. There is a faithful plodding forward, not without mishaps, not without falling, "For a just man falleth seven times, and riseth up again" (Proverbs 24:16). Thus forward progress is maintained. Progress into God can come to a point where the soul is established, where no desire can be stirred within that soul to turn from Him. A spiritual height is gained where there is an unusually close relationship with the Lord. But there is a danger in this. If the danger does not exist at the height to which I just referred, it certainly exists somewhere near it. The soul may feel no further spiritual needs. There may be the sense that one has arrived, and all is well, and will forever be well. Satisfaction sets in, satisfaction and contentment with one's particular position and condition. No longer does it become necessary to seek the Lord. The soul has lost its sense of need. That is dangerous, since we will always be in need in the realm of our spirits. King Uzziah sought the Lord, and as long as he sought the Lord, the Lord made him to prosper. Then, in his strength, his heart was lifted up, and he sought not the Lord any longer (II Chronicles 26:5,16). And so Uzziah began on this Bethaven business and backed down from God. He became leprous, an indication of the true state of his heart.

Spiritual giants are seen and known in our day. They have been active in the work of the Lord in public ministry. They have their heyday, and then seem to decline. A friend of mine in the ministry left his wife for another woman. Other pitiful situations and conditions in the ministry prevail. Lying, hatred, cheating, stealing, I've seen the frightening lot among the clergy. When such conditions followed a high point in God, I have seen no recovery. Remember, I have been watching this for over half a century. There may be repentance, but recovery seems to be out of the question. I hope I am wrong. Still, I have never seen a recovery. Certainly Judas repented, but did not recover. Esau repented and did not recover. Moses was sorry he struck the rock the second time, but there was no recovery, he still could not get to lead the Israelites into the Promised Land. Elijah may have repented from his waywardness, but he did not recover; Elisha had to finish his ministry. There never seems to be a getting back to that particular height in God once a particular low is subsequently reached. Therefore never start toward Bethaven if you can help it. If you do find yourself in the Wilderness of Bethaven, don't go any further; get back to God immediately.

A TENDER HEART

To every danger factor in our relationship with God, there is a safety factor. For this occasion the safety factor is a tender heart, "The sacrifices of God are a broken spirit: a broken and a contrite heart, O God, thou wilt not despise" (Psalm 51:17). God can always move a tender and humble heart. If you do not have such a heart, ask God to create it in you (Psalm 51:10). Once you have it, always keep It. Then, If you ever go out the back door of Bethaven, the Lord can reach you before you get three steps into the wilderness. Like butter, you will melt under the heat of His dealings. Be so submissive, so broken before Him, so tenderhearted that He can successfully correct you at any time, in any situation. This will keep you on a forward progression. Never continue in disobedience. Do not ever continue in any type of deceit or wrongdoing. Always be willing for God's correction.

PRAYER

Father, we are grateful to You. We want to surrender ourselves to You for Your constant dealings with us. We do not want to become complacent in our positions with You, Lord. We want to ever move forward in Your love and in Your mercy, that we may learn to trust You more. We want to come into the inheritance which is yet to be ours. May You bring us to our high places. Help us to journey day by day into Your fullness. Teach us Your way for Your glory. Amen.

Chapter Twelve
Meeting with God
in the Wilderness of Sinai (Part One)

———∞∞∞———

"In the third month, when the children of Israel were gone forth out of the land of Egypt, the same day came they into the Wilderness of Sinai," states Exodus 19:1.

The Hebrew word "Sinai" means "miry," as in "miry clay." Another meaning is "thorn bush." This second meaning relates to the call of Moses at a thorn bush in Sinai.

Even a surface glance at the wildernesses discloses the obvious fact that the wilderness is a place where great and wondrous things happen. Here is where the greater part of the action is in this Christian life. It is a place of personal benefits. It is a place of prosperity, success, and victory. It is where most of the believer's vision, strength, and faith are developed, and where most of his learning takes place. Here he gets stretched out.

Pack your suitcase and come along into the wilderness and stay a while. It is a good place. If you do not spend much time there, you will miss much. It is the place of the burning bush and many other marvelous events.

Three months after leaving Egypt the children of Israel arrive at the Wilderness of Sinai. They camp here and remain for almost one year. This gives time for things to happen.

Numbers 10:11 reads, "And it came to pass on the twentieth day of the second month, in the second year (eleven months after they first arrived), that the cloud was taken up from off the tabernacle of the testimony, and the children of Israel took their journeys out of the Wilderness of Sinai." They had camped in this wilderness one year, less a week or two. At the end of this time God said, "You have encamped around this mountain long enough."

After "long enough" in God's judgment we are to move on. Sometimes we are glad to move on. At other times we are reluctant to move on when God urges us to make a change. We become adjusted and accustomed to one particular place. Perhaps our roots have penetrated deeply. Things have at last worked out, and all the loose ends are tied together. Enjoy! And so we settle down to relish our situation. But the cloud lifts, and we are to follow. "Please, God, not now!" But God ignores our cries, and urges, "Now! Get moving!" With reluctant obedience we drag ourselves in the direction the leading of God indicates. At least I hope we do.

WHERE THE ACTION IS

The Wilderness of Sinai was the most important stop in all of the journeys of the children of Israel. Many essential things occurred here—the giving of the Ten Commandments, the plan of the tabernacle was its construction. Here the priesthood and the sacrifices were instituted. This is where Moses saw the glory of God. No wonder some people actually like the wilderness.

Get accustomed to the fact that tremendous things happen in the wilderness. Some of these wonderful experiences cannot be gained in any other place. When Jesus went into the wilderness, He returned from it in the power of the Spirit. If it were not for the wildernesses and the experiences we have there, we all would limp through this Christian life as weaklings.

Too many things happened in the Wilderness of Sinai to trace each one through its ramifications. Thus this text will deal only with that which transpired in the Scriptures in which Sinai is actually mentioned. Most of the Pentateuch was given by God to Moses, written during the eleven months spent at Sinai. This span of material is too vast to treat in this work. Yet we can gain an accurate message by sticking to the references which mention Sinai by name. Happenings can occur in the Wilderness of Sinai without being directly related to it. But when the Word expressly ties in the name with the incident, then there can be gained an accurate message as related to the place.

TO MEET WITH GOD

The Wilderness of Sinai is a place of meeting. It is a place where the people have an opportunity to meet with God. Previously, the Israelites had not met God. Moses first met God at Sinai and received his orders to return to Egypt. Most of us must enter the wilderness to meet with God. Usually difficult situations, such as no water or food, no money or house, fire, death, and other calamities occur in order for God to get an audience with some. Otherwise their appointment books are too full to include God. Upon rising in the morning, it's a rush to get to work on time. A busy day follows. Evening activities and weariness crowd out God. "Could I have an appointment with you?" asks God. "I'm busy right now." "Oh, so you're too busy, are you?" So God brings you into the wilderness in hopes of meeting with you. If the wilderness is tough enough and long enough, you may be glad to meet with God. There, in distress and trouble, you will find time for God in your busy schedule.

In the Wilderness of Sinai, "Moses brought forth the people out of the camp to meet with God" (Exodus 19:17). What could be better than meeting with God, even though it means time in the wilderness? Moses brought them out from their coverings and comforts, away from their conveniences in the camp, for the purpose of meeting with God. Some time earlier Moses had met with God. It had been away from his comforts and conveniences in Pharaoh's court. Because of his past experience, it was easier for Moses to understand the Israelites' meeting with God than it was for the people themselves. Actually, the people did not desire such a meeting.

Since the beginning, God has been calling mankind to Himself. In most cases there has not been a favorable response. God invites man to His nearness and into His confidence, but most refuse to attend.

THE UNKNOWN

Exodus 20:18-19

"All the people saw the thunderings and lightnings and the noise of the trumpet and the mountain smoking. And when the people saw it, they removed and stood afar off.

And they said to Moses, 'You speak with us, and we will hear. But let not God speak with us lest we die.'"

Under the circumstances, the Israelites had no desire to approach God. There are people who will approach God under certain circumstances, yet will not approach Him otherwise. God may manifest Himself to certain individuals who will not respond. Here at Sinai God approached the people with manifestations which they could not understand and therefore they feared. When God does things to fit our understanding, we more readily accept Him and His work. We are likely to feel uncomfortable with the unknown. Suppose you are out walking alone and suddenly come upon a five-foot bright blue creature with crumpled skin walking like a man. Would you readily and comfortably approach him? Doubtful! Most of us would avoid extremely strange creatures, and probably shun totally strange circumstances. This is why some believers cannot readily accept certain truths, truths which are foreign to them.

While teaching a certain class in a Bible school, I horrified some students by saying that God demands restitution. One student expressed the fact that he did not understand that. My response was, "Don't be horrified at this simply because you do not understand it." If we can conveniently fit truth new to us into our present way of life, then understanding is not too difficult.

In any given level of spiritual growth, the believer will meet truth which he cannot handle. He can find no place in his present life into which it will fit, and he is not as yet willing to have it worked into his life. Sometimes it is quite convenient for the believer not to understand truth. It is less troublesome not to understand certain things than to understand them. Here we can apply the oft repeated statement, "The truths which I do not understand do not bother me; it's the truth I do understand which disturbs me."

There is one way in which you can approach the unfamiliar without fear. In 1973 the Lord led me in a very strange way. It was so strange that I did not recognize it as His leading. I approached it with a great deal of hesitancy. I was not certain of direction, and thus I did not feel I was on solid ground. It all began with someone suggesting to me that I go to Europe to minister in Germany and the British Isles. Although I did not have what I would then term a "leading," I felt as if I had no choice in the matter, and that I had to go. But to go without a familiar leading was distressing to me. There was only one thing I could do. I would put aside the "leading" as solid ground, and take God instead. I knew I could depend upon Him, and that He would be solid ground enough.

So I told Him that I was going, and that I would depend upon His faithfulness to me to correct me if this direction was not wholly according to His will and purpose. In the absence of hearing anything different from Him, I went. The ministry went well; people were helped. But all during that trip I had no confirmation from Him that I was moving in His perfect will. At the very end of the trip, just as the wheels of the 747 touched the runway, the Holy Spirit strongly rose within me and spoke these words, "Thank you." Tears rolled down my cheeks. I was grateful that the unfamiliar had not caused me to miss God's will.

All through your Christian life you will meet the unfamiliar, things you do not understand. You cannot afford to make your approach to the things of God on the basis of understanding. Doing so will lead you nowhere. All you need is a desire to hear God, to obey Him, and to know Him. These people whom Moses brought to meet with God did not want to hear Him. In Jesus' parable of the sower, hearing becomes the foundation of receiving. Understanding comes later. Some people want to understand all about it before they make their approach. What are these thunderings and lightnings? What do these things mean? Why is the trumpet blowing and why all this smoke? If we do not understand all these things, we cannot meet with God. Too bad! So sad! There is no faith. There is no approach.

Can God Himself be understood by mere man? No! He must be approached by faith. God is eternal. Eternity cannot fit into man's small mind. The extensive greatness of God's love and grace cannot be contained in this restricted human understanding. God will always be drawing man into the unknown. Man, responding to God, will always be learning. No matter how far into the unknown we are taken to experience revelation and understanding, we will always have the unknown before us.

BE STILL AND KNOW

The unknown is frightening to most individuals. In the case of the spiritual realm, any approach by God which is not understood frightens most believers. The Lord Jesus made an unusual approach to over 200 assembled Bible school students. The entire student body became still and silent. Although the Lord could not be seen, He was heard walking in the chapel. He walked down the middle isle, across the front, and started walking up the right-hand aisle. As He approached the fifth row of seats, a girl sitting at the row's end heard the rustling of His garment and screamed in fear. She could not understand what was happening. That ended that manifestation of the Lord. The Lord cannot bring very much from the unknown to the believer fearing it. The Lord can visit you with an unusual manifestation. If there is not a proper response in such a visitation, the Lord will not hang around for long.

While in language study in Costa Rica in 1962, I became the sickest that I had ever been in my life. I was in constant pain, and I could not sleep more than five to ten minutes at a time, day or night. On the third night of my intense sickness and pain, as I lay on the bed resting, the Lord came and stood beside me. Fear would have sent Him on His way. But I did not fear. His glory and beauty were so great that it did not occur to me that I was sick and in pain. If I were aware of my condition, I would have asked Him to heal me. But that would have been the wrong response, and He would have left immediately. As it was, He lingered in an atmosphere of silent awe and worship. By the Spirit, and not by our own understanding, can we give Him the responses He seeks. But peace must reign instead of fear, and faith must unite us with Him.

Not all manifestations of the Lord are dramatic and spectacular. Some are so prosaic that most believers would not recognize them as manifestations of God. But revelation will be brought to that one who wholly seeks and desires the Lord.

Care must be taken not to place your desire in the wrong areas. A wrong area may be to desire God to do something for you, or to give you something for self-satisfaction, or to know and understand certain things to satisfy your curiosity. The right area is a desire for Him alone. This desire will be the foundation upon which much revelation is brought to you. God's heart responds to the heart desiring Him.

A hunger and thirst for righteousness characterize this desiring heart. The heart of God desires this same thing—righteousness in human hearts. Thus, kind is answering to its own kind. Remember this basic principle, since it will determine the extent to which you will progress in God. Kind is attracted to kind. This principle is true, not only in the spiritual realm, but also in the social realm and in the animal realm. As much as you desire what God desires, to that extent God brings you into Himself, and you become more like Him.

Man was created in the image of God. To some extent that image is maintained. Basic in every heart is a god-likeness. As man gives this instilled awareness attention, it is projected and manifested in a variety of ways, from idol worship to a walk with the wonderful living God. This god-likeness in every man is attracted to its own Kind. There is a lack of satisfaction in the heart of man until he finds his own Kind.

HAVE IT YOUR WAY

God permits the desires of men to take their own intended directions. Jesus said, "Don't be like these Pharisees who seek honor from man. They pray in the street corners and make fasts to be seen and honored by man. They have their reward" (Matthew 6:2,5). God allows even the Pharisees to have the desires of their hearts. Don't forget it. God will allow men to have their desires fulfilled, in spite of their lack of true faith, sincere prayers, and humble fasting.

Hezekiah was thirty-nine years of age when God said to him through the prophet Isaiah, "Set your house in order for you will certainly die; you will not live" (Isaiah 38:1). Who wants to die so young? Hezekiah wept and prayed for his own desire. God gave him his desire at the detriment to himself and the nation (II Chronicles 32:25).

Judas Iscariot followed his own desires. Did Jesus relieve him of his treasurership? No! Judas was permitted to continue to dip his hand into the common funds for his own personal use (John 12:6). That's what he wanted, and God gave him the desire of his heart.

In certain situations God may actively prevent fulfillment of certain desires. But in most cases God does not go around wrecking man's own arrangements designed to bring the desired objectives. Quite the contrary! God does not interfere. "You want it? You can have it!" is this world's philosophy which has invaded the church. And God allows it to be, and may even take an active part in its fulfillment. But remember, "They have their reward."

The two-year-old son of a mother in Philadelphia was seriously ill. He grew worse. The doctors could do nothing. The believing mother prayed. But God left no doubt in her heart as to what He wanted. He wanted to take her baby through death. But the mother would not go along with God's desire. She began to fast and to pray more earnestly. She wept before the Lord day and night. Finally God said, "Okay, if that's what you want—." He healed her son. Twenty years later her son died in the electric chair for murder.

I do not wish to insist upon having my own way. I do not have enough knowledge, understanding, and wisdom to go that route. God's desires will always be better than mine, for He has the vision and understanding and all the other qualities necessary to entertain desires of the greatest value and highest worthiness. To follow your own desires contrary to God is very foolish. Follow them, and the danger is that you might receive them.

Jesus had His own desires. He did not insist upon fulfilling them. On at least three occasions did His own desires pop to the surface. This shows us how the Son of Man moved in relationship to God. The first time was at age twelve when He desired to be about His Father's business (Luke 2:49). At that early age He began to pursue this desire's fulfillment. But Mary and Joseph were God's agents to keep Him in the harness for further learning and training. When we see Jesus eighteen years after desiring to be about His Father's business, we do not see Him even beginning to pursue His own desires. Thus, "though he were a Son, yet learned he obedience by the things which he suffered," states Hebrews 5:8.

The second time we might be able to see His own desire is in the case of Lazarus. Jesus had great care and concern for Lazarus. Lazarus became sick. This news was sent to Jesus. The message was,

"Lord, behold, he whom thou lovest is sick," in John 11:3. The word translated "lovest" is "phileo" which means to be fond of. Lazarus was Jesus' close friend. Jesus, in His own desire, would wish to get to Lazarus as soon as possible. But we see in verse 6 that Jesus tarried two days before starting for Bethany, Lazarus' home. He restrained His own desire in order to move in the desire of His Father.

The third time we plainly see His desire. It is in the Garden of Gethsemane. There He addresses the Father, "O my Father, if it be possible, let this cup pass from me: nevertheless not as I will, but as thou wilt," in Matthew 26:39.

We cannot move in response to our own desires and expect everything to come out for the best. The fulfillment of the desires of God will always be for our very best.

COMMUNICATION

If your desire can focus upon the Lord, communication with Him will be open. Moses had a great desire for God. "Show me Your glory," he desired in Exodus 33:18 (NIV). We have evidence that this desire moved in his early life. There must have been communication from God to Moses when he was young, for he was aware then that God wanted him to deliver his brothers from Egyptian bondage (Acts 7:23-29).

At the burning bush in Exodus, chapter 3, we see a marvelous method of communication from God to Moses. At Mt. Sinai God called Moses to Himself for the purpose of a very lengthy communication. Moses ascended the mount and waited there six days, as stated in Exodus 24:16, "And the glory of the LORD abode upon mount Sinai, and the cloud covered it six days: and the seventh day he called unto Moses out of the midst of the cloud." This extensive communication lasted thirty-four days, probably without interruption day or night, since Moses did not eat nor drink during that time (Deuteronomy 9:9).

I believe that Moses did not sleep during this time; it would be hard to sleep with God that close. I believe that Moses did not urinate nor defecate during those thirty-four days. He was cleaned out during the six days he waited for God. This constant communication produced most of the Pentateuch. God called Moses and led him to the Wilderness of Sinai upon two different occasions to communicate with him.

God may call you to the wilderness to meet with Him. Communications follow the meeting. Suppose you fail to meet with God due to fear or some other personal reason? Then the communication which God intended does not occur. He stands at the door and knocks. If anyone hears and opens the door, extensive communications can follow. Do you desire Him enough to open the door or go to the wilderness to meet with Him?

Communication is established. A messenger is born. The messenger becomes God's mouthpiece to those who have not met with Him. Jesus testifies of this in John 5:19-20, "The Son can do nothing of himself, but what he seeth the Father do: for what things soever he doeth, these also doeth the Son likewise. For the Father loveth ["phileo"] the Son, and sheweth him all things that himself doeth: and he will shew him greater works than these, that ye may marvel." If there is no communication, how can Jesus know what His Father is doing? If He doesn't know what His Father is doing, how can He do His Father's will? Communication is necessary. We need it. We must have it, even if it means living in the wilderness.

Communication is necessary, for God needs messengers. He communicates to the angels [messengers] of the seven churches in Revelation, chapters 2 and 3. He does not communicate directly to these seven churches. God uses messengers. It is the same today. We do not go to church, sit down, and wait till God shows up to speak in person to us. No, we hear His messenger. He used prophets to speak to the nation of Israel. There will be no messenger if there is no communication.

Without communication, how can anyone know the will of God? I heard much about the will of God in the 1950s. I heard less about it in the 1960s. After eleven years as a missionary under a mission board, I resigned in 1971 to teach in a Bible school. Soon I received a questionnaire with eighty listed reasons why I left the mission field. In vain I searched for my reason. Sadly, I added number eighty-one to the list, "the will of God." By the 1970s hardly anyone was concerned with the will of God. Was this because there was a breakdown in communications with God?

God still seeks messengers and prophets. Are they getting as scarce as they were in Isaiah's day? "Whom shall I send," God cries out in Isaiah 6:8, "And who will go for us?" God desperately seeks those with hearing ears. He can put His word into them. His word can possess them and accomplish the purpose for which God sends it. Let us prepare our hearts to meet with God to hear His communications.

"Be ready in the morning," God said to Moses in Exodus 34:2. "Early [earnestly] will I seek You" (Psalm 63:1). "Those who seek Me early [diligently] will find Me" (Proverbs 8:17). All things must be laid aside. God wants hearts ready to meet with Him and to receive that which He has for them. "Come up unto Mount Sinai in the morning," God continued to say to Moses, "And present thyself there to me in the top of the mount."

The meeting and communication are necessary. God worked through human instruments, and continues to do so. Therefore, in order to accomplish the will of God there must be the meeting of the mind of God with the mind of man. Moses is called to the top of Mt. Sinai in order to receive specific instructions from God for the children of Israel, as well as God's foundational directions for mankind. God gave Moses the plans for the Tabernacle and its instruments and furniture and priestly arrangements. This included specific instructions concerning Israel's involvement in worship. It also held the typology of today's Christian revelation.

The importance of this meeting between God and Moses goes further. God provided the wherewithal to prepare Israel for a successful conquest of the Promised Land. The means of preparing their hearts was presented to Moses, which he, in turn, presented to the people. But they did not respond correctly. They were rebellious. They had no faith.

As the right relationship to God develops, the desire to walk in the will of God grows. As obedience increases, faith does likewise, and conquest is certain.

PREPARATION

Our hearts are to be prepared to receive even the most fundamental of God's truth. To prepare one's heart is to turn from that which would hinder the will of God to that which would enhance

211

it. This is well put by Peter. "Rid yourselves of all malice and all deceit, hypocrisy, envy, and slander of every kind. Like newborn babies, crave pure spiritual milk, so that by it you may grow up in your salvation," he writes in his first epistle (2:1-3, NASB). If there is to be a continual receiving from God, there must be a continual turning from all which is contrary to the known will of God. The will of God is paramount in His dealings with man. He persists in presenting His will to man, and in working it into his heart.

In the Wilderness of Sinai the will of God was broken by the Israelites in a double fashion. The children of Israel were below the mount moving into idolatry (worshipping the golden calf), and at that sight Moses broke the stone upon which God had written His will with His own finger (Exodus 31:18). But now, in Exodus 34:4, God persists in getting the pieces together again, so to speak. At this point we read, "And he (Moses) hewed two tables of stone like unto the first; and Moses rose up early in the morning, and went up unto mount Sinai, as the Lord had commanded him, and took in his hand the two tables of stone." God made the first set of stone tablets, and wrote on them. Moses had to hew the second set himself.

Correction may be part of preparing your heart to meet with God. Moses broke the first set of tablets. He must pay the price. Even though the people were breaking God's commandment, there is no excuse for Moses' doing so. But he allowed those rebellious people to vex his spirit. Now he must spend his sweat to fashion stone tablets. This was to serve as a lesson to Moses for a future occasion of greater magnitude. But he did not learn the first lesson very well. On the second occasion of bringing water out of the rock (Numbers 20:11), Moses struck the rock instead of speaking to it as God had instructed. The reason he did this is given in Psalm 106:32-33, "They angered him also at the waters of strife, so that it went ill with Moses for their sakes: Because they provoked his spirit, so that he spake unadvisedly with his lips." This resulted in Moses' not being able to enter the Promised Land (Numbers 20:12).

When correction and preparation of the heart are not effected in the first teaching of a lesson, a second teaching of the same lesson is given. To insure better learning of the second presentation, the tuition is raised.

Where correction is possible it should be made. A heart properly preparing itself will make corrections where possible. If such corrections are neglected, it is a sign that there is not a proper heart condition. While in high school I regularly stole merchandise from a variety store. Before going to Bible school I had to make restitution by paying the manager an approximation of the amount stolen. I also had to correct a bet I had made and won by cheating. Other corrections were made.

Everything that can be reconciled between you and man must be. "Owe no man anything," urges the apostle Paul in Romans 13:8. The Old Testament is full of directions concerning restitution. The New Testament does not require less than the Old, but more. Grace is greater than law. Grace requires more than law. Grace is abundance. Trace the word "charis" (5485 in *Strong's* numbering system) and see for yourself.

"Seek ye first the kingdom of God and His righteousness," urges Jesus in Matthew 6:33. You cannot have righteousness and not do right. Defend not your own position. Do not rationalize. Seek the fulfillment of God's righteousness in your being and in your doing.

GOD GETS DRASTIC

In the case of Ananias and his wife Sapphira in Acts 5:1-11, Peter moved with God in drastic measures. In Leviticus we see God's extreme action against that which is not correct.

Leviticus 10:1-3

"And Nadab and Abihu, the sons of Aaron, took either of them his censer, and put fire therein, and put incense thereon, and offered strange fire before the LORD, which he commanded them not. And there went out fire from the LORD, and devoured them, and they died before the LORD. Then Moses said unto Aaron, 'This is it that the LORD spake, saying, "I will be sanctified in them that come nigh me, and before all the people I will be glorified."' And Aaron held his peace."

If there is to be a continual approach to God, there must be a concern for holiness in all areas of your life, "I will be sanctified in them that come nigh me." As God instructed Moses, you must prepare yourself to meet with God. Peter attempts to press this into our hearts when he wrote, "But just as he who called you is holy, so be holy in all you do; for it is written: 'Be holy, because I am holy'" (I Peter 1:15-16, NIV). And consider the words in Hebrews 12:14, "Follow peace with all men, and holiness, without which no man shall see the Lord." This urging to prepare one's heart is so frequent in the Word of God that I would be afraid to ignore it.

How can one assume to continually approach God for an ongoing and growing relationship, and yet always bring with him elements contrary to the righteousness of God? Divine order must be maintained. Otherwise your communion with God will be hindered, and you will not be able to progress ever upward in Him. Even in the wilderness you must maintain divine order, ever seeking the righteous character of God to become the very core of your life and activity.

"Blessed are the pure in heart, for they shall see God," said Jesus in Matthew 5:8. "Follow righteousness, faith, charity, peace, with them that call on the Lord out of a pure heart," Paul instructs Timothy (II Timothy 2:22). And there are more such urgings, too many to ignore.

If you are to walk with God, the two of you must be in agreement. "Can two walk together, except they be agreed?" we read in Amos 3:3. If you have one attitude and God has an opposing attitude, you better straighten out yours. God is not going to change. If you want His best, something must take place to cause you to correct your ways in order to conform to God's ways.

If correction is not forthcoming, God may take a rare extreme measure. A friend of mine pastored a church in New Jersey. He was given much trouble, and the spiritual progression of the church was being hindered by three individual believers. John began to pray that these three be removed. Within thirty days they were removed, but not in a way John had anticipated. The three died!!

God's actions may be very drastic at times. But He would like to avoid such harsh measures. "A bruised reed shall he not break, and smoking flax shall he not quench" (Matthew 12:20) does not mean that God enjoys a broken reed, and loves smoke in His eyes. St. Matthew continues to quote from Isaiah, "Till he send forth judgment unto victory." What Matthew is conveying is that God has patience with wrongs, but hopes for correction or victory through the judgment He sends. God does not want destruction, He wants correction. But if there can be no correction effected, then He must go to the extreme harsher measures. Proverbs 29:1 warns, "He who being often reproved hardens his neck, shall suddenly be destroyed, and that without remedy" (Amplified).

The judgment of God for correction will always and continually be applied to those who are correctable, no matter how evil they may be, and no matter how long it takes. Read the life of King Manasseh for an example of this. If God cannot get correction in one place under one type of judgment, He will try another place under another type of judgment.

The longer correction is withstood, the greater the hindrance to spiritual growth, and as one continues in the wrong path, more and more of his spiritual life is chipped away. For example: Some believers refuse to apologize to others, or to make wrongs right, and therefore grow bitter toward these individuals. The increasing bitterness chips away at their spiritual lives, and no spiritual growth is realized. There are believers (believe it or not) who do not want to correct wrongs and straighten out their crooked paths. Are they waiting for the harshness of God?

A refusal to walk a straight path causes personal problems. Believers have come to me with these problems. When I ignore their problems and deal with that which has caused the problems, then I become their problem. Your so-called problem may simply be a manifestation of the real problem.

A minister friend of mine, in dealing with problems, often asks a standard question, "Have you been baptized in water since you have been saved?" If the answer is "no," he then ceases to deal with their problem until they are baptized in water. Jesus was baptized in water to fulfill all righteousness (Matthew 3:15). Is your problem really the problem? Or is it a manifestation of an unwillingness to fulfill all righteousness?

Basic righteousness must be fulfilled. There is no way to skirt this issue and yet achieve progression in spiritual living. People who are operating in the gifts of the Spirit come to me with their problems. Usually I discover unfulfilled basics. These cause problems. Some do not believe even the most basic Scriptures. Others are more interested in their ministry than in the Word of God. GET BACK TO BASICS!

God is after correction. He brings His people to the Wilderness of Sinai to iron out the wrinkles. The Children of Israel spent many months in this wilderness. God brought them to a long halt in their journey in order to enhance their progression. If you feel like you have been stopped in your tracks on your spiritual journey, it may be for correction and instruction, in order that your spiritual journey will be what it ought to be.

IMPARTATION

If you find yourself stopped in your tracks in the Wilderness of Sinai, look up. Apart from correction, it may be a time for impartation, "And it came to pass, when Moses came down from mount Sinai with the two tables of testimony in Moses' hand, when he came down from the mount, that Moses wist not that the skin of his face shone while he talked with him" (Exodus 34:29). The impartation here in the wilderness is the glory of God.

Impartation is the reason for God's drawing us unto Himself. He desires us to wait in His presence for the purpose of imparting His glory and power. He must accomplish this impartation in order to express Himself to others through the one receiving the impartation. A minister who waits in His presence before the service carries God's glory and power with him into the service. During the meeting, that impartation is manifested.

In Exodus 33:18-23, Moses expressed his desire to see the glory of God. He said, "I beseech thee, show me Thy glory." If this becomes the prayer of your heart, you may have to be brought to a standstill in order to have your prayer answered. Be still and know Him.

In response to Moses' prayer, God said, "I will make all My goodness pass before you." It took more than Moses' natural vision to see the qualities of God. It is one thing to see the manifestations of God's mercy, love, grace, etc., and quite another thing to see the qualities themselves. If your prayer is to see the invisible, then you must expect God to bring you to a halt and bring you apart from some natural and spiritual involvements. Moses was separated from all natural involvements. He did not eat, drink, or sleep. God actually waited six days for Moses' system to be cleaned out so that Moses would not have to excuse himself for nature's call.

That which is impossible for man to see will be brought by God to man's spiritual vision. The unseen beauty of the Lord will be seen with the eyes of man's spirit. You have eyes in your spirit. When your body falls to the ground dead, leaving your spirit standing over it, your spirit will not be blind. You will then see more than you ever saw with your physical eyeballs. I remember on two different occasions seeing the presence of God. Never mind what it looked like. On both occasions I saw two different things. Others may see it in yet different forms. But you actually see a form. Only the eyes of your spirit can do this.

Moses actually saw form. "I will show you My goodness, and I will proclaim the name (character) of the LORD before you," God promised Moses. In the fulfillment Moses saw goodness in form, and heard its identification. Moses was not able to explain what he saw. It is beyond language, testified the apostle Paul (II Corinthians 12:4, Moffatt, Goodspeed, Phillips). It is so far above the natural that there is nothing in the natural realm to which it can be related. And it happens in the wilderness. It does not happen in green pastures. It does not happen every day.

Most of the time God works with us on lower levels. In fact, Scripture is in the lower form, even in the natural and physical form. That way, we all have opportunity to see. "There went forth a sower to sow seed," is very physical and natural. This can be seen and translated into spiritual parallelism. Things of God must be reduced for us children and fools. Otherwise we would never grow into wise adults. So God must say, "I am your Banner; I am your shield; I am the LORD Who supplies all your needs." Almost everything from God moves on this level so that we can grasp His truth.

Hidden in this lower level language is the spiritual sublime. God will bring us through and beyond the lower level into the unknowable. He will transcend all that is high and noble in our culture and language, and bring the unknowable to the heart of man. He will instill within man such mysteries of the Kingdom of God that man is at a loss to explain them. But that which man cannot speak will be communicated as light flowing from that life. That which God has shared of Himself will be manifested in that human life and seen and felt by others. The love of God, His mercy, the grace of God, His faithfulness, cannot be translated into terms. But God's qualities can be translated into a life. That which is not understood and not able to be known by the human mind is expressed by a life. Jesus, the character ("charakter," 5481, in the Greek, meaning "impress," "engraver") of God, becomes the greatest example of this.

Language and man's mind will limit communication of God's glory. The inner spiritual being of man breaks through this limitation. But even with this breakthrough, the glory of God is still limited to man. The reason for the limitation is that man, in all of his spiritual qualities, is finite and God is infinite. Man does not have the capacity to contain the capacity of God.

God will give to in relationship to our ability to hold His things. Strong meat will kill an infant, just as revelation was Adam's downfall. He was not able to handle all that the tree of knowledge of good and evil brought to him. Jesus said to His disciples (John 16:12), "I have many things to say unto you, but ye cannot bear them now." They were not able to walk under such a load; they could not carry nor sustain such sublimeness. The Greek word (941) translated "bear" means "lift," "raise," "bear," "carry," "sustain," and a few other related words. Moses, in his limitations, would not be given such a fullness of God as to render him inoperative. Little by little will God bring the infants into the strength to sustain heavier revelations.

Revelation is progressive. This progressiveness can be seen and traced in the Bible from Genesis through Revelation. The revelation of God to man is like an ascending stairway, one step up, next step up, next step up, and on it goes, one step at a time. This method is most suitable for man. This is why God said to Moses in so many words, "You will see only so much at this time, and no more." "Now I know in part," the apostle Paul wrote in I Corinthians 13:12. He also wrote, "Holding the mystery of the faith," in I Timothy 3:9. We are to be content to have something which is a mystery, without pressing to know that which God has no intention of revealing at this time.

As it is to our advantage to know certain things, it is to our advantage not to know certain things. The unknown things will be revealed to us when we are in the proper place in God, and with the suitable strength to receive and properly carry them.

Chapter Thirteen
The Proper Place in God
in the Wilderness of Sinai (Part Two)

———— ∞ ————

THE CLOSER TO GOD, THE GREATER THE REVELATION

The Lord said to Moses, "There is a place by Me" (Exodus 33:21). There is always a place for revelation. About a half century ago the songwriter Cleland B. McAfee penned, "There is a place of quiet rest Near to the heart of God." There is a place for such a revelation of rest that it changes the life. The children of Israel did not move toward this place, near to the heart of God. Their history portrays them moving more away from God than toward God. Here at Sinai they withdrew from God. But Moses came toward God.

In our approach toward God, we, at first, see and know very little. We do not know of the existence of a place near His heart. When we do learn of it, we do not see, perceive or understand it, "Moses drew near unto the thick darkness where God was" (Exodus 20:21). In our progression in God we constantly move toward the unknown. Some believers today are just like most of those people under Moses' command, afraid of the unknown.

The unknown is usually the place to which God calls one for revelation and impartation. The unknown is a place where you meet very few people. But it is the place of greater and clearer revelation. There is a place near God where He talks with man face-to-face. It is a place where visions and dreams are laid aside for more direct communications. It is there the picture of the shield and banner fade. There He is seen to be that which natural things cannot portray. In that place there is no symbolism or parable. Face-to-face! Communication there is in the realm of the Spirit, not in words of any language. Almost nothing of this high realm

221

can be explained. God reaches down to pull a few up, beyond the known. I cannot explain any further as to how it takes place and what it is. It transcends the knowledge of man. "There is a place by Me," God said, "And you shall stand upon a rock."

The standing upon a rock is very significant in this context. The danger of not being able to stand up under revelation has been mentioned. The need of a rock or stability underneath the person is necessary. Without it God would not give such intensive revelation as He gave to Moses. Far less revelation than Moses had has swept away to ruin more than one preacher. Even revelation which can be expressed in language was taken by some and carried into paths of error. We need something unmovable under our feet; "On Christ the Solid Rock I stand."

The solidity and immutability of the Word of God is certainly a rock upon which one can stand. "All His commandments are sure. They stand fast for ever and ever" (Psalm 111:7-8). There is somewhat of an echo of this in the words of St. Paul in I Corinthians 15:1, "I declare unto you the gospel which I preached unto you, which also ye have received, and wherein ye stand." The value of the Word is focused upon in Psalm 119. Consider just a few verses.

Psalm 119

"How can a young man keep his path pure? By heeding thy word" (verse 9, Goodspeed).

"Thy word have I hid in mine heart, that I might not sin against thee" (verse 11).

"This is my comfort and consolation in my affliction, that Your word has revived me and given me life" (verse 50, Amplified).

"If your law had not been my delight, I would have perished in my affliction" (verse 92, NIV).

"From Thy precepts I get understanding; Therefore I hate every false way" (verse 104, NASB).

"Thy word is a lamp unto my feet, and a light unto my path" (verse 105).

"Great peace have they which love thy law: and nothing shall offend them" (verse 165).

PASSAGE OF DANGER

There is a rock. God will provide, "While My glory passes by, I will put you, Moses, in a clift of the rock, and will cover you with My hand while I pass by" (Exodus 33:22). God will continually shield us from and sustain us in the dangers present in the glory of high revelation and impartation.

Peter was exposed to danger in the manifestations on the Mountain of Transfiguration. If he had his way, that would have been headquarters, with Moses and Elijah sharing the headship with Jesus (Luke 9:33). But God protected Peter from himself by redirecting him (34-36). Peter saw this tremendous manifestation with his natural senses. Even on that high level there is danger and a need for protection. How much greater the danger and need for protection on the higher level of seeing with the spiritual senses.

One of the greatest dangers in revelation and manifestations is presumption. Peter presumed. Presumption is based upon a lack of the awareness of certain things, or not seeing the "big picture." That is, one does not usually consider that which he does not know; revelations and manifestations which, in themselves, become a directive to certain people. A person can easily be mislead by this, since the whole picture is rarely, if ever, seen. This is why we must depend upon the leading of the One Who knows all. When Peter saw all that glory and manifestation, he thought he was seeing the whole. That was the most he had ever seen. It was so great and glorious, that there was no thought in Peter that there could be more to this than meets the eyes. Thus, the danger of presumption.

Not many escape the danger of lofty heights. Not many individuals can ascend the Mount of God and handle it all perfectly the rest of their lives. Moses failed. He struck the rock in presumption, instead of speaking to it as God ordered. King Uzziah found lofty heights in God, only to lift up his heart (to become presumptuous) and fail (II Chronicles 26:5, 16-21). Although it is difficult to maintain a lofty level in God, it is not impossible. For with God all things are possible.

223

THE SAFETY FACTOR

The difficulty is not so much in maintaining the lofty height as it is in maintaining lowliness in the lofty height. Can humility be maintained in exaltation? There can be no greatness in God without humility. So-called greatness without humility stinks.

Man ascends to great heights in God, thinking that he has traveled a great distance. Actually God has come down to him, traveling a much greater distance than the man has. God must greatly humble Himself in order to exalt man. This is seen in Jesus. He became a servant. He was highly exalted, but He came down. He was rich, but He became poor in order that we, through His poverty, might be made rich (II Corinthians 8:9) and be seated in heavenly places.

It would help us to keep in mind that every exaltation God brings to us entails a great humiliation or descending upon His part. In order to bring Moses into a sublime spiritual experience never before known to man, God had to come most of the way. Moses had to climb Mt. Sinai, but God had to come down all the way from Heaven to the top of Sinai. How high is Heaven? How high is Mt. Sinai? There is a vast difference. God has humbled Himself. "The LORD **descended** in the cloud, and stood with Moses" (Exodus 34:5). May we learn humility from Him.

Peter puts it in proper perspective in his first epistle, "Humble yourselves therefore under the mighty hand of God, that he may exalt you in due time" (5:6). If God brings you into the wilderness to communicate and to impart His glory to you, it will help if you have humility. When Moses came from the glory of God with his face lit up, he could have walked proudly because of it. But humility is needed.

Perhaps the wilderness is necessary in order to bring us to humility. It would be nicer if God brought us to Heaven (or at least to green grass with softly flowing water) to impart His riches to us. But He usually brings us to the wilderness. And that is necessary in order to help us with our pride.

If pride continues to be characteristic in the life of a believer, he will not be able to carry God's truth properly. This implies, among other things, that the believer's communications to others would be seriously hampered. Most of that which God imparted to Moses was to be shared with others.

If some of God's communications through you were beyond the realm of words, pride would hinder your life from expressing such communications. What God has given you is to be given to others without its being contaminated. God seeks open and clean channels through which to flow toward others. There is a desire in most believers to be used of God. But a desire which should supersede the desire to be used of God is the desire to be right and pure before Him. The condition of heart has much to do in receiving from God.

Peter may have missed much on the Mount of Transfiguration, but God worked effectually in him (Galatians 2:8). Peter was taken through trying circumstances when Jesus was crucified. His hopes and dreams were shattered into a million pieces. He was so devastated that he had to find a place near God in order to survive. (We all walk this path.) Peter had to find something solid. He did, and he became stable. In fact his very name, "Petros" (4074), is an adjective, from the noun "petra" (4073), meant to describe his stability. "There is a place by Me," God said in Exodus 33:21, "And you will stand upon a rock."

Peter, in spite of his weaknesses, was brought to this place of revelation, communication, and impartation. He knew from experience the words he wrote in I Peter 5:10, "After you have suffered awhile God will make you perfect, establish, strengthen, and settle you." Not long after the ascension of Christ, Peter was receiving from God and giving it to others. Peter addressed the lame man in Acts 3:6 and said, "Silver and gold have I none; but such as I have give I thee: In the name of Jesus Christ of Nazareth rise up and walk." Where did Peter receive "such as I have?" There is a place near God. At that place God imparts. Are you willing to go to the wilderness to find that place?

Remember that most of the Pentateuch came to Moses in the Wilderness of Sinai. Most of what faithful believers receive from God comes to them in the wilderness. Our times of blessings in green pastures beside still waters do not etch in our spirits and natures the character and glory of God as deeply as do those times we spend in the wilderness.

The only time I have ever seen with the eyes of my spirit something of the character of the Lord was when I was my sickest. It was at a time when I did not understand, and questioned God more than at any other time. It was at a time God did not deliver me from my pain and agony in spite of my pleas. I could not sleep day or night. The hours of trial and testing slowly dragged relentlessly from day to night, night to day. There was no provision which I could discern for my weary, weak soul. What I wanted seemed to be unreachable. Yet in the midst of all this the Lord came. I found myself in a place near Him, in the desolate wilderness. You need not know the details in my personal experiences. You will have your own. In your darkest hour, in your deepest despair, God will come and give you the treasures of darkness.

The Wilderness of Sinai was the leading of God in the lives of the children of Israel. He continues to lead us onward, forward, into these unlikely situations, for He wants to impart to us His unlikely treasures. He will give you treasures unlike any earthly wealth in existence. In the wilderness He brings to you His ways and His glory. His intentions are revealed in the Wilderness of Sinai. His truth is made known in the wilderness.

Whenever you see the richness and glory of God flowing in another, clearly mark in your mind that he has been through three hells. It is the foolish youngster who looks up in awe and admiration to a man of God of richness, and wishes to be like him. It is a sober man who gazes into a life of spiritual wealth and glory, and prays that God gives him the grace and strength to be made as wealthy. Refined gold is not the first thing in your life; fire is before that. The gold is admired and desired. The process is not so admired and desired. But we must know the ways of God, that we may be willing to walk in His processes.

KNOW AND LIVE

God gives direction that we may know His ways. Pay attention! "These are the statutes and judgments and laws, which the LORD made between him and the children of Israel in mount Sinai by the hand of Moses" (Leviticus 26:46). Here are the instructions, not for the Israelites only, but also for us today. This is the setup, in shadow for them, in reality for us. This is the direction; their direction then, our direction now. "This is the way; walk ye in it."

"These are the commandments, which the LORD commanded Moses for the children of Israel in Mount Sinai" (Leviticus 27:34). The directions of life are received by Moses for God's people, "All the commandments which I command thee this day shall ye observe to do, that ye may live" (Deuteronomy 8:1). "That you may live" is the purpose of God's commandments. And in verse 3, "He humbled thee, and suffered thee to hunger, and fed thee with manna, which thou knewest not, neither did thy fathers know; that he might make thee know that man doth not live by bread only, but by every word that proceedeth out of the mouth of the LORD doth man live." Experience is to teach that the Word which God gives is life to man.

The law was not given to kill the people. God said this in Leviticus 18:5, "Ye shall therefore keep my statutes, and my judgments: which if a man do, he shall live in [by] them: I am the LORD." All that God gives His people is designed to lead them into the fulfillment of life. Both the path leading to life and the path leading to death were revealed to His people.

The path which you follow will be the path of your own choice. The blessings of life are set in the path of God, "And all these blessings shall come on thee, and overtake thee, if thou shalt hearken unto the voice of the LORD thy God" (Deuteronomy 28:2). "But it shall come to pass, if thou wilt not [your choice] hearken unto the voice of the LORD thy God, to observe to do all his commandments and his statutes which I command thee this day; that all these curses shall come upon thee, and overtake thee" (Deuteronomy 28:15). God's choice and provision are that you might have His life and benefit from its blessings. But your choice is that which determines your final outcome. You determine the path which will lead you to your eternal dwelling place, whether in God's glory or in the lake of fire (Revelation 20:15).

HIS DWELLING PLACE

Dwelling places are important to God. In the Wilderness of Sinai there is a dwelling place, "And the LORD spake unto Moses in the Wilderness of Sinai, in the tabernacle of the congregation"

(Numbers 1:1). The Tabernacle of the congregation served as God's dwelling place. This is what God told Moses in Exodus 25:8, "Let them make me a sanctuary; that I may dwell among them." God was willing to live in the wilderness. For forty years He lived in the wilderness without complaining about the provisions. God said, "I have not dwelt in an house since the day that I brought up Israel unto this day [time of King David]; but have gone from tent to tent, and from one tabernacle to another. Wheresoever I have walked with all Israel, spake I a word to any of the judges of Israel, whom I commanded to feed my people, saying, Why have ye not built me an house of cedars?" (I Chronicles 17:5-6).

In the wilderness God gave Moses the plans for His dwelling place. This dwelling place for God was built and set up in the wilderness. And in the wilderness God inhabited it. If the wilderness was good enough for God to live in, it should be good enough for His children. I would like to live where God is living. If He is living in Heaven, I want to be there. If He is living in the wilderness, I want to be there. If He is living in the valley, I want to be there. If He is living on the mountaintop, I want to be there. Location is very immaterial to me. It always has been in this earth. It doesn't matter where God is; that's the place for me. Many believers sing C. F. Butler's hymn, "Where Jesus is, 'Tis Heaven." But very few will believe it.

God's desire for a dwelling place is amazing in itself, since we think that Heaven should be sufficient for Him. But when we read what God said in Isaiah 66:1, "Heaven is my throne and the earth is my footstool" (NIV), we get the picture of His feet dangling outside of Heaven. And that is just the picture God intends to portray. For in this same verse in Isaiah He goes on to say, "Where is the house you will build for me? Where will my resting place be?" He is saying, in other words, "What is there that will be big enough for me?" Then, in verse 2, He answers his own question, "To this will I look," in the literal Hebrew. "This" (2088) is a demonstrative pronoun for a person, place, or thing. Since the question is, "Where is God going to live?" a place is in consideration here. "To this [place] will I look, to the poor and wounded of spirit and trembling at my word," to put it in its literal Hebrew.

This roomy place which God seeks in man is very illogical to our finite minds. But remember what the apostle Paul wrote, "The Lord said unto me, 'My strength is made perfect in weakness'" (II Corinthians 12:9). The strength of the Lord was mightily manifested in creation. Yet that was not the fullness of His might. He needs man in which to demonstrate His greatest output of strength. He needs man in which to spread Himself out in living space greater than Heaven. Such extent of truth is not for the natural mind to understand; it is for the spiritual man to hold and allow to grow.

This desire of God to live in man is not only revealed in the Old Testament, but is also expanded in the New Testament. Jesus said, "If a man love me, he will keep my words: and my Father will love him, and we will come unto him, and make our abode with him" (John 14:23). Paul expresses this quite adequately in Ephesians:

Ephesians 2:19-22

"So then, you are no longer foreigners and pilgrims, but fellowcitizens with the saints, and the household of God, being built upon the foundation of the apostles and prophets, Jesus Christ himself being the cornerstone, in whom the entire edifice, being fitted together, grows into an holy temple in the Lord, in whom you also are being built together into a dwelling for God by the Spirit" (Greek text).

This desire of God is one of His ultimate biblical purposes seen in Revelation 21:3, "And I heard a great voice out of heaven saying, 'Behold, the tabernacle of God is with men, and He will dwell with them.'" The mystery here is found in the use of the two prepositions, "with" and "in." "In" applies to the tabernacle of God "in" which God dwells, and refers to the saints in the above Ephesians text. The men "with" whom God dwells in the Revelation 21:3 reference are people different from those "in" whom God dwells.

God wants to get as close to people as possible. First He wants to dwell "in" them. That will not be accomplished over the entire population. There will be some that will be suitable only for God's dwelling "with." God does not always get the entirety of that which

He seeks. He is not willing that any should perish, but some do. He will be content to get what He can. He looks to certain quality people for His dwelling place, forever.

Some people want to live in Heaven forever. But the forever situation is you in God and God in you. Even the new earth may not be a forever situation. The geographic location is of no importance. God could camp in Hell. Even in that place He would be your shield. The powers of Hell have no adverse effect upon God. There is no power greater than God's. There is no power which can burst into God and wreck everything there. Earthly circumstances cannot destroy that arrangement of God in you and you in God. In this present world, in tribulation, in distress, in anguish, in despair, in trouble, God wants to live in you, and wants you to live in Him. He intends this to be a constant and permanent arrangement. He does not want you to leave Him. He says, "I'll never leave you."

Some individuals whom God brings into the wilderness will leave God because of the situation. God doesn't want that. He wants you to stick with Him, for He has brought you into the wilderness in order to make you His dwelling place. Be content to live where God lives, so that He can live in you.

MORE ABOUT OBEDIENCE

Part of this indwelling life is obedience. One of the reasons for which God brings us into the wilderness is to learn obedience. The first lessons in obedience are not difficult. God did not immediately tell the Israelites to go up and possess the Promised Land. But one of the first lessons was relatively simple. The Passover was instituted while they were still in Egypt. Once they were in the Wilderness of Sinai, the Lord commanded them to keep the Passover (Numbers 9:1). In this they could exercise obedience. And they did, as stated in verse 5, "And they kept the passover on the fourteenth day of the first month at even in the wilderness of Sinai: according to all that the LORD commanded Moses, so did the children of Israel."

If obedience was not learned in the wilderness, the children of Israel would not enter the Promised Land. They did fail in obedience, as did even Moses himself by striking the rock when God told him to speak to it (Numbers 20:8-12). Moses and those adults, except for Joshua and Caleb, did not go into the Promised Land to possess it. The New Testament refers to this with these words in Hebrews 3:18, "And to whom did He swear that they should not enter His rest, but to those who were disobedient?" (NASB).

The first relatively simple lessons in obedience soon fade into the background in light of more difficult lessons thrust upon us as we progress in our schooling. Obedience in the glory of His presence, when there is water aplenty, is not too hard. What is much more difficult is obedience in darkness without water. In our difficult terrain we learn the most about obedience. Thus it is necessary that God takes us over rough roads to train us properly.

Proper training in obedience prepares us (it is hoped) to obey without questioning. When God speaks and leads, He does not usually say why or explain the purposes. If we learn our lessons well, we will walk in His commands without asking, "Why?"

I finally learned not to ask, "Why?" But then I came up with another trick. When the Lord wanted me to leave Peru and the mission work there (in which I was involved for eight years) and teach in a Bible school in Pennsylvania, I made stipulations. After some weeks I finally learned not to do that, and repented in tears. We must learn to follow Him without questions and without stipulations and without deals. Obedience should be based upon nothing but that which God commands.

Immediate obedience may save your physical life or preserve you from other dangers. For more important reasons than our physical well-being God wants us to learn obedience. This is why in the school of obedience God gives us a very rough course.

Usually one does not know what's going on in the realm of obedience until it is completed. Little did King Saul realize that failure in his test of obedience would cost him his kingdom (I Samuel 15:11-23). In disobedience there is loss. In obedience there is gain, not just for the one, but for many others, "By one man's disobedience many were made sinners" (Romans 5:19); "By the obedience of one shall many be made righteous" (Romans 5:19).

"Obedience is better than sacrifice," said Samuel to King Saul (I Samuel 15:22). There is no substitute for obedience. Some folks will pray rather than obey. A friend of mine was visiting friends in California and was alone at the house playing the organ. God spoke to her to take tracts and pass them out from door to door, beginning with the nearest neighbor. But she was so taken up in her playing and singing and tearful worshipping and the presence of God, that she ignored God's directive. Again the Lord urged her. Still she continued to play the organ. After about two hours she heard sirens and a great commotion outside. She looked out the window and saw at the nearest neighbor's house an ambulance, a fire truck, and police. She later found out that the neighbor, alone at home, had committed suicide. Obedience is better than worshipping God at the organ. Obedience is better than the tearful joy of basking in the presence of God. Nothing will take the place of obedience.

Obedience is of great importance. It goes beyond yourself into an ever-broadening area. If you were the only one involved in your own obedience, the importance would be greatly diminished. Consider the case with the disciples of Jesus. Their obedience has reached out two thousand years to touch our lives. Consider the life of Paul. It was not just Paul's life and well-being which were at stake. Today we have great benefits because of him. Look at what comes out of Paul's obedience. Out of the twenty-seven books of the New Testament, he wrote thirteen. If it were not for Paul, the Christian world today would be saddled with circumcision and other points of the Mosaic Law.

Consider also the life of Joseph, the son of Jacob. He learned to follow the Lord in obedience without complaining. He was tried and tested. He went through trials. He remained faithful. And through his faithfulness to God, Egypt and her neighbors were spared from death through starvation.

You are just one grain of wheat, one seed. You come into God's life and obedience. You fall into the ground and die to self. Now there is a production which touches the lives of many. Where does it end? It never does. And this is just your obedience, no one else's.

The total effect that our lives have upon others will not be known in today's age. Some of the effect, however, can be seen. The ten spies discouraged the hearts of the Israelites by their evil report. The people said, "How can we go up to possess the land? Our brothers have discouraged our hearts saying, 'The people are greater and taller than we. The cities are great and walled up to heaven'" (Deuteronomy 1:28). Without this report, the people would have had no reason to be discouraged. There would not have been reason for their unbelief. There would not have been reason for their disobedience. But they were infected by the ten. Instead of the adults going up to possess the land, they died in the wilderness, infected by ten men. How fearful!

ORDER OF RESPONSIBILITY

You are not responsible for the whole world. Jesus Himself fulfilled that responsibility. Your responsibility lies within your own awareness and control. In the Scriptures, the responsibilities of a daughter or wife before the Lord, through a vow, could be nullified by the father or husband. In that case the Lord did not hold the lady responsible (Numbers 30:5,8,12,13). Responsibilities are limited. Paul wrote to Timothy, "If anyone does not provide for his relatives, and especially for his immediate family, he has denied the faith and is worse than an unbeliever" (I Timothy 5:8, NIV).

Personal responsibility cannot possibly move out to an unlimited extent. You cannot be responsible for going to Africa if you have to neglect your responsibility to provide for your immediate family in order to go to Africa. Perhaps God has led you to go to Africa. But the leading of God is not in question. The question is, "Have you fulfilled your basic responsibility?" "First things first" is God's arrangement.

If in our obedience we have God's priorities straight, we will bring the glory and honor to Him which He intends. If these priorities are not in order, we bring shame to Him. If a wife prophesies and disobeys her godly husband, it brings shame to the Lord. If a husband preaches but does not provide for his family, it brings shame to the Lord. If a teenager is a helper in the local church but is rebellious at home, it brings shame to the Lord. If a man is a Sunday school teacher and fights with his wife and children, it brings shame to the Lord. Take care of first things first.

Obedience, and in its proper order, is God's prime concern in the lives of His children. Thus, He brings us under training in order to accomplish this. Training may first begin in natural and mechanical things. Once obedience is learned on this lower level, then it is less difficult for God to get it moving on the spiritual level. The Lord used my dad to get obedience into me on the natural level.

When our daughter, Brenda, was about four, she got into something and made a big mess. I called her to me, but she refused to come. So I went and corrected her. Then I returned to my former place and called her to me. Still she did not come. Again I corrected her. Again I called. Still she would not obey. A third time I corrected her. Now when I called her the fourth time she came. She did not come to the punishment; she came to love. That is, when she finally came to me, rather than spanking her further, I embraced and kissed her. From then on she was always obedient. That has translated into her present spiritual life and walk with the Lord.

Chastisement is training. The Lord does not delight in chastening His children. He does delight in obedience. Thus He continues to chasten in order to bring us to a place of broad benefits. Through the obedience of Abraham all nations become blessed (Galatians 3:6-9). God calls each of us to this same faithfulness, that our lives may richly flow out to others throughout all the ages to come. The far-reaching effect of your faithfulness in obedience is staggering, even unbelievable. God trains you for this. We must learn to obey. For this reason we come to the school of obedience in the Wilderness of Sinai.

Once we make proper progression along the lines of obedience, we become responsible enough to begin to fulfill God's call into service. This is the time we receive our orders and directions to participate in the work of God. The call of God into service is upon every developed saint, without exception. In the Wilderness of Sinai the call into service was to those men twenty years of age and upward. Children and infants were not pressed into service. We should remember this in our churches.

Listen to the development Paul mentions in Ephesians 6:10-11, "Finally, my brethren, be *strong* in the Lord, and in the *power* of his *might*. Put on the whole armour of God, that ye may be able to stand against the wiles of the devil." The armor of God is not for the weakling. Not all believers are able for it. God is not going to call you into His active service unless there is some ability in you to fulfill that calling. I do not refer to natural ability, but rather to the ability which God has been able to implant within you. We are called into battle. But before we go, there must be obedience and strength instilled within us.

The reason for the need of inner God-given ability and strength is the battle itself. Paul states this reason in Ephesians 6:12, "For we wrestle not against flesh and blood, but against principalities, against powers, against the rulers of the darkness of this world, against spiritual wickedness in high places." Who are the wrestlers in "*we* wrestle?" They are not infants.

Before Israel went into possess the land they had training battles. In the wilderness they fought and defeated, within a forty-year period, about six kings. In Canaan Land they fought and defeated thirty-one kings in one year. King David was a man of war, but first he was trained. His first training took place in the sheep field. His second phase of training was on the battlefield with Goliath, at a time when he was not yet able to handle armor. His third phase of training came when he was a renegade, on the run from King Saul. From there he went into full-scale battle as king, with full armor, subduing kingdom after kingdom. In our training we sometimes feel as if we are in full-scale battle. That intensity in training is necessary to prepare us. Some believers never succeed in their training. Therefore they never come into the fullness of the battle.

All the men of Israel participated in the battles. The priests took part. There was a diversity of functions. This is true today. If someone does not function in the same assignment in battle as you, do not consider him not in the battle, or that he is shirking his duty. On the spiritual battlefield one may subdue through prayer. Another may conquer through being kind to others. The spiritual enemy is defeated by many means. He may be defeated in the life of a husband by the wife's good housekeeping (I Peter 3:1).

Every Christian is called into the Lord's service (I Corinthians 12). But every Christian does not make it. The unfaithful are not pressed into service. There is no ability in the unfaithful to properly function in a God-appointed office. He who is unfaithful in little things is also unfaithful in the more important things (Luke 16:10-12). An unfaithful man is not able to be a proper steward. This is why Paul writes to the Corinthians, "It is required in stewards, that a man be found faithful" (I Corinthian 4:2). The requirement is not that a steward be found faithful, but that a man be found faithful before he is brought into stewardship.

God does not press children into service. The immature Christian does not have the ability to function properly. I know this statement will make the immature angry. The very fact that they become angry is sure proof that they are not ready for service. There is both Old Testament and New Testament evidence that God does not press children into service. Do not misapply this biblical principle. God can and does use children. God may even use a donkey. This biblical principle is not referring to that which God may use. God has used sinners. This biblical principle is referring to **service**. The one being used of God can be anything. But service is for the qualified.

The apostle Paul wrote to Timothy concerning God's service, "Not a novice, lest being lifted up with pride he fall into the condemnation of the devil" (I Timothy 3:6). The novice does not have the necessary strength. You do not put a novice into a responsible role in the work of God, no more than you would put an eight-year-old in a steel mill to operate a crane. The Greek word "neophutos" (3503) is translated "novice" in the King James Bible; it is translated "new convert" in the NASB; and "recent convert" in the NIV. "Neophutos" (adjective) means "one newly planted." Only in this passage is "neophutos" used in the New Testament. We must consult the Old Testament to understand Paul's inference.

In Leviticus 19:23 a fruit tree is planted; this tree is "newly planted." After some time the tree begins to produce fruit. Three yearly fruit productions were left alone; it was not eaten (went to waste?). The fourth year of this tree's fruit was offered to the LORD (verse 24). Not until the fifth yield was the fruit eaten (verse 25). This message from the mouth of God to Moses moved in the life of Paul and was presented to Timothy. This message is still moving today, and should serve us with its wisdom. The message is "not a novice," not one who is "newly planted." The wisdom of God has a definite reason for this piece of advice.

John Mark was a young man whom Paul and Barnabas took with them on a missionary journey. But John Mark was not strong enough to endure the rigors of such service. He left the work. Before a Levite could be accepted for the priesthood, qualification was the central issue. The one with a crooked nose was disqualified. If you had a bald head you could not get into the priesthood. In today's spiritual realm God is not looking at your nose or lack of hair, but qualification is still necessary. God has specific order and arrangement for everything. Any specific order or arrangement is not a purpose in itself, but is so arranged that it may fulfill the purpose God intends for it. Thus it is absolutely imperative that we adhere to His order.

Chapter Fourteen
Divine Order
in the Wilderness of Sinai (Part Three)

———∞———

"Order" was God's big delivery to the children of Israel in the Wilderness of Sinai. There, God gave order to the worship and the life of these people. Order was given to their manner of traveling. Order was given to their manner of eating. It seems that in the Wilderness of Sinai everything was set in order. Looking at it in retrospect from our time, we can see the New Testament set in order in the Tabernacle in the wilderness. Redemption is set in order in type in the Tabernacle. This would not be difficult for God to do, since redemption was set in order before the foundations of the earth. Order! Order! Order! God is still pounding His gavel, calling for order.

Truth is not helter-skelter. Truth has as much, if not more, order and arrangement than we find in nature itself. And the Truth, entering and working in our lives, will bring divine order to our living and doing. Truth regulates and relegates, adjusting each item and bringing it to its assigned slot. Truth makes you what you ought to be and puts you where God wants you to be. It is divine order, and is often contrary to our own order. It's divine order, apart from which nothing endures.

If your life is to fulfill God's intentions, it must come under that which God has ordained, or ordered (both words English are from the same Latin stem). Your inner life cannot be in disarrangement and you still be effective in the service of God. When God first finds us, we are out of order. He first must take time to tear us apart, if we are not already torn apart. Next, He must reassemble us in proper order, His order. He brings us to the Wilderness of Sinai for this job.

It would make God's task of getting us in order much easier if we could learn well some of the principles of order from the revealed Word of God. For example, learn that evening comes before morning in God's arrangement. This is the first of God's orders revealed to us. It is found in Genesis, chapter 1, "And the evening and the morning were the first day." Night comes before day. Joy does not come first in God's well-ordered Truth. In God's order, sorrow is before joy. Esther 9:22 states, "The month was turned unto them from sorrow to joy, and from mourning unto a good day." In Psalm 126:5 we read, "They who sow in tears shall reap in joy." Some may not be willing to learn God's proper order from the revealed Word of God. Maybe they will learn correct arrangement in the wilderness school. But even there, some do not learn. This may lead to death in the wilderness.

Disorder brings nothing but confusion, defeat, and ultimate death. Thus, it is extremely important that we pay close attention to God's order. Learning God's divine order and adjusting to it will lead to victory and abundant living.

Just because you are brought into the wilderness to learn, does not guarantee your success. Success is not guaranteed by any particular arrangement which God brings about. Jesus died for the world. Does that guarantee that the world will be saved? That which God provides is absolutely necessary for success. But that which guarantees the success God intends is a person's relationship to God's provision.

Obedience to the will of God guarantees success. Even though Israel was delivered from Egypt and called by God to possess the Promised Land, this did not guarantee success. We read concerning these very ones who were told to possess the Land, "And there was not left a man of them, save Caleb and Joshua" (Numbers 26:65). They did not obey. This is clearly stated in Numbers 32:11-12, "Surely none of the men that came up out of Egypt, from twenty years old and upward, shall see the land which I sware unto Abraham, unto Isaac, and unto Jacob; because they have not wholly followed me, save Caleb and Joshua: for they have wholly followed the LORD."

God may call you into His service, but that in itself does not mean that you will fulfill it. This is why Peter urges us, "Give diligence to make your calling and election sure: for if ye do these things [obedience]), ye shall never fall [the guarantee]" (II Peter 1:10).

In our learning of God's arrangements, we do not have to see the whole from beginning to end in order to experience victory in our lives. But we must align ourselves to that which we know God is requiring, and move with it in His timing. If we do not understand what the order is, we at least will have a great advantage if we become obedient to what we know God is requiring. If a child had to understand everything about his food and his digestive system before he could eat, he would die. Although understanding in the spiritual realm would bring certain advantages, we can live without it through obedience. Obedience, not understanding, is your guarantee for success.

God does not make the guarantee. He provides the basis for it. You write your own guarantee, every day of your life. While the men failed and died in the wilderness, Caleb wrote his own guarantee. Look at the words of Caleb in Numbers 13:30, "Let us go up at once, and possess it; for we are well able to overcome it." This is a heart of obedience to and faith in that which God commanded. This is the response to His Word which God seeks. We are often told that the Word of God guarantees it. It never did so in the Bible. In God's own words, with His own mouth, He said to go up and possess the Land. But these to whom He spoke died in the wilderness without fulfilling His Word.

Suppose God said to me, "During February and March you will minister around the world in seven different countries." I could ignore it and not go. Just because God told me I would go, does not guarantee it. But if I take the foundation which God laid, and be willing to go, and prepare as much as possible, then I have guaranteed the fulfillment of His word to me. There is within the Word which comes out of the mouth of God tremendous power, enough to allow me to write the guarantee. But in spite of all the power God has provided, many leave the Truth lying untouched and unfulfilled in their lives.

The promise God spoke to the Jews through Peter, "The promise [the gift of the Holy Ghost] is unto you, and to your children, and to all that are afar off, even as many as the Lord our God shall call," has been, for the most part, left lying untouched and unfulfilled, generations dying without it. Truth must be embraced and put into practice in order for it to be fulfilled in the life. God is not willing that any should perish. But they perish. The Truth must be embraced.

TWO IN ONE YOKE

"Take my yoke upon you," Jesus said. The yoke is for two. Truth always has two aspects. The believer must always be tied in to God. It is strange, this hookup between God and man. The Amalekites were killing the Israelites. But when Moses held up his hand Israel prevailed; when he dropped his hand Amalek prevailed (Exodus 17:11). It was not just Moses swaying the battle, and it was not just God. It was both yoked together. God is not going to plow the whole field alone.

King Herod Jr. (actually, the grandson of Herod the Great) takes James, the brother of John, and throws him into prison. One would think that God would deliver James. But He did not, and James had his head chopped off (Acts 12:2). Herod saw that his game pleased the Jews. So his next action was against Peter. Unlike the case of James, the Church prayed without ceasing when Peter was in jail. God delivered Peter. Why did He deliver Peter, but not James? Because the Church plowed in the yoke with God.

When the Egyptian army had the children of Israel pinned between the mountains and the Red Sea, God **did not** part the sea. Moses cried to God, "Help!" God's response was (Exodus 14:15,16), "Why are you crying out to me? Lift up your staff and stretch out your hand over the sea and divide it [**yourself**]." Yet in verse 21 we read, "The LORD caused the sea to go back." Did Moses divide the Red Sea or did God divide it? Neither. Both of them divided it.

Take His yoke upon you and learn to move together with the Lord. The Lord knows His place in the yoke. "The Lord worked with them," records Mark in 16:20. Mark doesn't say, "They worked with the Lord." The reason why the Lord can work with them is that they are in the yoke. The reason why the Lord cannot work with some is that they are not in the yoke. The Lord does not work alone. Jesus and God occupied the same yoke during Christ's earthly ministry. It takes two—God and you.

A covenant is made between two parties. It is to be kept by both sides. Both parties are responsible. If either party fails to comply, the covenant will not work. The correctness of one party in the covenant does not insure the correctness of the other party. God is faithful. That does not guarantee the faithfulness of the other party. The very fact that God made a covenant with so and so does not guarantee its success.

The apostle Paul speaks of two covenants in Galatians 4:24. One, he says, is from Mount Sinai, "giving birth to bondage." But when God instituted this covenant in the Wilderness of Sinai, He did not intend it to lead to bondage. Nevertheless the covenant failed. God did not fail. God completed all His responsibilities in this situation. Even though God accomplished His part, the very thing He instituted for life brought death. Why? Because the children of Israel did not keep their part of the covenant.

The common theme of every covenant which God made with anyone was life. Outside God's covenant there is no life. If one chooses to negate his part in the covenant, he has forfeited life, and has gone into bondage. For him there is no fulfillment of the covenant of God. The failure on man's part destroys the full intentions of the covenant of God, resulting in bondage and death. God never fails; upon this foundation man can write his own guarantee.

God is sure. "And I give unto them eternal life; and they shall never perish, neither shall anyone pluck them out of my hand," Jesus assured in John 10:28. The success of the covenant between you and God does not depend upon what an enemy does. The third party, the enemy, or even your brother in the Lord, has not the power to make your covenant with God succeed, nor does he have the power to make it fail.

You are responsible for making God's covenant with you a success or a failure. The fulfillment of your responsibility will be found in a dedication to the Lord. If you remain dedicated to Him, rather than to the world, rather than to yourself, your success is assured.

The difficulty in maintaining your dedication is in the trials, the difficult situations, the testings, the training. There is one thing to keep in mind. The trials, the testings, the training are not permanent situations. We are in constant transitions. This is graphically portrayed in just a very few words from Numbers 33:15-16, "And they departed from Rephidim, and pitched in the Wilderness of Sinai. And they removed from the desert of Sinai." It was a temporary arrangement.

All the mechanics of your spiritual training, the circumstances, the difficult times, the testings, the fire, are on the scene for only a short time. They are tools used by God to bring you onward to greater spiritual heights. When the job is done, the tool is put away, but the work the tool did is taken with you. When the children of Israel left Sinai, they left behind all their trials and testings, but they took with them all that God had established.

God may have you under pressure where there is no water, no spiritual blessings. You are there for a special work. When God completes this work in you, you leave behind all the unpleasantries, and take with you God's work of art, which is eternal. We do not carry His paintbrushes with us. Upon completion of a set of fine kitchen cabinets, the cabinetmaker installs the finished product in your kitchen. He does not bring his tools to mount them in your kitchen as showpieces; his tools have been put away. When you purchase a lovely piece of needlework, you do not find the needles attached to it.

The trials and tribulations are not going to last forever. They are simply tools used to build something which will last forever. Paul puts it all in proper perspective when writing to the Romans, "For I reckon that the sufferings of this present time are not worthy to be compared with the glory which shall be revealed **in** us" (8:18).

THE CHANGING OF THE PATTERN

When God, in training you, calls you from a particular situation, do not be too overjoyed. He may be calling you to even more difficult situations. Read slowly and meditate upon the following passage.

Deuteronomy 2:3-7

"Ye have compassed this mountain long enough: turn you northward a [particular direction]. And command thou the people, saying, 'Ye are to pass through the coast of your brethren the children of Esau, which dwell in Seir; and they shall be afraid of you: take ye good heed unto yourselves therefore: Meddle not with them; for I will not give you of their land, no, not so much as a foot breadth; because I have given Mount Seir unto Esau for a possession. Ye shall buy meat of them for money, that ye may eat; and ye shall also buy water of them for money, that ye may drink.' For the LORD thy God hath blessed thee in all the works of thy hand: he knoweth thy walking through this great wilderness: these forty years the LORD thy God hath been with thee; thou hast lacked nothing."

God will bring you from one pattern to another. The children of Israel never had to buy water; they never had to buy meat. But now they do. Things are not as easy as they used to be. A friend of mine said to me, "When I was first saved, God answered every prayer I prayed. But it did not last long." The bottle is not to be in your mouth forever. You are not going to be hand-fed all your life. One of these days the Lord is going to wean you, and you will discover what it means to buy your meat, prepare your meals, and, in general, work. No more the easy pickings of manna. You will think God cruel, mean, and a deserter. He is non of these things; He is still training you. Training does not get easier; it gets harder. But, as you are being trained, you are gaining strength and are growing in Him.

Do not allow changing patterns to discourage your dedication to the Lord. Changing patterns are absolutely necessary. Today you wear size 10. Tomorrow you will wear size 12. God will change your patterns to suit your growing needs. In addition to pattern changes in circumstances and training, even prayer patterns will change. As there are changes in the outward natural and physical patterns, there will be changes in the outward and inner spiritual patterns. Through it all, hold to your dedication to God. He is holding to His dedication to you, which is called "love" ("agape").

The Lord's dedication to His people in the Wilderness of Sinai is stated in terms of love in Deuteronomy 33:3, "Yea, he loves his people" (Goodspeed). This is a picture of the Lord embracing His people and drawing them close to Himself. The Hebrew word ("khawbab" 2245) translated "loves" in this passage relates to the word "khobe" (2243) meaning "bosom." This picture of the Lord's love is expanded when applied to the tribe of Benjamin in verse 12, "Let the beloved of the LORD rest secure in him, for he shields him all day long, and the one the LORD loves rests between his shoulders" (NIV). Here the Hebrew word "dowd" (1730) is the word translated "beloved." (The words "the one the LORD loves" are inserted as understood in the Hebrew text.) This word "dowd" is used in family settings. It denotes intimacy and fondness. The picture of the Lord's dedication and concern for His people is vividly portrayed throughout the Old Testament. But in the New Testament it reaches a brightness not seen in the Old Testament. Upon this love, which the Lord has for you, can rest a faithful dedication.

This love of God for His people contains a tremendous desire to give. His ultimate giving is not seen in the things He provides, but in His giving Himself. God wants to share Himself with His people to such an extent that we become partakers of His divine nature. This is what the apostle Peter expresses, "Whereby are given unto us exceeding great and precious promises: that by these ye might be partakers of the divine nature, having escaped the corruption that is in the world through lust" (II Peter 1:4).

This is quite a task God has, getting into us His own character. Partaking of the divine nature lays the foundation for the partaking of His character. Partaking of the divine nature is instantaneous at the new birth, the rebirthing by the Holy Spirit. The partaking of the divine character, however, takes a lifetime. It's a grind. God must put a divine character in one who is filled with "undivine" characteristics. In order for the love of God to become characteristic in you, hate must be eliminated. In order for the dedication of God to become characteristic in you, dedication to self must be eliminated. In order for God's spirit of giving to become characteristic in you, selfishness must be eliminated.

For this reason, God puts the squeeze on us, to squeeze out certain juices in order to make room for other kinds. If we know what God is up to when the pressure is on, when the fire is burning the dross, we can better maintain our personal dedication to Him. When we understand what God is doing and why, we will more readily endure the fire and the valley of the shadow of death.

God's peace will not characterize one in whom there is unrest. In order for God to work divine trust into you, He must squeeze out that "undivine" doubt. This is the reason for the wilderness and the trials. Every trial, every circumstance, every experience will be tailored to your personal being and needs. Through all the testings and difficult times God is translating truth into your life and living. Know this, and be faithful to Him. Know the Truth, for the Truth will set you free to live it.

There is so much to know of the things of God. But knowing is not enough. Someone may explain faith to you. You may read six books on faith. But all that does not cause you to live it, nor even to have it. God by His Spirit must translate that truth to your life. No man can do this; no book can do this; only God can work it into your life. Do not be too concerned about how He does it. Just be willing to endure whatever it takes to get these things of God into your everyday living.

God's work within us, in order to develop us into His image, may at times be unpleasant. Some believers consider these unpleasantries evil. For example, they think "though I pass through the valley of the shadow of death" as evil. They think suffering is evil. I wonder where they get this. It does not come from the Bible. The thinking that adversity is evil comes from certain logical conclusions drawn from particular truths. But God does not operate on logical conclusions. The apostle Paul certainly did not come to such a logical conclusion. Paul saw glory in the suffering, rather than evil. He said that the suffering works a very great glory in us.

KEEP IT SIMPLE

We must simply believe the Bible, and take it for what it says. Man seeks a nicely laid out arrangement of answers, exactly defined. That arrangement is illusive in the Bible, as the Bible itself tries to communicate. Proverbs 26:4 states, "Answer not a fool according to his folly." The very next verse is, "Answer a fool according to his folly." There is not much in the Bible that is neatly packaged to fit into man's logical arrangement. Man cannot find a set of rules which will satisfy his intellectual mechanism. Each application God makes will move under its own set of circumstances, as Proverbs 26:4-5 implies.

Just because someone is afflicted, does not in itself reveal to anyone the conditions relating to it. In fact, when a person refers to the word "afflict" in the Bible, he does not really grasp the idea—no fault of his. There are no less than twelve different Hebrew words in the Old Testament which are translated "afflict" and its derivatives. The word "afflict" could mean "discomfort" or "humbled" or a number of other meanings. If someone is sick, does that mean that he was afflicted? Maybe he ate spoiled meat. Affliction can be many things brought about by many causes and for different reasons. The only way you will know what's going on is for the Lord to tell you.

Sickness in one case may be related to biblical affliction as a result of what God must accomplish in the person. The very same sickness in another person can be directly from the enemy with no relationship to its being in God's arrangement, but contrary to the will of God. The complexity of life transcends the simple mind of man.

God shared with Adam the knowledge of good and evil. Adam was told what he should do (good) and what he should not do (evil). But when the knowledge of good and evil came through another source, it was sin. Moses numbered the people. That was obedience. King David did the very same thing, and that was sin (Numbers 1:19; II Samuel 24:10-17).

Many believers seek to know the complexities of the Kingdom of God through rules and definitions. Since man has had little success in living a natural life through attempting to know its complexities, there is little hope for the believer's success in the spiritual life when using this same method. If it's eternal life you seek, lay aside a quest to know its complexities, and seek to know the Giver. Jesus said, "This is life eternal, that they might know thee the only true God, and Jesus Christ, whom thou hast sent" (John 17:3). Keep it simple.

"Let Reuben live, and not die." This is God's concern for life as expressed in Deuteronomy 33:6 in the wilderness. It was God's concern even for Ishmael when he was in the wilderness, threatened with death (Genesis 21:14-20). God is the Giver of life. He is not out to kill anyone. Sometimes you imagine that He is out to kill **you** when He is trying to kill your flesh. But if God doesn't kill your flesh, your flesh will kill you. Your flesh is your worst and most dangerous enemy. The prayer for Judah in Deuteronomy 33:7 was, "Be thou an help to him from his enemies." The theme of help is carried further in verse 11, "Smite the loins of those who rise up against him [Israel]; strike his foes till they rise no more." Given a chance, God will kill the enemies within you, and insure you life. If you do not fight against God in His destruction of your own flesh, you will be able to live in victory.

There is no defeat in God, only victory. If there is defeat in the life of a believer, it must come through unbelief, disobedience, or some such condition. God ordains victory in the lives of His children. He does not ordain defeat; that is not part of His arrangement for you. You bring about your own defeat. Once defeat comes to your life, God will work with the situation the best He can, and try to use that defeat to teach and strengthen you. Hopefully, He will be able to bring you out of defeat into victory.

This theme continues in Deuteronomy 33, verse 12, "The beloved of the LORD shall dwell in safety by him; and the LORD shall cover him all the day long, and he shall dwell between his shoulders." His divine care and dedication toward us insure us a life of victory.

As the theme continues in verse 13, we see emerging from it spiritual wealth, which is always the case in spiritual victory, "Blessed of the LORD be his land, With the wealth of the heavens above (Goodspeed)." Blessings upon blessings are directed by God toward Israel at the end of their wilderness experiences. Through the rest of chapter 33 of Deuteronomy they continue to be stated.

Various blessings from the earth are mentioned in verses 14-16. From the spiritual blessings, we are led into the material blessings. Spiritual blessings are first in God's order. The apostle John keeps this order in the opening remarks of his third epistle, "Beloved, I wish above all things that thou mayest prosper and be in health, even as thy soul prospers." Many believers insist upon claiming this greeting to Gaius as their own personal promise. Some who are doing this would lose if God fulfilled this greeting in their lives.

Personal glory is projected in verse 17. Although some may insist that there is no personal glory, the Bible disagrees with them. Paul, in Romans 8:18, mentions the "glory which shall be revealed **in** us." In II Timothy 2:10 he writes of our "salvation which is in Christ Jesus with eternal glory." In II Corinthians 4:17 he writes of the glory for us. The righteousness of God and its results are brought out in verses 18-19. Growth is the subject in verses 20-21. Strength is the theme in verse 22. In verse 23 fulfillment and fullness are the focal points.

BLESSINGS BELONG TO YOU

God is attempting to release many blessings to His people. But quite often these blessings are missed. A believer may bog down in the means which God uses, rather than focusing upon God's intentions. If such be the case, the treasures are ignored while the methods fill the believer's vision. The apostle Paul learned to focus upon the purposes of God. Others with him focused upon the hardships, and therefore left the work of God. Leaving the work of God, they forsook the purposes of God.

When God brings you into the wilderness, do not forsake the hardships. They are the workings of God. If you see only the hardships which you are experiencing, you will never see the possessions God has for you. Like the children of Israel, you may get so bogged down with the wilderness conditions that you never see the Promised Land. Forget about conditions as much as you can, and allow God to do a work within you. The more God can do in you, the more He can do for you.

God is attempting to make you a fruitful believer. This is the thought in verse 24, as we continue through the rest of Deuteronomy 33. In verse 25 God establishes. In verse 26 He helps, and fills your vision with Himself. He is your refuge in verse 27. A life of safety, free from fear, is portrayed in verse 28. In chapter 33's last verse (29), a life of constant victory is promised.

The purpose of God is to fill your life with victory all the time. Lelia N. Morris, who lived a hundred years ago, caught this vision and wrote the hymn "Victory All The Time":

Victory! victory! blessed blood-bo't victory!
Victory! victory! vict'ry all the time;
As Jehovah liveth, strength divine He giveth
Unto those who know Him, vict'ry all the time.

Another lady gifted in song was Deborah. She too saw and experienced God's victory. She was a judge of Israel in the days before the kings of Israel. After her victory against the oppressing king of Canaan, Jabin, by name, she sang the lead part in a duet with Barak, her general. Some of these words are recorded in Judges 5:5, "The mountains melted from before the LORD, even that Sinai from before the LORD God of Israel." Even as the difficulties in the Wilderness of Sinai melted for Joshua and Caleb, so God melted them for Deborah.

For God, there is no insurmountable mountain. "The hills melted like wax at the presence of the LORD," records Psalm 97:5. Any difficulty will melt before the Lord. A believer may so focus upon difficulties that they are enlarged, magnified. This is expressed in the cliché, "Some people make mountains out of molehills." Most of the older generation in the wilderness was like this. But there are yet the Joshuas and Calebs today who so walk with God that they "make molehills out of mountains."

When the generation of Joshua and Caleb saw and heard about all the difficulties involved in possessing the Promised Land, it overwhelmed them. This prevented them from possessing the land. God attempted to communicate to these people that His greatness was sufficient to surmount any and all difficulties. Whatever it is that must be faced in life, God is bigger. Nothing can stand against the greatness of God. Hear the voice of the prophet Nahum coming to us through twenty-five centuries:

Nahum 1:5-6

"The mountains tremble and quake before Him and the hills melt away, and the earth is upheaved at His presence, yes, the world and all that dwell in it. Who can stand before His indignation? And who can stand up and endure the fierceness of His anger? His wrath is poured out like fire, and the rocks are broken asunder by Him" (Amplified).

Imagine a power of such immensity being your ally. You can't lose. Just the thought ought to double you over with laughter. There is no power that can compare to God's. No power—nothing—exists apart from God. He created all. No power, no circumstance, no situation can operate apart from and independent of God. The very existence of Satan cannot be without God. God could even now snuff out his existence and activities. All things have come out from God. He is over all.

He translated the power of His greatness to Joshua when He said to him, "No man shall be able to stand before you all the days of your life" (Joshua 1:5, Amplified). No power, no king, no nation, no city, no doubt, no discouragement, defeated Joshua. There is nothing and no one able to defeat you. If you experience defeat, it has been your own making. You and you alone hold the seeds of your defeat. "No one," Jesus said in John 10:29, "is able to snatch [them] out of the Father's hand" (Amplified). No one possesses such power.

We each have our own views of life. When we meet horrible situations, we see everything breaking apart. Our view of life is warped. We see things outside of God and beyond His control. So we attempt to fix things and get the pieces together again for God, so that once again He will be in control. Who are you trying to fool?

Don't kid yourself. God is in control, always. He is still on the throne, always. Allow God to reveal life to you, instead of badly botching its meanings through your own misunderstandings. Your mind is not built for such a task as understanding life. But the revelation is in God; there you can discover it.

Suppose you meet with an accident. How do you interpret that? How do you interpret death? Your understanding of God's values and purposes in these things will help you in properly understanding and living in peace and harmony with so-called tragedies. How can one understand God's point of view? Not by reading books, but by knowing God. How can one know God?

By spending time with Him and filling oneself as much as possible with His Word through the Bible.

REST IN HIM

I lay on a macadam road in Florida bleeding from my ears, nose, and mouth. No pulse or breath could be located by the doctor. I had just had an accident while riding a moped. My three daughters and son-in-law who were also riding mopeds, gathered round me and began to pray in the Spirit (I Corinthians 14:14-15). The police officer quickly arrived. He approached my children and asked if anyone spoke English. My pulse started to beat and I started to breathe. The Lord spared my life, and I woke up in the hospital in the intensive care unit in great pain. There were between fifteen and twenty breaks and fractures in the right side of my body. But the overwhelming sensation was the presence of God. I had a very strong awareness of well-being. I had great peace and knew that I was in the will of God. I was aware of His nearness and knew that He was greater than my situation. I rejoiced. Not for a moment did I feel discouraged or grieved because of the situation.

The three Hebrew children were thrown into the fiery furnace by Nebuchadnezzar (Daniel 3). Before going into the furnace they seemed to care little whether God would deliver them or not (verses 17-18). Their trust was in God, not in what He would do. Regardless of how things went, God would continue to be their focal point of worship and relationship. He did not have to prove anything to them. What God would or would not do seemed insignificant to them.

If a situation is significant to God in a certain way, then it can be significant to the believer in the same way. But if it is not significant to God in a particular way, and the believer is trying to make it so, he is out of the divine path. That which touches our flesh is usually significant to us in a negative way. But it may be significant to God in a positive way.

The believer becomes more content and comfortable as he walks more and more in God's way. His greatest problem is his own way. To avoid this problem he must learn to know God and His ways. His great hindrance to this learning is his great fascination in learning the works of God.

Once he learns the works of God, his next fascination is that of the naturally and physically inclined people in John 6:28. They wanted to know what they had to do in order to work the works of God. Behind that search was a natural satisfaction which the works of God could fulfill. They experienced it when Jesus fed them bread and fish. They sought Jesus for a continuation of this natural feeding. When Jesus refused, they sought the means of doing it themselves. So actually they wanted the ability to make the works of God work when they wanted them to work, and upon what they wanted them to work. This is true today. Very often the believer desires the miraculous in his hand so that he can do what he wants for himself. But two very important elements are missed. If anything is to be a work of God, it must also be in His time and in His will.

In learning God well enough to know His times and will, one must spend time before Him and draw near. One must become what the Old Testament calls a "seer." Simply stated, it is one who sees. As the prophets and others, such as Paul and John, saw the Lord, so we must desire to see Him. The more you can see Him, the clearer the knowledge of His ways and will. Seeing the Lord is quite unusual. But I am referring to it in a broad sense. Seeing the Lord may mean different things to different people. All I wish it to mean here is an insight into His being, regardless of what may or may not be seen with your physical eyes.

THE PURE IN HEART SHALL SEE GOD

The prophet Habakkuk makes a very strange statement concerning seeing God, "The mountains saw thee, and they trembled" (3:10). Relative to this is a statement from God's own mouth in Exodus 33:20, "...there shall no man see me, and live." But Jesus comes along and says, "Blessed are the pure in heart: for they shall see God" (Matthew 5:8). There is a possibility of seeing God.

There is a possibility of seeing God after death to self. Everything that looks into the eyes of God must melt and die. It is still true that you cannot see God and live. Yet it is also true that the pure in heart can see God. The heart must be purified from selfishness. One must die to self. In the very process of learning God by being with Him and ingesting His Word the believer comes to a gradual dying. When the dying is sufficient in the sight of God, He can have a trust in the believer not to spend His resources on the desires of the flesh, "And when you do ask he doesn't give it to you, for you ask in quite the wrong spirit—you want only to satisfy your own desires" (James 4:3, J. B. Phillips). The more we move away from self as the center, the greater the opportunity to see God as the center.

In seeing God, we are able to see what is in Him. That is, we get a view of His character which transcends the ability of language to describe. We see His purposes. We see a heart which is indescribable. We see His intentions. Learn God well enough to move with Him on His pathway.

If we can learn to walk God's pathway, living in His will, we, like the Hebrew children in the fiery furnace, will not be concerned about what God will or will not do. The reason for this lack of concern is that we have learned God well enough to know that He is concerned for us. Thus we can "cast all our care [not cares] on Him, for He cares for us," as we see in I Peter 5:7.

Shadrach, Meshach, and Abed-nego knew God well enough that they were certain of their deliverance. God could deliver them outside the fiery furnace, keeping them from ever going into it. God could deliver them out from the fiery furnace, bringing them out once they were thrown into it. God could deliver them in the fiery furnace, through physical death. They never questioned God about their situation or about what He would do, because they knew Him.

If I wanted to sell you a used car, you may have many, many questions about it if you do not know me. But if you knew me to be a person of openness and integrity, you may not ask any questions. Those who question God are those who do not know Him very well.

If we knew God well enough, we would know of His greatness and unlimited power, we would know of His love and care, and of His mercy and kindness and longsuffering. There would be no room for questions or doubt. In learning to know God, we can become so full of Him that it leaves room for nothing ungodly. The Bible does not say, "Love casts out fear." But it says in I John 4:18, "Perfect love casts out fear." Love which is complete enough crowds out elements contrary to it. We can become so full of love that fear cannot find any room in us.

God gave the provisions necessary for learning to know Him. In referring to the time in the Wilderness of Sinai, Nehemiah writes in 9:13, "You came down on Mount Sinai; you spoke to them from heaven. You gave them regulations and laws that are just and right, and decrees and commands that are good" (NIV). As man reaches for all that God provided, and continually takes in as much as he can, he will learn to know God.

The importance of knowing God is seen in God's efforts to reveal Himself to man. Nehemiah's statement, "You came down on Mount Sinai," illustrates God's effort. For God to "come down" on Mount Sinai would mean that He traveled an unimaginable distance. He left Heaven and came to the Wilderness of Sinai. Or did He bring Heaven with Him? "The chariots of God are twenty thousand, even thousands upon thousands. The Lord is among them, as He was in Sinai" (Psalm 68:17, Amplified). In the Wilderness of Sinai Heaven comes down.

Conclusion
Heaven on Earth
in the Wilderness of Sinai (Part Four)

———— ∞∞∞ ————

There is more Heaven here on earth than most people suspect. "The angel of the LORD encamps around those who fear Him, And rescues them," writes the psalmist in Psalm 34:7 (NASB). "Encamp" would indicate a lifestyle of place and condition. "Around those who fear Him, And rescues them" would indicate the place to be earth. "For He will give His angels charge concerning you, To guard you in all your ways" (Psalm 91:11, NASB). The Word indicates that there is a lot of Heaven with us in the here and now. When you are taken into the wilderness, Heaven goes with you. For heavenly beings to stay with us, they must live here. For the sake of the prophet Elisha, "the mountain was full of [heavenly] horses and chariots of fire" (II Kings 6:17).

A missionary I personally know arrived in a cannibal's village uninvited and unannounced. They put him in a hut and the elders met. Late that night the missionary heard a commotion moving toward his hut. He went out and stood before the crowd of cannibals carrying torches, beating drums, and yelling. The missionary raised his hands to God and prayed with his eyes closed. The crowd moved closer to him. He could feel the warmth from the torches. Suddenly the crowd stopped dead in its tracks as if on cue. All noise stopped. There was absolute silence for a moment. The silence turned to screaming and the crowd fled. The next day the missionary was called to meet with the elders. They asked him, "Who were those men of fire surrounding you last night?"

I traveled many roads in the mountains of Peru. They leave much to be desired. I came close to putting my car over a 3,000-foot drop. One missionary lost the brakes on his vehicle on his

257

downward way in the Andes. He was able to hold to the curving road and felt he was in no danger since he knew the road leveled just ahead at the bridge. But when the bridge came into view he realized the danger. Heavy rains further up in the mountains had gathered force and washed out the bridge. The missionary could not stop and there was no place of escape. He bowed his head on the steering wheel and prayed, "Jesus." The peace of God flooded his soul and Heaven came down. He was so caught up in praising God that he lost all sense of motion and time. When he finally lifted his head and opened his eyes he saw that the vehicle was stopped and was on the other side of the washed-out bridge.

Of what are you afraid? "Are they [angels] not all ministering spirits, sent forth to minister for them who shall be heirs of salvation?" (Hebrews 1:14). There is nothing to fear. The provisions of God for you are more than you can possibly imagine. Even food was brought from Heaven to the wilderness to feed the needy people, "He rained down manna upon them to eat, and gave them of the corn of heaven. Man did eat angels' food" (Psalm 78:24-25). God can provide for you food, water, chariots, soldiers, safety, shelter, light—whatever is needed.

Most believers have the dream of going to Heaven. But before that happens, God brings Heaven, with all its appropriate provisions, to us, "Say not in your heart, 'Who shall ascend into Heaven?'" (Romans 10:6). Rather believe that God has brought Heaven to you. Your ascension to Heaven will be soon enough. There is no need to live there now. For the present you are stuck on earth. Live in God's presence and enjoy Heaven in the wilderness.

If we deny ourselves the nearness of Heaven, then where is God? Where are the angels of God? Where is the work of Christ? Where are the provisions of God? If Heaven were not near us, all these would be out of reach. As in the Wilderness of Sinai, God has brought Heaven down among us. If salvation is in Heaven, how are you going to receive it? If you need physical healing and it's in Heaven, what good is it going to do you? If you need deliverance and it's in Heaven, how are you going to get it? But it all comes down and touches our lives right here on earth. My contemporary, John W. Peterson, expresses it in his song, "Heaven Came

Down and Glory Filled My Soul." God Himself expresses it in Deuteronomy 11:21, "...as the days of heaven upon the earth." This is God's intention for us. He is doing His utmost to get Heaven down to man.

The purpose of the wilderness is to get Heaven into your soul. Heaven came down in the Wilderness of Sinai. If that truth is worked into your living, then your hardships, your trials, testings, and temptations, as well as your sufferings, fade into nothingness. The glory of Heaven overwhelms the situations, circumstances, and difficulties. It brings down to us the victory we need. In it we can see God and learn of Him and His ways. In it we partake of His provisions. Come, let us follow the beckoning of God toward the wilderness that we may experience **HEAVEN ON EARTH**.

AS I WALK THIS EARTH BELOW
Charles A. Haun

As I walk this earth below,
It is difficult, I know,
But my God would have it so,
As I walk this earth below.

As I put my trust in Him
As I walk a path so dim
He will lead through thick and thin
As I put my trust in Him

In the daylight or in dark
We are not at all apart,
I am happy as a lark
In the daylight or in dark.

Tribulation is for me;
That's the way it out to be;
Jesus hung on the tree;
Tribulation is for me.

Reigning in eternity–
He who suffers here with Me;
Tried and tested shall he be,
Reigning in eternity

When the morning break so clear,
When God wipes away each tear
In His rulership we'll share,
When the morning break so clear.

So encouraged is my heart,
For in every trail I start
'Tis, I know, His work of art,
So encouraged is my heart.

As I walk this earth below,
Toward His glory I must go;
I can see the Heavenly glow
As I walk this earth below.

About the Author

Charles Haun

—∞∞∞—

Charles Haun was born June 18, 1929, and reared in a Christian home. He came to know the Lord as his Savior before he was old enough to remember. During his youth, Charles attended Robert Morris Business College in Pittsburgh, Pennsylvania, and later joined the Air Force where he began his call to teach Bible on a regular basis. After finishing with the military, Charles attended Eastern Bible Institute where he met and married Violet Fields. The newlyweds immediately went to Norman, Oklahoma, to attend the Summer Institute of Linguistics, later returning to Pennsylvania where they served as pastors for about three years in Bedford County.

Subsequently, the husband and wife were appointed missionaries under the Assemblies of God church and served eleven years, ministering in Iquitos, Peru, along tributaries of the Amazon River and among native tribes of headhunters south of Ecuador. From Peru, the Haun family (now with four daughters, Telva, Renay, Brenda, and Cindy) returned to Pennsylvania where Charles taught at Western Pennsylvania Bible Institute for seven years.

In 1978 the Haun family (except for Telva, who was attending Evangel University) relocated to Jerusalem, Israel, where Charles attended The American Institute of Holy Land Studies, and taught Bible regularly.

Returning to the States in 1980, Charles traveled full time, teaching the Word and writing books till the time he passed away in 1996. He left behind a legacy in his recorded teachings (168 tapes/CDs), books, and the lives that he touched.

Other books by Charles Haun: *Becoming the Expression of the Father; Spiritual Suggestions: Genesis 1 Through 5; Feeding on the Gospel of John: Chapter One; Feeding on the Gospel of John: Chapter Two & Three; and Feeding on the Gospel of John: Chapter Four.*

Further information can be found on the website, teachingall-nations.com or email TeachingAllNations4Him@gmail.com.

Charles embraced life and loved capturing it with his camera.

▲ *Air Force, early 1950s*

▲ *Amazon tribal dress*

Charles, Violet and daughters in 1969 ▶

▲ *Charles' family with the Murato Indian tribe, off of the Amazon River in Peru.*

◀ *Charles and Violet on a casual canoe ride on Lake Rimachi.*

▲ *First trip up the Amazon took sixteen days in this wooden houseboat. Daughters, Telva and Renay, are playing on the side of the canoe. The other upgraded houseboat was later given by the youth of Speed the Light (AG).*

Violet and Charles (1994) ▶

263

Brenda Haun

—✺—

The Lord placed it on Brenda's heart to take her father's "Wilderness" booklets and have them published in one book as *Life in the Wilderness*. Brenda was born a missionary kid in Iquitos, Peru, then at age five moved to Pennsylvania and later spent two years living in Jerusalem, Israel, with her parents (1978-1980). She herself has been a missionary to Trinidad, Mexico, and Africa.

Brenda has an AA Degree in Commercial Arts, and a Bachelor of Arts in Biblical Studies from Zion Bible College. She also has twenty years' experience in the publishing field as an assistant production manager, art director, and designer. Brenda has been an award-winning graphic designer for over twenty-five years (Charlie Awards: 2003, 2004; Florida Hospital: Aster, Healthcare Advertising, and Communicator Awards).

Brenda designed and produced the cover of *Life in the Wilderness*.

To contact Brenda Haun, please email her at: brendahdesigns@ gmail.com or visit her website at brendahdesigns.com.

www.ingramcontent.com/pod-product-compliance
Lightning Source LLC
Chambersburg PA
CBHW051946090426
42741CB00008B/1301